Lecture Notes in Computer Science

Lecture Notes in Computer Science

Edited by G. Goos and J. Hartmanis

128

Paul Branquart
Georges Louis
Pierre Wodon

An Analytical Description
of CHILL, the CCITT
High Level Language

Springer-Verlag
Berlin Heidelberg New York 1982

Authors

Paul Branquart
Georges Louis
Pierre Wodon
Philips Research Laboratory
Avenue Emile Van Becelaere 2, Box 8
B-1170 Brussels, Belgium

AMS Subject Classifications (1979): 68 B 99, 68 F 99
CR Subject Classifications (1981): 4.12, 4.22, 5.23

ISBN 3-540-11196-4 Springer-Verlag Berlin Heidelberg New York
ISBN 0-387-11196-4 Springer-Verlag New York Heidelberg Berlin

CONTENTS

FOREWORD : ON DESCRIPTIVE METHODS FOR ALGORITHMIC LANGUAGES

0. INTRODUCTION

0.1. GENERAL

This report is a description of the programming langage CHILL, the CCITT standard language whose official definition is contained in Recommendation Z200 [1]. This report uses a largely original method for describing algorithmic languages. Both the general structure of this description of CHILL and its notations are unusual and therefore should be justified. This is the purpose of this Foreword.

There were two basic reasons for building still another set of tools. Firstly, our method took shape during the actual design of an algorithmic language [5]. Design is a dynamic process which we considered an engineering task, hence a rather pragmatic form for the objects dealt with and for the notations representing them. Roughly, this system is halfway between the abstract view of theoreticians and the loose jargon of some practicians.

The second reason was our intention to produce a description suitable for implementors. This accounts for two important aspects of the method : completeness at implementor's level and compiler oriented general structure. Too often, reference manuals of programming languages show holes which implementors have to plug, each of them in his own way. We tried to avoid that by being precise in definitions and formal in notations. Furthermore, the information was organized in a form easily usable for compiler writing.

0.2. BACKGROUND

At the end of 1974, we found ourselves involved in the preliminary discussions on CHILL specifications and the method used here was developed during the design of a complete software programming language [5], our prototype for CHILL. We had an Algol 60-68 background, experience with compiler writing [7] and attribute systems [3,8], and the language had in its specifications that its implementation should produce efficient object code. For these reasons, we naturally started, in 1975, with a context-free grammar, context conditions, static semantics, and dynamic semantics, all more or less separated. At that time, we used formal notations only for syntax rules, the rest being in hopefully correct English.

During the progress of a design, things have to be reconsidered, rephrased, made more precise, etc. We soon found English texts inadequate in that process : not precise enough, too verbose, etc. This has been discussed elsewhere e.g. in [4]. Step by step, we found ourselves using shorter more systematic notations for more and more stereotyped objects and properties, until we decided to take the plunge and use as much as possible precisely defined objects and a systematic formal system of notations. The result is reported in [5].

In 1979, we undertook to apply the same method to CHILL itself, then in a draft form. This had two purposes, tidying up CHILL and testing the usefulness of our method. At that time, the definition of CHILL was incorporated in [2] and completed with a number of progress reports. The

committee in charge was faced with the task of producing a coherent
definition. We agreed to help. This is the work reported here, which had
some influence on Z200, especially on its consistency.

Finally, in 1981, as a further test, the method was applied to an existing
language, Pascal as described by ISO Draft Proposal 7185 [9]. This work is
unpublished since ISO Pascal has not stabilized yet.

In the three cases, a point was made to write a complete description of
the complete language, with the only exception of explicitly identified
details such as the spelling of numbers or the possibility of optimizing the
evaluation of Boolean expressions.

0.3. FORMAL SYSTEMS

In the first chapter of [4], P. Lucas classifies systems for describing
semantics as mathematical (denotational), operational, and axiomatic.
Already in 75, all three families of systems had been described. An
axiomatic, although partial, description of Pascal was available [10], PL/1
and Algol 68 had both been precisely defined, and yet we have been using a
different method.

In fact, we did not choose to use a formal system, it was forced upon us
by necessity, when our work was well advanced. Since the language under
design was to be a software programming language with an efficient
implementation, it was necessary to ascertain that every introduced feature
besides fitting neatly with the rest, did not imply troubles for the
compilation. This led to a separation between static and dynamic semantics
and to a rather operational expression of the latter. This structure was
there before we decided to use formal notations. At that point we borrowed
as much as possible but without changing our point of view.

It is difficult, if not pointless, to find out now which method of
description we would have chosen, had we decided from the beginning to use a
formal system. Let us only repeat that we saw our task as an engineering
task, not a theoretical one, and, with the possible exception of VDM [4], all
formal systems have a strongly theoretical orientation.

An interesting problem, which is occurring at this moment with both Ada
and CHILL, is that of validating an official formal description with respect
to a not less official reference manual. We did not have to face that
problem formally since our descriptions have no official status but of course
we had to deal with it. For [5], there is not other description and
therefore no problem. For CHILL, the "Language Definition" [1] and this
report were produced in a rather close cooperation, so that we feel that we
know the few minor points were they are in disagreement. For Pascal, the
language is sufficiently simple and well known to make the problem more
manageable.

In any case, this problem is the wrong one in that reference manuals
should be written from formal or quasi-formal descriptions and not the other
way around. Three steps are necessary : a draft, a formal description, a
reference manual. It is simpler, faster, and more secure to paraphrase a
formal text than to formalize an informal one, usually not meant for that
purpose. In the case of a compiler-oriented formal description, it can, to a
very large extent, be validated for internal consistency by a working
compiler written from it.

1. OVERVIEW

1.1. GENERAL

Most language descriptions are centered on a context-free syntax around
which semantics is informally described. If the description takes care of
implementation problems, static and dynamic parts of the semantics are
separated. We have followed this scheme but with formally expressed
semantics and precisely defined mappings.

Informal semantics tends to be expressed in a more or less stereotyped
language. This has been systematically replaced by formal notations. The
technical terms of an informal description are often described, if at all,
where they are used. Here, technical terms are precisely defined, their
meaning being an object or a property of an object. When terminated, the
description has two parts, the first one contains definitions and properties
of objects. the second part describes the language itself in terms of these
objects. During the design, both parts take shape together.

1.2. LEXICAL AND CONTEXT-FREE STRUCTURES

Although a good lexical structure is important in practice, its
description gives neither practical nor theoretical problems. The spelling
of identifiers, constants, standard operators, etc, given in [1], is not
repeated here. In the context-free syntax, these lexical units are
considered terminals with a special notation (different type font) and an
adequate semantics.

The context-free syntax itself is written in BNF with one extension, the
list. Besides shortening the syntax, the list notation often makes the
semantics easier to express. For example, there is no inherent recursivity
in a list of formal parameters.

We have chosen to use a concrete syntax, with keywords and separators
included and ambiguities avoided. This is quite convenient since the
semantic description supposes that a context-free analysis has been performed
and refers to the syntactic trees of programs, not to their texts. Then, a
concrete syntax is very much like an abstract one for all practical purposes,
with the advantage that it is immediately usable for writing programs as well
as compilers and the disadvantage that there are more rules.

1.3. STATIC SEMANTICS

The static semantics, which defines type control, declaration handling,
and other textual properties not dealt with by the context-free syntax, is
described by synthesized and inherited attributes [3,8] associated with each
context-free rule. This technique showed itself very convenient during the
design since it is flexible when not allowing to easily overlook something.
Furthermore, it is very much compiler oriented [7]. Static environments,
modes, context information for coercions, etc. are all there, neatly
displayed with each context-free rule.

This may look like fastidious repetition for someone reading the
description sequentially, but it is very useful to catch inconsistencies when
designing as well as to quickly find all information pertaining to a
construct when reading.

An attributed grammar can be seen as describing "decorated" syntactic trees, and this was our point of view. The semantics is mapped on the syntax by considering that each non-terminal represents a node of a syntactic tree. This has several advantages, among them compiler orientation, ease of understanding, abstract-like syntax, etc.

Each attribute is written as a formalized, usually short, expression which, given a program syntactic subtree described by the context-free rule under consideration denotes an object, like a mode or an environment, associated with the root of the subtree. The predicates which these objects must satisfy are also written formally.

These objects, which given a particular construct in a particular program are unique, are either CHILL objects, e.g. values, or objects used for descriptive purposes only, e.g. environments. This aspect resembles denotational semantics.

1.4. DYNAMIC SEMANTICS

The dynamic semantics defines in a rather operational way the effects of program execution. It is described by means of elaboration procedures which, like attributes, are associated with the syntactic trees described by the context-free rules. These procedures have arguments, one of them being the "dynamic environment" which models the dynamic effect of declarations.

Again, this is compiler oriented. In particular, the description is on purpose operational (keyword "Step"), although in many but not all cases it need not be. Replacing "Step" by the keyword "Let" is often possible and would give a functional flavor to the very same semantics. It is not always possible however. Furthermore, operational views are more usual for implementors.

Apart from the use of steps, an elaboration procedure is written in much the same way as an attribute but its interpretation is different. Given a particular syntactic tree, an attribute denotes an object statically "decorating" a node. An elaboration procedure denotes, if anything, an action which, whenever executed, produces an object and/or an effect modifying an object. This execution depends dynamically on objects given as arguments to the procedure and on the execution of elaboration procedures associated with the subtree whose root is the considered node.

2. OBJECTS, FUNCTIONS, AND PREDICATES

2.1. GENERAL

"The major problem in establishing the mathematical semantics for a given language is to find suitable mathematical objects, that can serve as the denotations." (P. Lucas, in [4])

This is indeed the case. In fact, a major trouble with semantics expressed in natural language is the lack of precise definitions for the objects dealt with. A systematic description has to choose suitable objects and functions and cannot avoid completely defining each of them. Common sense is not sufficient.

The objects on which the described language operates obviously appear in the description. In the present case, they are values, locations since

storage allocation and pointers are explicit, and more specialized objects
such as procedures which can be arguments of procedures.

Although they cannot be operated upon as such, objects like modes,
declarations, environments, etc., appear more or less explicitly in CHILL and
therefore also belong to its description. Giving them an appropriate
structure is not always simple however.

Finally, in order to link objects and functions with the syntactic
structures, nodes of syntactic trees and texts of some terminals like
identifiers are treated as objects with specific properties, and, whenever
needed, very ad hoc objects are freely introduced, e.g. "addressability",
"packing", etc.

2.2. STRUCTURES OF OBJECTS

Objects are classified as simple or structured, the distinction being
often a matter of notational convention.

Among the simple objects, only the numbers with arithmetic and the logical
values with predicate calculus can be taken for granted : their properties
are used without being described. All other sets of simple objects are to be
explicitly defined, by extension or by specification.

From simple objects, structured ones are built. They are sets, lists,
tuples, and "labelled tuples". They are structured in that they are
presented as being made of components. In other words, a structured object
is one for which an explicit operational model is exhibited. For example, an
array base mode is defined as a labelled triple whose components are an index
mode, a component mode, and a packing information.

An alternative way of describing an object is an axiomatic definition.
This is used also whenever suitable. For example, a pointer is presented as
a value which "refers to" a location in such a way that the location referred
to can be obtained, together with some of its properties, etc. Such objects
are, rather arbitrarily, seen as simple.

Sets, lists, and tuples have known properties. Only the labelled tuple is
a specially introduced kind of object, which was found very convenient.

2.3. FUNCTIONS AND PREDICATES

A language description uses many mappings from sets of objects to other
sets of objects, as "the value of a variable", "the index mode of an array
mode", etc., which are mappings respectively from locations to values and
from array modes to discrete modes. It was rather natural to model that by
functions with specified domains and ranges.

Part I contains many function definitons, which include a function name f,
a domain D, a range R, and a description of the mapping y=f(x) for each x in
D. The latter part is either operational, i.e. is an algorithm, or
axiomatic, i.e. is a set of properties uniquely defining y given x.

Similarly, the different properties which objects must satisfy are
expressed by predicates, also defined in Part I.

In fact, the bulk of Part I is made of such definitions. Besides giving a
precise basis on which to build the language itself, the functions in Part I
provide a useful interface when designing : like procedures in a program,
they tend to decrease the amount of change to be made when modifications are
introduced. They also make the description shorter. On the other hand, a
reader must often refer to both parts to understand a particular point. To
minimize this problem, "meaningful" names, like "is assignable", were given
to functions and predicates.

2.4. CHOICE OF NOTATIONS

In practice, manageable notations are very important. In our way from
traditional to systematic description, we were very often led by notations.
English sentences, being too long, were progressively replaced by
abbreviations which in turn looked more and more formal until a precise
definition for formalized notations became necessary.

Let us take array modes (base modes in CHILL) as examples. An array mode
is specified by an index mode I, an element mode E, and a representation
information R, i.e. by a triple of objects. It is much quicker to write a
triple [I,E,R] than a phrase like "the array mode whose index mode is I,
element mode is E, and representation is R". The trouble with a notation
like [I,E,R] is that it does not suggest at all that the object thus
represented is an array mode. This led to the use of "labelled tuples",
array(I,E,R) in the present case, in which the tuple is prefixed by a
"label", an identifier written in a special type font to make it conspicuous.
This practice, amounting to explicit typing, proved itself very serviceable,
in particular to shorten and thus make more legible many formulas. For
example, to check that a mode M is an array mode, we write

   Test M = array(-)

instead of a classical predicate of the form

   Test ∃ I,E,R : M=[I,E,R] ∧ P1(I) ∧ P2(E) ∧ P3(R)

The advantages of the shortest form are obvious.

It should be remarked that representing objects either by notations of the
described language itself or by non-terminals of the description can only
lead to trouble.

2.5. AXIOMS OR OPERATIONS

The example of stack specification has been used so often that it can
serve once again. An operational definition will present the stack as e.g. a
list and describe pop and push in terms of modifications of this list. An
axiomatic definition will achieve the same purpose in terms of properties.
If the same object, a list, is used in both cases and if some care is taken,
both definitions are equivalent for all practical purposes. Which method is
clearer depends on the reader's background and on the case at hand.

Usually, programming languages have an operational description : to each
construct is associated an algorithm expressing what the execution should do
with the data to produce the result. Being more traditional, such methods
seem easier to understand. Often, they suggest a method of implementation or
at least show that an implementation is possible. On the other hand, they
are prone to overspecification, which can be cured, and difficult to handle
with traditional mathematics. For proof purposes, axiomatic methods
describing the neat effect of an execution by initial and final conditions
are more manageable.

We have chosen the way we found easiest for each particular object or
construct. It turns out that our descriptions have an operational
appearance.

3. VALUES AND MODES

3.1. GENERAL

It is clear that the definition of a typed language should classify values
according to the types, called here "base modes", which are present or
definable in the language itself. This however is about the only obvious
choice which can be made. The association value-mode in CHILL, as well as in
Pascal, raises several problems which have four different sources :
(i) a mode is a partly dynamic affair, whereas we would like type control to
be static,
(ii) a mode is partly syntactic, in particular there are distinctions
possible between modes with entirely equal properties,
(iii) the representation of values in memory is shown in the language and
mode control must deal with it, and
(iv) there exist possibilities of mode transformations (coercions), usually
depending on the context only.

3.2. STATIC AND DYNAMIC PROPERTIES OF MODES

In general, a mode determines a set of values and a set of properties for
these values. Purely static modes can be attached to expressions of the
language. This is the ideal situation with completely static control. There
are however such things as dynamic indexing in arrays, A[i], and worse,
arrays with dynamic bounds. Their control is necessarily dynamic whether or
not it is part of mode control. For the description, a choice must be made
between having dynamic modes, as done in [1] and in [9], or to exclude
dynamic properties from modes as done here.
This description emphasizes static properties as far as possible,
inherently dynamic properties being factored out. For example, an array
premode is a labelled tuple in which a component is either stat or dyn
indicating if an expression with that premode delivers arrays with static or
dynamic bounds. In the latter case, the indicated index mode I specifies
only an upper bound for indexes. It is only in that case that dynamic
control for size is necessary and that problems for storage allocation
appear. This is expressed in the elaboration functions and is not part of
the mode control as such.
Thus, modes are statically attached to expressions and consequently to any
value which the expression may deliver. Obviously, the mode can then appear
as a static attribute. On the other hand, any elaboration produces a value
with a mode, and the association value-mode must be described taking into
account that one same value may have any number of modes.

3.3. WHAT IS A MODE ?

In CHILL, as in Pascal, two modes which have exactly the same definition
in a program and the same structure in the language can nevertheless be
different. Thus, if a mode uniquely specifies a set of values, the converse
is not true. In CHILL and Pascal, modes are linked to the occurrence of text
which defines them, not to the meaning of the text, as in Algol 68. The
description has to take care of that. An object like array(I,E,R), which
only specifies structural properties, is unsufficient.

To model this purely conventional distinction, a CHILL mode contains among its components a so-called "novelty" N. This object is the root node of the syntax tree of the text defining the mode in a program. This achieves the distinction in a neat way. The same method is used whenever an object in the description cannot be separated from the program text which constructs it.

It remains to decide where the association between a value and its mode is to be defined. In Part II, a value is defined by an elaboration function, its mode by an attribute of the same node. The association is thus rather implicit. To make it more explicit and also because modes cannot be ignored by Part I functions, any value that is an argument or result of a function is always accompanied by a mode. This is sometimes useless but always consistent. For example, the definition of indexing, V[i], is a function with three arguments : the array V, its mode M, and the index i whose mode can be deduced from M. The result is a value whose mode is explicitly specified.

3.4. THE REPRESENTATION OF VALUES

To take care of the fact that the memory representation of compound values can be programmed, base modes like array[I,E,R] have a slot R for that information. But what sort of object is a value of that mode ? According to this description, an array value is a list of n values of the same mode. This is hybrid in that, from the triple [I,E,R], it only shows E and the cardinality of I. It works since a value is always accompanied by a mode, containing the rest of the information, including the low level "representation". Another possibility, which was tried out but abandoned, is to see a value as a pair "representation-mode".

We feel that showing the hardware in a programming language, however slightly as in Pascal, is a burden for its definition. It is lenghtened, values which are similar except for their representation have different properties which must be described, and it is made less satisfactory from an aesthetic point of view. On the other hand, this was an explicit requirement for CHILL.

3.5. DESCRIBING MODE CONTROL

The mode system of CHILL does not appear simple in [1], and the same occurs here. Both descriptions still show traces of their evolution. This however has no influence on the general structure of the description : static mode control clearly is to be defined by attributes. A synthesized attribute defines the "premode" collecting all mode information in the described construct itself, and an inherited attribute describes the "postmode", i.e. context conditions indicating possible coercions.

In principle, it could be possible to have a larger part of the mode system described with the syntax rules, in Part II, since this is a syntactic affair. Part I in that case would contain mainly mathematical descriptions of sets of values. This was found impractical mainly because value representations have also to be dealt with. The definition of the mode system is therefore spread over Parts I and II, each property being defined where it was found most convenient to do so.

4. LOCATIONS, STORE, AND ENVIRONMENT

4.1. GENERAL

The description of declarations, especially variable declaration, the "environment", and the description of assignment of values to variables, the "store", is a well known snag for mathematical descriptions. Stores and environments have a dynamic aspect, they can be modified while remaining themselves, whereas mathematics only deal with permanent properties.

In a sense the compiler orientation of this description makes the problem simpler : we have used the same system as well structured compilers, with more abstract notations however.

The static and dynamic effects of declarations are separated, and the description uses a static and a dynamic environment to model that. Locations are presented as modifiable objects, whose identity is preserved when their contents is changed.

4.2. STATIC ENVIRONMENT

Because of the elaborate visibility rules for the declarations of CHILL, an axiomatic description was preferred to an operational one for the static environment. In Part II the latter is an inherited attribute the structure of which is never apparent. For descriptive purposes, this was found simpler than an operational explicit structure. On the other hand, this had at least two drawbacks. Firstly, it was for us less simple to ascertain the consistency of the system, and, secondly, implementors would have to reconstruct an operational system from the axiomatic one.

In any case, a static environment is a set of static declarations with a set of properties. In turn, a static declaration, in its simplest form, is a pair text-node. The text is that of the declared identifier and the node the syntactic node of its defining occurrence. The identification process of an applied occurrence has then to uniquely produce that node. All static properties of the declared object are attributes of that node. If the declared object is static, it is itself one of these attributes.

This basic idea is very simple but, unfortunately, CHILL has different visibility rules for its different sorts of declarations, so that the predicates and functions describing the static environment are rather clumsy.

4.3. DYNAMIC ENVIRONMENT

A dynamic environment is made of dynamic declarations, and a dynamic declaration is a pair node-object. The node is that of the corresponding static declaration and the object the declared object, when it is dynamic. The dynamic part of the identification process is then given the node and has to produce the object.

The dynamic environment is defined partly axiomatically and partly operationally, its operational structure being compiler oriented even in the terminology. A dynamic environment has a "stack" and a "display", the stack is a list of "locales", one for each entered block, etc. This is a classical structure, less complicated than the static one.

4.4. LOCATIONS

CHILL has generators to allocate storage and pointers to deal with that storage, hence the explicit appearance of locations as objects containing values. Since mode control applies to locations as well, they are given a mode, handled in the same way as that of values. In fact, the physical representation of values of a given mode is that of locations. This is the reason for the introduction of "referability".

Another problem for locations is the definition of their "lifetime". For declared variables, this is controlled by the block structure. For dynamically allocated locations, the problem is in general less simple. In CHILL, such locations also have their lifetime controlled by the block structure. This simplifies the description but not the task of properly handling pointers in programs.

5. PARALLELISM

5.1. GENERAL

When CHILL was designed, there was no well accepted set of operators for controlling parallel processing and no well accepted method for dealing with the description of such operations. This is still the case, and more than elsewhere, language designers have to innovate.

CHILL has processes, which are pieces of text, instances of processes, which are activations of those texts in some environment, descriptors of process instances, which behave like values. Process instances can be active or delayed on some queue.

We have chosen to describe these things as flatly as possible, with a mixture of axioms and operations.

5.2. EVENTS, BUFFERS, AND SIGNALS

Being a language for all seasons, CHILL has a very redondant system of synchronization, in which implementors are invited to choose their own subset. There are three sorts of synchronization objects, the events, the buffers, and the signals. All three are defined in terms of queues, waiting queues on which delayed processes are waiting for data, and data queues where data exchanged between processes are placed.

In turn, a queue is a modifiable object which can be lengthened or shortened without loosing its identity. This is not too difficult except for one point : one same delayed process instance can be waiting on several queues. This has caused descriptive problems, showing implementation problems very likely. A process instance waiting on several queues can be reactivated on any of them but must be taken out from all of them, thus triggering much activity since overflow conditions may disappear. The functions describing that have a rather formidable aspect.

5.3. PROCESSES, INSTANCES, AND DESCRIPTORS

A process text can be activated any number of times, hence the distinction between a process and its instances. An instance may be either active or delayed on any number of queues, and may disappear, i.e. become non existent. The conditions under which these changes of state are legal are expressed in very general terms in [1] and in this description as well. The same is true for the handling of shared resources. CHILL offers means for handling them but their description is unable to suggest how to use them consistently.

Descriptors of process instances do not exist in [1]. They have been introduced here for descriptive purposes. Indeed, CHILL permits dynamic manipulation of process instances, and it was found better to do that with descriptors as the implementation will do anyway.

6. CONCLUSION

The complete description of a language, especially a hardware oriented language, is a formidable task, very often underestimated by the various committees undertaking it. It is also essential, no language being actually defined unless it has such a description.

A complete definition also shows how deadly complex modern programming languages can be even if, as for CHILL, the preliminary specifications forbade the inclusion of unproved features. We do not know if such complexity can be avoided. In fact, even Pascal is more complex than it superficially looks.

Although its formal appearance is different from most others, our description has a classical structure resembling e.g. that of Algol 68. It is compiler oriented in the way informations are grouped and repeated whenever needed, and because of its operational view based on primitives of an intermediate code level. Furthermore, it describes how to recognize correct programs, and not how to generate them, as does the two-level grammar used for Algol 68. Finally, its analytical nature makes it rather longish.

Remarks

In this report, such things as lexical structure, character set and some syntactic alternatives have not been included since they have no special interest for our purpose.

Implementation options, such as partial evaluation of expressions and "receive-case actions" have not been described. They are not easily amenable to formalisms.

Syntactic ambiguities of Z200 have been included in our context free syntax, e.g. slicing in a character string obtained by concatenation is ambiguous, and some location conversions can be parsed as value conversions as well.

There are some minor differences between the language as described in Z200 and in this report; they may be considered side-effects of the respective descriptive methods and could be mended if necessary:

- this description does not make any difference between a discrete mode and a subrange thereof containing the same values, whereas there is a slight difference in Z200
- this description does not make the same distinction as Z200 between bit strings of length 1 and Boolean values
- this description does not allow the "seize all" operation on identifiers granted by a surrounding module.

It should be noted that this work has been complicated by the fact that, during its production, CHILL has undergone many changes, as shown by the various progress reports. As a consequence, parts of the description are more complex than necessary or less structured than possible and desirable. To save time and energy, the original structure was sometimes only adapted to follow CHILL's variations whereas, ideally, it should have been changed. Now that CHILL has stabilized, this could be corrected but, since our primary goal has been reached, this has not been done.

Finally, our terminology is sometimes different from the one in Z200.

Acknowledgement

Marcelina Salgado has shown much skill and patience in typing and editing the successive versions of this work with the editing system PDG [6].

PART O : METHOD OF DESCRIPTION

1. OBJECTS

(1) The description is in terms of objects, properties of objects, and
functions taking objects as arguments and delivering objects as results.
   The basic objects used in the description are the natural numbers, the
logical values, in general the objects of the language itself, with, in
addition, more ad hoc objects, specific to the description, such as "modes",
"program nodes" or "program texts".
   From basic objects, compound ones are constructed : they are "sets",
"lists" (also called "strings"), "tuples", and "labelled tuples".

*

(2) In the description, notations for objects are introduced by the phrase
"is written", as in "the set of integers is written int". Conversely, a
notation "represents" an object. Most of the time however, the distinction
between object and notation is not made explicitly, as in "the set int".
   There are four classes of notations for objects : constants, variables,
patterns and forms. These four classes taken together are called
"expressions".

*

(3) A constant represents one single basic object. Natural numbers are
represented by decimal notations : 0,1,2,... . The logical values are
represented by true and false. This description specifies how the other
basic objects are written. As a rule they are written as identifiers in a
distinct type font : int, stat, etc.

*

(4) A variable, which is an identifier possibly with a sub- or superscript,
may represent any object in its "range". The "scope" which is the part of
the description in which the variable can be used, is at most the "paragraph"
in which the variable is defined.

*

(5) A pattern, if it is entirely written with constants, represents a unique
object. If variables and/or dashes appear in it, then it may represent any
object in its range. For example, {true, false} represents the set of
logical values, whereas {1,N} may represent any set obtained by replacing N
by an object in the range of N. Patterns are, like the objects they
represent, classified as being sets, lists, tuples, and labelled tuples.

*

(6) Sets, in the classical sense, are represented in the usual fashion :
   - by a phrase in English, as "the set of positive integers",
   - by an enumeration of its elements (between braces), as "{true, false}",
   - using predicates and/or functions, as "{a|P(a)}" or "{f(a)|P(a)}", etc.
   An interval of a totally ordered set, defined by $\{a|m \leq a \leq n\}$, is itself a
totally ordered set, written {m:n}. If m>n, {m:n} represents the empty set.
   The notations used for sets are :
- {}   : the empty set,
- $\cup, \cap, \setminus$: union, intersection, difference of sets,
- $\subset, \subseteq$: proper inclusion, inclusion,
- =, $\neq$: set identity and its negation,

- ∈   : membership,
- 2**S   : the powerset of set S,
- #S   : the number of elements in set S,
- S{i}   : the ith element of the totally ordered set S,
- min(S)   : the smallest element of the totally ordered set S,
- max(S)   : the largest element of the totally ordered set S.

                                *

(7) Between two elements of a set, the relations = and ≠ with their classical
meaning are defined; similarly, the relations <, ≤, >, ≥ are defined between
two elements of an ordered set.
The elements of the set of integers are written ... -1,0,1,2,... and the
operators +,-,*,÷, mod,rem are defined for them with their classical meaning.
The elements of the set of logical values are written true and false, and the
operators ¬, ∧, ∨ and xor (also noted +) are defined on them with their
classical meaning.

                                *

(8) A list is an ordered enumeration of occurrences of elements from a given
set, indexed from 1 upwards. List notations use the bracket pair ⊀⊁ where
set notation use the pair {}. List are written
    - as a phrase in English, as "the list of bit positions in location L",
    - as an enumeration of its elements, as "⊀true,true,false⊁",
    - using predicates and/or functions in such a way that the ordering is
      clear, as
      "⊀f(a)|a∈S⊁", with S an ordered set,
      "⊀a|a∈L ∧ P(a)⊁", where L is a list and P a predicate.
The other notations used for lists are :
    - x∈L : membership, meaning precisely : "there is an occurrence of x in
      list L",
    - =,≠ : list identity and its negation,
    - L⊀i⊁ : the ith element of list L,
    - L⊀i:j⊁ : the list constituted from the elements of L whose indexes are
      in the interval {i:j}; if i>j, L⊀i:j⊁ is the empty list,
    - ⊀⊁ : the empty list,
    - L||M : the concatenation of lists L and M,
    - #L : the length of list L.

                                *

(9) On lists, the elements of which are elements of an ordered set, the
relations <,≤,>,≥ are defined with their classical meaning i.e. :
    - the longest list is the greatest one,
    - when lists have the same length the elements with the smallest indexes
      have the biggest weight.

                                *

(10) A tuple is an element of a Cartesian product of sets. It is written as
    - a phrase in English, as "the pair constituted by the set int and the
      parameter attribute inout",
    - an enumeration of its constituents, enclosed in square brackets :
      "[stat,true,int]".
    - using predicates and/or functions in such a way that the ordering is
      clear, as
      "[f(a)|a∈S]", with S an ordered set,

"$[a|a\epsilon L \land P(a)]$", where L is a list and P a predicate.

If T is a tuple, $T[k]$ is its kth component.

*

(11) A mapping (or function) is, as usual, a set of pairs such that no two
different pairs have the same first constituent. More precisely, this
description uses the word "mapping" for those functions that are seen and
described as set of pairs.
    Pairs belonging to a mapping are written "$[a \rightarrow b]$" instead of "$[a,b]$". The
other notations are, for a mapping S :
    - $dom(S)=\{a|[a \rightarrow b]\epsilon S\}$, i.e. the domain of S,
    - $range(S)=\{b|[a \rightarrow b]\epsilon S\}$, i.e. the range of S,
    - $S[a]$: the object b such that $[a \rightarrow b]\epsilon S$.

*

(12) A labelled tuple is an element of a set P constructed from one or more
other given sets $S_1,S_2,...,S_n$. A labelled tuple is written as
    - a phrase in English, such as "the discrete basemode with lower bound 1,
      upper bound 7, and root int",
    - a "label", followed by an enumeration of the constituents of the tuple,
      between parentheses : "discr(int,1,7)".
A label, which is an identifier written in distinct type font, represents the
same set of labelled tuples, in the whole description.
    A label P constructed from sets $S_1,S_2,...,S_n$ behaves like a function in
that it has a domain, which is the Cartesian product $S_1 \times S_2 ... \times S_n$, and a
range. There is a difference : the range is a newly constructed set, and not
an already existing one.
    S_i will be called the ith domain of the label P.

*

(13) A form is the application of a function or operator to arguments. It
represents an object, or may represent any object in its range.
    A form is constituted by
    - a phrase in English, such as "the mode of V",
    - a "function name", followed by an enumeration of the arguments, between
      parentheses : "element(i,V,M)",
    - a unary operator followed by its operand : "-7",
    - a binary operator between its operands : "a=7".
Function names, which are identifiers, and operators represent the same
function in the whole description.

*

(14) A constituent of a pattern or an argument of a function may be a dash,
as in discr(int,1,-) or element(-,V,M). The dash behaves like an unnamed
variable ranging on the corresponding domain of the pattern or of the
argument of the function.

*

(15) Two constants, udf and unused, have a particular role. The first one,
udf, represents the undefined object. For example, if a function is applied

to an argument outside its domain, the value thus obtained is undefined and written udf whenever this description wants to make that explicit. The operations written x=udf, x≠udf are defined and have the value true or false. Any other operation on udf gives again udf.

The second constant unused is written in the description to point out situations that never occur.

*

(16) To avoid two-dimensional notations, the following conventions are used :

$$\Sigma(i \epsilon S){:}X_i \text{ means } \sum_{i \epsilon S} X_i$$

and similarly for the operators

$$\cup, \cap, \forall, \exists, \|, \Pi$$

where Π stands for the Cartesian product of sets.

2. CONVENTIONS FOR PART I

(1) Part I describes the objects of the language, together with the operations on them. Other objects and operations that are used in the description itself are also described in Part I.

*

(2) Part I is organized into sections. In turn, each section is divided into "paragraphs", separated by stars, like the one which follows.

*

(3) The first paragraph of a section defines the basic concepts (axioms) of the section; it is written in English. Comments and redundancies are frequent.

Example 1
(1) A discrete basemode is specified by a finite totally ordered set S and
    an interval {L:U} such that {L:U}$\subseteq$N. It is written discr(S,L,U).
(2) The values of basemode discr(S,L,U) are the values in the interval
    {L:U}.

In this example, S,L and U are variables. Their range is explained in words and their scope is the paragraph. The domains of the labelled tuples of the form discr(-,-,-) or in short discr(-) are thus well defined.
    Another role of such paragraphs is the introduction of technical terms, as seen in the following example :

Example 2
(3) The premode of a value is specified by
        a "class", which is either vclass, dclass, refcl, null or all.
        a "staticity", which is either stat or dyn,
        a "regionality", which is ...

*

(4) The other paragraphs of a section have a more formal appearance. Their role is to define properties of objects, written as predicates in "prop-phrases", and to describe operations on objects, written as function definitions in "def-phrases".

Example 3
For   each basemode BM=discr(S,L,U)
Prop   L$\leq$U
Def   min(BM)=L

This example states that the lower bound L is less than or equal to the upper bound U. It also defines a function of name "min", defined on the discrete basemodes and delivering the smallest value of the argument basemode.

*

(5) A "def-phrase", which starts with the keyword "Def", contains one or more function definitions.
    Each function definition has the following format :
        $f(X) = Y$

defined by P(X,Y)

in which "f" is an identifier which becomes the function name, "X" is an
n-tuple of variables whose range has been defined elsewhere in the paragraph,
"Y" is a new variable, or a pair of new variables written "V' of premode M",
and "P(X,Y)" a set of predicates defining the value of the function for each
n-tuple of objects in its domain.

Example 4
Def   string slice(V,i,j,P) = V' of premode P'
           defined by V' = V{i+1:j+1},
                      P' = string slice premode(P,j-i+1)

This format is however replaced by a shorter one whenever this is more
convenient, as in
Def   min(BM)=L
instead of
Def   min(BM)=X
           defined by X=L.

*

(6) In the description, the same function name may appear in several function
definitions. This is e.g. the case for "basemode" in Example 5.

Example 5
For   each mode M=mode(-,BM),
       each denotated mode DM=[-,M],
       each premode PRE=val(-,-,-,M)
Def   basemode(M)=BM,
       basemode(DM)=BM,
       basemode(PRE)=BM

In such a case, the domains which are specified in the several definitions
are disjoint, although similar in their meaning. If the same function name f
appears in several functions definitions with domains $D_1, D_2, \ldots, D_n$, this must
be seen as a piecewise definition for f in the domain $D_1 \cup D_2 \cup \ldots \cup D_n$.

*

(7) The function definitions in each formal paragraph use variables whose
ranges are specified by "for-phrases" and "let-phrases", these variables may
be linked together. In Example 3, the variables BM,S,L, and U are linked
together by the equality BM=discr(S,L,U) which expresses, among other
properties, that L and U must represent values in the set S. Such linkages
are specified in each paragraph by "for-", "let-" and "prop-phrases".
    Any object which the variable may represent must satisfy all the
properties that are specified for the variable in the whole scope of the
variable. For example, objects represented by U and L must satisfy L≥U.

*

(8) A "for-phrase", which starts with the keyword "For" usually followed by·
"each", contains one or more definitions of universally quantified variables.
    Each definition introduces one or more variables, specifies their range
and partially their linkage. The variables thus introduced are those used in
the paragraph for stating properties of objects (in "prop-phrases") or
defining functions on objects. This is done with English phrases, functions
and predicates as in

For   each basemode BM

where the range of the new variable BM is specified by the phrase "basemode".
If this variable definition is followed by

For   each value V of basemode BM

in the same paragraph, then V is a new variable with obvious range, but BM is
the variable already defined, V and BM being linked by the fact that any
object denoted by V must have the basemode denoted by BM.

A newly defined variable in a for-phrase is recognized as such only by the
fact that it has not been defined previously in the paragraph.

In Example 3, appears the phrase

For   each basemode BM=discr(S,L,U)

in which the four variables BM,S,L and U are defined at once, together with
their range and linkage as given by the properties of discrete basemodes.

A for-phrase is a place where dashes can be used in labelled tuples :

For   each basemode DM'=discr(-)

defines BM' as having the same range as BM (base modes) without defining
variables ranging over the components of the labelled tuples, as done for BM.

*

(9) A "let-phrase", starting with the keyword "Let", contains one or more
definitions of auxiliary variables.

Each definition in a let-phrase has the format

     "X ≡ expression"

  or "X such that predicate" (predicate which any value of X has to
     satisfy)

where X is a new variable, a labelled tuple containing new variables, or more
generally a pattern containing new variables.

Example 6

For   each premode PRE_1=val(-),

    each premode PRE_2=val(-)

       such that are compatible(PRE_1,PRE_2)

Let   PRE ≡ resulting premode(PRE_1,PRE_2)

Def   ...

If the variables are introduced in a pattern as in

Let   [RD,M] ≡ DENMODE,

it is assumed that the expression has a range containing only objects of the
stated pattern. Otherwise the variables denote udf.

*

(10) A "prop-phrase", which starts with the keyword "Prop" contains one or
more predicates.

The interpretation of these predicates is that the language is, and its
implementation must be, such that these predicates are satisfied.

*

(11) A "case-construct", has the format :

  Case C_1:S_1,

  Case C_2:S_2,

    ...

  Case C_n:S_n

often enclosed in parentheses.

Each S_i is a construct that could appear alone where the case-construct is used; all S_i's have the same range. All C_i's are predicates having the same domain and such that exactly one of them is true for any tuple in that domain.

In the last alternative of the case-construct, "<u>Case</u> C_n" is often written "<u>Case</u> <u>else</u>", and "<u>Case</u> <u>else</u> : unused" or "<u>Case</u> <u>else</u> : true" are omitted.

<u>Example 7</u>
<u>For</u>   each pair RD_1, RD_2 of readonlynesses

<u>Def</u>   most restrictive(RD_1, RD_2)=the readonlyness RD

defined by RD=(<u>Case</u> rdo$\epsilon\{RD_1, RD_2\}$:rdo,

<u>Case</u> <u>else</u>:write)

In some cases, a condition C_i is also defining new variables whose scope is the pair $C_i:S_i$. Again, a new variable is recognized as such by the fact that it has not been defined previously. Furthermore, if C_i is an equality condition, $\equiv$ is used instead of the equal sign.

<u>Example 8</u>
<u>For</u>   each pair of basemodes BM_1 and BM_2

<u>Def</u>   f(M)=a logical value T
        defined by T=(<u>Case</u> array($I_1,-,-$) $\equiv BM_1$

$\land$ array($I_2,-,-$) $\equiv BM_2$)

In this example, the case-condition is true if BM_1 and BM_2 are array basemodes, and at the same time variables I_1 and I_2 are defined with their range and linkage.

*

(12) The next paragraph uses the conventions which have been explained to define two functions. (Other definitions at the same level of simplicity will be made less pedantic.)

*

<u>For</u>   each list of lists LL=$\{L_i | i\epsilon\{1:n\}\}$
<u>Def</u>   flatten(LL)=the list L_1

defined by $L_1 = \|(i\epsilon\{1:n\}):L_i$
<u>For</u>   each non empty list L
<u>Def</u>   head(L)=L$\{1\}$,
        tail(L)=L$\{2:\#L\}$
        reverse(L)=the list L_2

defined by
        (<u>Case</u> #L=1:L_2=L,

<u>Case</u> <u>else</u> : reverse(tail(L))$\|\{$head(L)$\}$)
<u>For</u>   each X in L
<u>Def</u>   index(X,L)=the smallest number <u>such that</u> L$\{i\}$=X,

```
take out(X,L)=L⦃1:index(X,L)-1⦄
              ‖L⦃index(X,L)+1:#L⦄
```

3. CONVENTIONS FOR PART II

(1) The second part of the description defines the language itself in terms
of a context-free grammar in which each context-free rule is associated with
a set of attributes describing the static semantics, and elaboration
functions, describing the dynamic semantics.

> Example 9
>   <conditional part>
>   → <*boolean* expression> *THEN* <serial option> <else part>

     Pass   ENV↓,
     With   PRE ≡ <*boolean* expression>.PREMODE↑,
            D_1 ≡ <serial option>.DECLA↑,

            D_2 ≡ <else part>.DECLA↑

     Test   basemode(PRE)=discr(bool,-,-)
     Def   DECLA↑ ≡ D_1 ∪ D_2

     Dyn   ELAB=(E%):
            Step 1 : B% ← <*boolean* expression>.ELAB(E%)
            Step 2 :
                (Case(B%=true):← <serial option>.ELAB(E%),
                 Case(B%=false):← <else part>.ELAb(E%))

3.1. CONTEXT-FREE GRAMMAR

(1) Terminal symbols of the grammar are written as strings of characters in
the italic type font such as *BEGIN* or *:=*, or as strings of characters not in
the italic type font but enclosed into angular brackets. The lexical
structure of the latter is not part of this description.
   Thus, in the grammar :
   - <identifier> is the terminal symbol representing all identifiers.
   - the terminals representing the dyadic operators are the elements of the
first column of the table below, they are given the attributes PRIOR↑ which
is an integer and OP↑ which is a function defined in PART I. (Columns 2 and 3
of the table below).

dyadic operator	PRIOR↑	OP↑
<OR>	1	or
<XOR>	1	xor
<AND>	2	and
<=>	3	equal
</=>	3	non equal
<<>	3	less than
<<=>	3	less or equal
<>>	3	greater than
<>=>	3	greater or equal
<IN>	3	in
<+>	4	plus
<->	4	minus
<‖>	4	concat
<*>	5	times
</>	5	divide
<MOD>	5	mod
<REM>	5	rem

- the terminals representing the monadic operators are <-> and <NOT>, they
   are given the attribute OP↑ which is "minus" and "not" respectively.
   Furthermore, the terminal written <empty> is an explicit representation of
the empty string.
   Whenever the exact representation of an occurrence of a terminal T in a
program is needed, for example for testing if an identifier has been
declared, the function text(T)" is used.

                                    *

(2) Nonterminal symbols of the context-free grammar are written as strings of
lower case italic letters enclosed in angular brackets, as e.g. "<*statement*>"
or "<*expression*>", the initial symbol of the grammar being the nonterminal
written "<*program*>".

                                    *

(3)
For   each occurrence of a terminal or non terminal symbol S labelling a node
         N of a program tree
Def   text(S)=the string of characters representing the terminal string
                    derived from N,
         node(S)=N,
         empty(S)=true if the terminal string derived from N is the empty
                    string, and false otherwise,
         successor(S)=the terminal symbol which follows the terminal string
                    derived from N in the program text,
         predecessor(S)=the terminal symbol which precedes the terminal string
                    derived from N in the program text,
         descendants(S)=the set of nodes of the program subtree issued from N, N
                    excluded.
The notation $\overset{*}{\Rightarrow}$ is used as a particular case of the classical relation of
production in the theory of context free languages in the sense that $S \overset{*}{\Rightarrow} \alpha$
means that the occurrence of the symbol S in the program tree produces the
string α. $S \overset{*}{\not\Rightarrow} \alpha$ is the same as $\neg(S \overset{*}{\Rightarrow} \alpha)$.

                                    *

(4) Between the angular brackets surrounding a terminal or nonterminal
symbol, underlined texts may appear, as in "<*discrete expression*>" or
"<identifier *one*>". As far as the context-free grammar is concerned, these
texts are to be ignored ("<*discrete expression*>" and "<*expression*>" represent
the same nonterminal).
   In the attribute system however, these texts are used to distinguish
several occurrences of the same symbol in a grammar rule. For example :
   Test text(<identifier *one*>) ≠ text(<identifier *two*>).

                                    *

(5) The context-free rules have the usual Backus-Naur form (BNF), with two
exceptions. The first exception is trivial : the meta-symbol "::=" is
replaced by an arrow :

Example 10
<*mode definition statement*>
     → <*newmode definition*>
     | <*synmode definition*>

The second exception concerns the repetition of the same string of symbols in the same rule. Let t be a terminal or the empty string, and ϕ a string of terminals and nonterminals. The notation "L(t){ϕ}" represents a hypothetic nonterminal X which would be defined by "X→ϕ|X$t\phi$". Thus "L(t){ϕ}" can be read as "list of one or more ϕ's separated by t".

Example 11
<set mode denotation> → <read> SET (L(,) {<set element>})
stands for
<set mode denotation> → <read> SET (<xxx>)
<xxx> → <set element>
     | <set element>,<xxx>

If t is the empty string, the parentheses are omitted : L{ϕ}, and if ϕ is a unique symbol, the braces may be omitted : L(,)<set element>.

*

(6) The context-free grammar is such that at most one list of the form L(t){ϕ} appears in each rule. Thus, in the attributes, "L" refers unambiguously to the list of ϕ's which are supposed to be numbered from 1 upwards, so that ϕ_i stands for the ith occurrence of ϕ. Furthermore, if $\phi = \phi'\alpha\phi''$, α_i stands for the occurrence of α in ϕ_i. Finally, as a shorthand, $i\epsilon L$ is written instead of $i\epsilon\{1:\#L\}$.

Example 12
<set mode denotation>
        → <read> SET (L(,) <numbered set element>)
...
Def $\forall(i\epsilon L):$(<numbered set element>$_i$.SMODE↓ $\equiv$ MODE,
                "   .SDECLA↓ $\equiv$ $\cup(i\epsilon L):D_i$)

*

(7) In each section of Part II, the context-free rules are labelled (a),(b),(c), etc.., whereas the different alternatives of a same rule are numbered (1),(2),etc.

*

(8) To shorten the description, a small part of the context-free structure of the language has been described by "when phrases" in the attribute system instead of being put in context-free rules.

A "when-phrase" is a list of predicates which must be satisfied for a program to be correct. These predicates either restrict the set of correct productions of a context-free rule (see Example 13) or disambiguate an otherwise ambiguous set of rules (see Example 14).

Example 13
<step attribute> → STEP (<pos attribute><comma><sizes>)
When empty(<sizes>) ⟺ empty(<comma>)
expresses that the comma is not present iff there is no "sizes".

Example 14
The two rules
<primitive value denotation> → <identifier>, and
<structure field> → <identifier>

give an ambiguity since a *<structure field>* also is a *<primitive value denotation>*. This is solved by using a when-phrase :
  <u>When</u> M≠with(-).
where M is deduced from the attribute system.

3.2. ATTRIBUTE SYSTEM

(1) The static semantics of each construct of the language is specified by a set of (static) attributes attached to the context-free (CF) rules which describe the context-free form of the construct. These attributes are expressions which, given a particular occurrence of the construct in a particular program, denote a set of objects, such as modes or static environments, attached to the construct occurrence.

                                     *

(2) Attribute expressions are attached to the symbols of the grammar. They are written in association with the CF-rules in which these symbols appear. Given a program in the language, the objects denoted by these attributes are then attached to the nodes of the syntax tree of that program.
   The inherited attributes are called "descending", the synthesized ones being either "ascending" or "declared", depending on the way they are used.
   All attributes have a name, constituted by the grammar symbol itself together with an identifier followed by an arrow, pointing upwards(↑) for ascending attributes, downward (↓) for descending ones, and by an exclamation mark (!) for declared ones. The names of attributes attached to right-hand side nonterminals are always written completely (*<boolean expression>*.ENV↑ in rule (a) below), whereas only the identifier is used if the attribute is attached to the left-hand side nonterminal.

   <u>Example 15</u>
   (a) *<conditional part>*
         → *<boolean expression>* THEN *<serial statement>*
            <else part>
   <u>With</u>   ENV↓,
           PRE ≡ *<boolean expression>*.PREMODE↑,
           D₁ ≡ *<serial statement>*.DECLA↑,
           ...
   <u>Test</u>   basemode(PRE)=discr(bool,-,-)
   <u>Def</u>   *<boolean expression>*.ENV↓ ≡ ENV↓,
           <serial statement>.ENV↓ ≡ ENV↓
           ...

   (b) *<serial statement>*
         → *<labelling><action statement>*
   <u>With</u>   ENV↓,
           D ≡ *<labelling>*.DECLA↑
           ...
   <u>Def</u>   ...
           DECLA↑ ≡ D

   (c) *<labelling>*
            → *<label identifier>*
   <u>Let</u>   T ≡ text(*<label identifier>*),
           N ≡ node(*<label identifier>*)

<u>Def</u>   DECLA↑ ≡ define(T,N)
        ...

The set of attributes associated with a CF-rule is described using
"with-phrases", "when-phrases", "test-phrases", "let-phrases" and
"def-phrases". Together, they form a "paragraph".

                          *

(3) The "with-phrases" make explicit the names of all the attributes that are
used with the rule, but whose expression is written elsewhere.
   In rule (b), the descending attributes ENV↓ is thus introduced. An
expression for it must be written wherever <*serial statement*> appears on the
right of a rule, as in rule (a).
   The ascending attribute <*labelling*>.DECLA↑ is also introduced in the
with-phrase of (b)' where, in addition, it is given the local name D. The
scope of such a local name is the paragraph. An expression for
<*labelling*>.DECLA↑ must be written, as a synthesized attribute, whenever
<*labelling*> is the left-hand side of a CF-rule, as in rule (c) of the
example.

                          *

(4) "When-phrases" and "test-phrases" are sets of predicates which must be
true for a program to be correct. When-phrases, already discussed, express
constraints on the context-free structure, whereas test-phrases express
constraints on the attribute values. For example, in rule (a), the predicate
"basemode(PRE)=discr(bool,-,-)" tests if the expression delivers a Boolean
value.

                          *

(5) A "let-phrase" is the definition of one or more local identifiers whose
scope is the paragraph.

                          *

(6) Finally, a "def-phrase" is the definition of one or more attributes.
Each attribute definition is constituted by the attribute name followed by
the dotted equal sign, followed by an expression.

                          *

(7) Declared attributes are synthesized attributes used for the description
of the declaration mechanism of the language : they express the static
properties of declared items. Their identifiers start with a D and end with
an exclamation mark : DDENMODE!.
   Given a particular syntax tree, their value is not transmitted upwards or
downwards, but from the node of a declaration to the node where the
definition is needed.
   This can be seen in the following example, where the mode associated with
an identifier is expressed as the attribute N.DDENMODE! (rule (a)) of the
defining occurrence of the identifier (represented by its node N in a tree),
and retrieved (rule (b)) from the applied occurrence via identification of
the defining occurrence (also written N).

<u>Example 16</u>
(a) <*mode definition*>
        → <identifier>=<*defining mode denotation*>

<u>With</u> ...
    DM ≡ <u>*<defining* mode denotation></u>.DENMODE↑,
    T   ≡ text(<identifier>),
    N   ≡ node(<identifier>)
<u>Def</u>   D ≡ define(T,N),
    N.DDENMODE! ≡ DM,
    ...

(b) <*mode identifier*> → <identifier>
<u>With</u> ENV↓
<u>Let</u>   T ≡ text(<identifier>,
    N ≡ identify node(T,ENV↓)
<u>Test</u> N.DCAT!=mode(-),
    N≠udf
<u>Def</u>   NODE↑ ≡ N,
    DENMODE↑ ≡ N.DDENMODE!

*

(8) As an additional convention, attributes attached to different symbols but
having the same range and the same purpose in the description usually have
the same identifier. This is the case for e.g. ENV↓, PREMODE↑, etc. For
example, <...>.ENV↓ denotes a static environment, whatever the three dots
stand for.

*

(9) For CF-rules with only one nonterminal on the rhight, two shorthand
conventions are used. Let <*x*>→<*y*> be such a rule. Then
    <u>Pass</u> A↓,
         B↑
is equivalent to
    <u>With</u> A↓,
        B ≡ <*y*>.B↑
    <u>Def</u>   <*y*>.A↓ ≡ A↓,
        B↑ ≡ B

The shorthand "<u>Pass</u>   A↓" is also used if the attribute A↓ is to be passed to
all non terminals on the right hand side, as is often the case for ENV↓.
Finally for a pair of grammar rules of the form <*u*>→<*y*>|<*z*>, <right>.B↑ means
at the same time <*y*>.B↑ and <*z*>.B↑.

3.3. ELABORATION FUNCTIONS

(1) The dynamic semantics of each construct of the language is specified by
"elaboration functions" attached to the context-free rules which describe the
context-free form of the construct.
    Given a particular occurrence of the construct in a program, an occurrence
of the elaboration function can be seen as attached to the node of the
construct in the syntax tree.   This occurrence of the elaboration function
denotes a sequence of actions which, if executed, produce an object from the
objects given as arguments.
    The name of an elaboration function has the form N.ELAB, N.PREELAB or
N.POSTELAB where N denotes a node, i.e. is, as for static attributes, either
a symbol of the CF grammar or a variable ranging over program nodes.

Example 17
<conditional part>
    → <boolean expression> THEN <serial option> <else part>
...
Dyn   ELAB=(E%):
       Step 1 : B% ← <boolean expression>.ELAB(E%)
       Step 2 :
           (Case(B%=true): ← <serial option>.ELAB(E%),
            Case(B%=false): ← <else part>.ELAB(E%))

                            *

(2) The main conventions used in writing an elaboration function attached to
a left-hand-side symbol of a CF-rule are as follows:
- Variables denoting objects which are produced dynamically are identifiers
followed by "%", as in "E%".
- E% is always a variable ranging over dynamic environments.
- Elaboration functions are introduced by the phrase
       "Dyn   F=(args):"
where F is ELAB, PREELAB or POSTELAB, and in which "args" stands for a list
of variables representing the arguments. In Example 18, the only argument is
"E%".
- The functions themselves are written as a list of "steps", numbered from 1
upwards, to be executed one after the other.
- The result of a complete elaboration function is the result of the last
step which is executed. In Example 18, the function constituting the last
step depends on the value of B% when the step is executed.
- Case- and let-phrases are used with the same conventions as for Part I.

- The notation "itself.ELAB" is the name of the elaboration function of the
left-hand-side symbol of a CF-rule. It expresses a recursive call of the
function being described.
- To specify the result of an elaboration function, its last step is
sometimes written in the format
       Step n : ← O%
where O% denotes the result.

                            *

(3) The execution of a program is the execution of the elaboration function
ELAB attached to the initial node of its syntax tree. This may involve the
"activation of process instances", which are parallel executions of
elaboration functions. Within each process, all executions are done one
after the other, as described by the elaboration functions.

                            *

(4) The execution of an elaboration function is a sequence of actions. The
actions involve objects from the objects given as arguments, and their
sequence of actions is the sequence of action of the execution of each of its
step in turn.

                            *

(5) Each step is either simple or composed of other steps. A simple step is
written in the format
       X ← F(A)

where X is a new variable, or a pattern containing new variables, or is empty, F is a function name, and A, a list of arguments for F. It expresses that the function F is to be applied to A and that the new variables in X, if any, are to denote the result or components of the result. Argument and result transmission is by identity, i.e. the parameters of the function denote the argument passed to it for the execution, and F(A) denotes the result of the execution of F with arguments A. F is most often the elaboration function of a right-hand-side symbol, as in Example 18 : <else part>.ELAB(E%). In this case, the execution of the step is the execution of the elaboration function. Otherwise, F is a function defined in PART I and its execution is any sequence of actions which has the prescribed effect and produces the prescribed object. However, the parallel execution of functions involving the same object (with dynamic property) can be undefined (see M-objects, computation state in PART I).

                                    *

(6) A compound step may be of three forms, called "serial", "random" and "choice".
    A "serial step" expresses that its components (substeps of steps are transitively called components) are to be executed one after the other in the specified order.
    A serial step, "Step n", may be a list of substeps, numbered from 1 upwards : "Step n.1", "Step n.2", etc.   , to be executed in that order.
    "Step n" may also be written in the format
        $S(i \epsilon S):X_i \leftarrow F_i(A_i)$
in which S is an ordered set or a list. It means that for each value of i taken in the order of S, the steps "$X_i \leftarrow F_i(A_i)$" are to be executed one after the other.

    Example 18
    <declaration statement>
        → DCL L(,) <declaration>

    ...
    Dyn   ELAB=(E%):
           Let   E%$_0$ ≡ E%
           Step : $S(i \epsilon L):(E\%_i \leftarrow$ <declaration>$_i$.ELAB(E\%$_{i-1}$))

                                    *

(7) A "random step" expresses that its components are to be executed one after the other in an order that is completely or partially left undefined. A random step has one of the two formats
        R(substep 1,...,substep n)
or
        R(i∈S):(substep(i))
In the first case, a substep of the form ∀(j∈S)∈α stands for #S substeps consisting of occurrences of α where j has been respectively replaced by the elements of S.
In each case, this specifies that the substeps can be executed in any order, but one after the other. However if substep n° k makes use of an object obtained in substep n° i, then the latter must take place before the former. The actions within a substep must be executed in the specified order.

Example 19
(a) <powerset tuple> → [L(,) <powerset element>]
Dyn   ELAB=(E%):
       Step 1 : R(i∈L):A%$_i$ ← <powerset element>$_i$.ELAB(E%)

(b) <value enumeration>
       → := <start value><step><end value>
Dyn   ELAB=(E%):
       Step 1 : R([L% ← <start value>.ELAB(E%),
                   S% ← <step>.ELAB(E%),
                   U% ← <end value>.ELAB(E%))

*

(8) A "choice step" is similar in meaning with a step in which the function
to be executed is chosen via a case-phrase (see Example 18). The format of a
choice step is
    (Choice((i∈S):C$_i$) : X$_i$ ← F$_i$(A$_i$),

    Choice else : X ← F(A))
The meaning of this is expressed by the case-phrase
    (Case C$_1$: X$_1$ ← F$_1$(A$_1$),

    Case C$_2$: X$_2$ ← F$_2$(A$_2$),

    ...

    Case C$_n$: X$_n$ ← F$_2$(A$_n$),
    Case else : X ← F(A))
A choice step is written whenever a case-phrase cannot, as in Example 21.

Example 20
<case statement>
    → CASE <case selector list>
    OF <range list>
    L <case part> <case else part> ESAC
Dyn   ELAB=(E%):
       Step 1 : V% ← <case selector list>.ELAB(E%)
       Step 2 :
           (Choice((i∈L):V%∈C$_i$) : ← <case part>$_i$.ELAB(E%),
           Choice else : ← <case else part>.ELAB(E%))

*

(9) In each execution of the elaboration function of a process instance, the
mechanism of execution is functional; functions are called, and when their
execution is terminated, an object is returned to the calling point.
    This mechanism can be seen as using a stack for functions that have been
called but are not yet terminated. This is not adequate for expressing the
dynamic semantics of "breaks" such as the "goto statement".
    To express such semantics, an "exit function" is used, whose name is exit.
    If the execution of an elaboration function calls exit(args), "args"
standing for a list of arguments, the effect is the following :
- all elaboration functions on the stack are considered in turn, in a "last
  called first considered" order,
- the considered elaboration function is entered at its "trap entry" with the
  arguments of the exit function,
- if the trap is successful, the execution of the considered elaboration
  function is continued from its "trap entry point", otherwise the next
  function on the stack is considered.
    Example 21 shows a partial description of the "goto".

Example 21
\<do body\> → *\<serial option\>*
Pass   D ≡ DECLA↑
Dyn   ELAB=(E%):
       Step : ← *\<serial option\>*.ELAB(E%,all)
       TRAP=(CLASS,NODE,E%$_e$,O%]):

       Case(CLASS=goto
             ∧ NODE∈labels(D)
             ∧ compatible(E%$_e$,E%)):

             Step : ← *\<serial\>*.ELAB(E%,NODE)

\<goto statement\> → *GOTO \<label identifier\>*
Let   T ≡ text(*\<label identifier\>*),
       N ≡ identify node(T,ENV↓)
Dyn   ELAB=(E%):
       Step : exit(goto,[N,E%])

A trap entry is either empty, i.e. does not appear at all, in which case
the trap is never successful, or has the following format :
    TRAP=(args):
    (Case C$_1$:F$_1$,

       ...
      Case C$_n$:F$_2$)

where "args" stands for the arguments.
    If one of the C$_i$, which are disjoint conditions, is true, the trap is

successful, and the subsequent execution is that of F$_i$, otherwise the trap is

not successful.

                                *

(8) {# In the whole description comments are put between special brackets
like this sentence #}.

PART I : SEMANTIC PRIMITIVES

0. GENERALITIES

0.1. HARDWARE

(1) The language CHILL is machine oriented in the sense that some hardware
    aspects are taken into account under the form of properties that
    implementations are assumed to satisfy.

(2) There is a memory M taken as a string of addressable units called
    "words". Each word has an "address" which is an integer.

(3) Each word is a string of bit positions of a length, written width, which
    is implementation defined. Words with consecutive addresses are said to
    be contiguous. If W_1 is a word with address A, and W_2 the word with
    address A+1, bit positions $W_1\{j\}$ and $W_1\{j+1\}$, $(1 \leq j \leq width-1)$, are said to
    be contiguous; so are bit positions $W_1\{width\}$ and $W_2\{1\}$.

(4) A "bit" in the usual sense is stored in each bit position. When a string
    S of bits is stored in a string of contiguous bit positions P, it is
    assumed that #S=#P and that $S\{i\}$ is stored in $P\{i\}$, $(1 \leq i \leq \#S)$.

(5) There are bit strings to which the hardware attaches special properties,
    in particular the strings representing hardware integers. The
    implementation defines an interval {minint:maxint} which contains those
    integers that can be efficiently handled. This interval is written int,
    it is the set of implemented integers.

(6) There are registers, which are strings of bit positions; the bit string
    stored in a register can generally be efficiently handled. Registers can
    be specified in some program parts by means of implemented identifiers :
    the register identifiers. These specifications are to be considered
    hints to the implementation.

0.2. OBJECTS, M-OBJECTS, COMPUTATION STATE

(1) The execution of a CHILL program consists of "actions"; actions involve
    "objects", mainly "values" and "locations".

(2) Some objects have dynamically variable properties (i.e. relationships
    with other objects); they are called "M-objects". E.g. locations are
    M-objects, their dynamic property is their contents.

(3) M-objects are put into existence by "creating actions"; existing
    M-objects are recorded in a "computation state" (abbreviated c.s in the
    sequel). Thus a creating action changes c.s.

(4) The c.s. also records the dynamic properties of the existing M-objects.
    Actions changing dynamic properties of M-objects thus also change c.s.

(5) Each M-object has a descriptor, i.e. another object allowing to recover
    the M-object and its dynamic properties. E.g. locations are described by
    references which are values.

(6) Actions changing the c.s. are said to have an "effect". The effect of an action changing the dynamic property p of an M-object O into v is written p(O) becomes v.

0.3 PROGRAM ELABORATION

(1) The actions which constitute the execution of a program are organized in "sequences of actions". At a given time, several sequences of actions can be executed simultaneously (in parallel); the number of sequences being executed can vary in time (it is dynamic).

(2) Each sequence of actions is specified by one "process instance" which is an M-object. A process instance has a "state" as its dynamic property.

(3) When the state of a process instance is active or reactivated(V), the execution of the sequence of actions it specifies is possible; otherwise no action of the specified sequence can be executed.

(4) The actions changing the state of process instances are called "synchronization actions". Some synchronization actions are indivisible, meaning that no other action involving the same objects may take place at the same time. An indivisible action A is written action:A.

(5) The effect or the object produced by the parallel execution of actions modifying the same M-object is undefined.

(6) A CHILL program is a sentence as defined in PART II of this description, mainly by means of a context-free grammar. To each CHILL program there corresponds thus a syntactic tree. A part of program "generated" by a node of the tree is called a program phrase. A program phrase may specify operations on objects and/or have effects; it may in turn "deliver" an object as its result.

(7) The execution of a CHILL program starts with the creation of a ("main") process instance from the root node of the program tree, the dynamic environment preenv% and an implementation defined argument list. Thus setting up the initial computation state is recording this only process instance in the active state.

1. VALUES

(1) A value is an element of some specified set such as the set of integers
    (written int) and the set {false,true} of Boolean values (written bool).

(2) Some program phrases such as expressions, when executed, deliver values,
    more precisely instances of values. Each such phrase is given a unique
    "value premode" specifying properties of the value instances it may
    deliver.   This premode is also attached to each delivered value
    instance. Generally, the premode specifies, for value instances,
    properties that are more restrictive than those of the values themselves.

(3) This description deals most of the time with value instances, they will
    simply be called values and a premode will be explicitly given to each of
    them; it will be called "the premode of the value".

(4) The premode PRE of a value is specified by
    - a "class" CL which is dclass, vclass, refcl, null, or all.
    - a "regionality" RG which is either reg or nreg,
    - a "staticity" ST which is either stat or dyn, and
    - a "mode" M.
    PRE is written val(CL,RG,ST,M).

(5) A mode M is specified by
    - a "novelty" NV which is either base or new(N) where N is the program
      node of a *new mode definition*, and
    - a "base mode" BM.
    M is written mode(NV,BM).

(6) Each value has a class, a regionality, a staticity, a mode, a novelty and
    a base mode which are those specified by its premode.

(7) - The class of a value restricts its use, especially according to its
      novelty when the class is vclass.
    - The regionality of a value restricts its use outside some "critical
      region".
    - The staticity of a value specifies whether or not some properties of
      (composite) values are known at compile time.
    - The base mode of a value is specific to some basic properties of the
      value.

(8) In general, the same value when delivered by different program phrases
    may be given different premodes and even different base modes.
    Conversely, each base mode BM specifies a set of values, those that can
    be given that base mode. This set is called the "set of BM".

(9) Values are classified according to their base mode as follows : a value
    is either
    - a "discrete value" and has a discrete base mode, or
    - a "powerset value" and has a powerset base mode, or
    - a "reference value" and has a reference base mode, or
    - a "general procedure value" and has a general procedure base mode,
    - a "composite value" and has a composite base mode, or
    - the "undefined value".

(10) A denotated mode is a pair [RD,M] where RD is a "readonlyness" and M is
     a mode; a readonlyness is either rdo or write.

(11) Notational conventions :
     wherever PRE=val(-,-,-,M), M=mode(-,BM) and DM=[-,M], PRE, M or DM may
     be used instead of BM, and PRE or DM instead of M.

*

For   each base mode BM
Def   set(BM) = the set of BM,

card(BM)=#set(BM)

*

<u>For</u>   each premode PRE₁=val(-,RG,stat,M₁),

each mode M₂

<u>such that</u> is value convertible (PRE₁,M₂)

<u>Def</u>   value conversion premode(PRE₁,M₂)=the premode PRE

defined by
PRE=val(vclass,RG,stat,M₂)

<u>For</u>   each value V₁ of premode PRE₁

<u>Def</u>   value conversion(V₁,PRE₁,M₂)=the value V₂ of premode PRE₂

defined by V₂= a value deduced from V₁ in an implementation defined

way,
PRE₂=value conversion premode(PRE₁,M₂)

*

<u>For</u>   each premode PRE₁=val(-,-,ST,-),

each mode M₂

<u>Def</u>   is value convertible(PRE₁,M₂)=T of premode dpre(bool)

defined by
T = (ST=stat)
∧ ¬ has the synchro prop(M₂)

∧ ∃ M:(size(M₂)=size(M)

∧ is comptatible with(PRE₁,M))

*

<u>For</u>   each function F∈{or, xor, and, equal, nonequal, less than, less or
equal, greater than, greater or equal, in, plus,
minus, concat, times, divide, mode, rem},
each pair PRE₁, PRE₂ of value premodes

<u>Def</u>   is operable(F,PRE₁,PRE₂)=T of premode dpre(bool)

defined by
T=(apply 2 premode(F,PRE₁,PRE₂)≠udf)

<u>For</u>   each function F₁∈{minus,not}

<u>Def</u>   is operable(F₁,PRE₁)=T₁ of premode dpre(bool)

defined by
T₁=(apply 1 premode(F₁,PRE₁)≠udf)

1.1. DISCRETE VALUES

(1) The values of a discrete base mode form an interval of a finite totally
ordered set S.

(2) A discrete base mode BM is specified by a finite totally ordered set S
and two values MIN and MAX in S such that MIN ≤ MAX. The values of base
mode BM are those in the interval {MIN:MAX}.
BM is written discr(S,MIN,MAX)
S is called the "root" of BM.
(3) A discrete base mode BM may have "holes", i.e. values in set(BM) for
which the program has no notation.
(4) The root of a discrete base mode is either
- the set of implemented integers written int, or
- the set of logical values written bool, or
- the set of CCITT characters written char, or
- a program defined set, written set(-).
(5) Accordingly, a discrete value is either
- an "integer value" and has a integer base mode of root int, or
- a "boolean value" and has a boolean base mode of root bool, or
- a "character value" and has a character base mode of root char, or
- a "declared set value" and has a declared set base mode, the root of
which is a declared set.

*

For   each premode PRE=val(-,RG,ST,mode(-,discr(-)))
Prop   RG=nreg,
         ST=stat

*

For   each base mode BM=discr(R,MIN,MAX)
Def   min(BM)=MIN of premode dpre(R),
         max(BM)=MAX of premode dpre(R)

*

For   each mode M=mode(NV,discr(S,X_1,X_2)),

         each pair of values V_1, V_2 of mode M such that V_1 ≤ V_2

Def   range mode(V_1,V_2,M)=mode(NV,discr(S,V_1,V_2))

*

For   each base mode BM=discr(-)
Def   no holes(BM)=true if BM has no holes, false otherwise
For   each value V of base mode BM
Def   is a hole(V,BM)=true if V is a hole, false otherwise,
         index(V,BM)=#{min(BM):V}

*

For   each value premode PRE
             such that base mode(PRE)=discr(R,-,-),
         each function F∈{succ,pred}
Let PRE_1 ≡ resulting premode(PRE,PRE)

Def   apply 1 premode(F,PRE)=PRE_1

For   each static environment ENV
Def   identify apply 1 exceptions(F,PRE,ENV) = an exception map XS
             defined by
                  XS=map(ENV,{OVERFLOW})

For   each exception map XM,
        each value V of premode PRE
Let   EXC ≡ select exception(XM,*OVERFLOW*),
        {MIN:MAX} ≡ R
Def   apply 1(F,V,PRE,XM)=V' of premode PRE₁

            defined by
              (Case F=succ :
                V'=(Case V=MAX:EXC,
                      Case is a hole(V+1,PRE):
                              apply 1(succ,V+1,PRE,XM),
                      Case else:V+1),
                  Case F=pred :
                    V'=(Case V=MIN:EXC,
                          Case is a hole(V-1,PRE):
                              apply 1(pred,V-1,PRE,XM),
                      Case else:V-1))

                               *

For   each pair of value premodes PRE₁,PRE₂

            such that basemode(PRE₁)=discr(-)

                    ∧ are compatible(PRE₁,PRE₂),

        each function F∈{equal, non equal, less than,
                         less or equal; greater than, greater or equal}
Def   apply 2 premode(F,PRE₁,PRE₂)=dpre(bool)

For   each static environment ENV
Def   identify apply 2 exceptions(F,PRE₁,PRE₂,ENV) = an exception map XS

            defined by
                XS=map(ENV,{})
For   each value V₁ of premode PRE₁,

        each value V₂ of premode PRE₂

Def   apply 2(F,V₁,PRE₁,V₂,PRE₂,-)=B of premode dpre(bool)

            defined by B=(Case F=equal:$V_1=V_2$,

                          Case F=non equal:$V_1 \neq V_2$,

                          Case F=less than:$V_1 < V_2$,

                          Case F=less or equal:$V_1 \leq V_2$,

                          Case F=greater than:$V_1 > V_2$,

                          Case F=greater or equal:$V_1 \geq V_2$)

1.1.1 INTEGER VALUES

(1) The base mode of an integer value is written discr(int,MIN,MAX) where
    int={minint:maxint} and {MIN:MAX} ⊆ int.

                               *

For   each integer base mode BM
Prop   no holes(BM)
For   each value V of base mode BM

<u>Def</u>   num(V,BM)=V of premode dpre(int)

                              *

<u>For</u>   each pair of value premodes PRE_1,PRE_2
           <u>such that</u> base mode(PRE_1)=discr(int,-,-),
                       base mode(PRE_2)=discr(int,-,-),
                       are compatible(PRE_1,PRE_2)
<u>Let</u> PRE_3 ≡ resulting premode(PRE_1,PRE_2)
<u>For</u>   each function F∈{plus, minus, times, divide, mod, rem}
<u>Def</u>   apply 2 premode(F,PRE_1,PRE_2)=PRE_3
<u>For</u>   each static environment ENV
<u>Def</u>   identify apply 2 exceptions(F,PRE_1,PRE_2,ENV) = an exception map XS
           defined by
                XS=map(ENV,{*OVERFLOW*})
<u>For</u>   each value V_1 of premode PRE_1,
       each value V_2 of premode PRE_2,

       each exception map XM
<u>Def</u>   apply 2(F,V_1,PRE_1,V_2,PRE_2,XM)=V of premode PRE_3

           defined by
           <u>Let</u>   V' ≡ (<u>Case</u> F=plus:V_1+V_2,
                       <u>Case</u> F=minus:V_1-V_2,
                       <u>Case</u> F=times:V_1*V_2,
                       <u>Case</u> F=divide:V_1÷V_2,
                       <u>Case</u> F=mod:V_1 <u>mod</u> V_2,
                       <u>Case</u> F=rem:V_1 <u>rem</u> V_2),
          V=(<u>Case</u> V'∈int:V',
             <u>Case</u> <u>else</u>:select exception(XM,*OVERFLOW*)

                              *

<u>For</u>   each premode PRE=val(CL,-,-,mode(NV,discr(int,-,-)))
<u>Let</u> PRE_1 ≡ val(CL,nreg,stat,mode(NV,discr(int,minint,maxint)))
<u>For</u>   each function F∈{minus,abs}
<u>Def</u>   apply 1 premode(F,PRE)=PRE_1
<u>For</u>   each static environment ENV
<u>Def</u>   identify apply 1 exceptions(F,PRE,ENV) = an exception map XS
           defined by
                XS=map(ENV,{*OVERFLOW*})
<u>For</u>   each value V of premode PRE,
       each exception map XM
<u>Def</u>   apply 1(F,V,PRE,XM)=V_1 of premode PRE_1

           defined by
           (<u>Case</u> F=minus:V_1=(<u>Case</u> -V∈int:-V,

                            <u>Case</u> <u>else</u>:select exception(XM,*OVERFLOW*)),
             <u>Case</u> F=abs:V_1=(<u>Case</u> V ≥0:V,

$$\underline{Case}\ V<0:apply\ 1(minus,V,PRE,XM)))$$

1.1.2 BOOLEAN VALUES

(1) The base mode of a Boolean value is written discr(bool,MIN,MAX) where
   bool={false,true}, ordered by false < true, and {MIN:MAX} $\subseteq$ {false:true}

*

For   each Boolean base mode BM
Prop no holes(BM)
For   each value V of base mode BM
Def   num(V,BM)=V_1 of premode dpre(int)

      defined by V_1 $\equiv$ ($\underline{Case}$ V=false:0,

                       $\underline{Case}$ $\underline{else}$: 1)

*

For   each pair of Boolean value premodes PRE_1,PRE_2

      $\underline{such\ that}$ are compatible(PRE_1,PRE_2),

      each function Fϵ\{and,or,xor\}
Let PRE_3 $\equiv$ resulting premode(PRE_1,PRE_2)
Def   apply 2 premode(F,PRE_1,PRE_2)=PRE_3

For   each static environment ENV
Def   identify apply 2 exceptions(F,PRE_1,PRE_2,ENV) = an exception map XS

         defined by
            XS=map(ENV,\{\})
For   each value V_1 of premode PRE_1,

      each value V_2 of premode PRE_2

Def   apply 2(F,V_1,PRE_1,V_2,PRE_2,-)=V of premode PRE_3

         defined by V=($\underline{Case}$ F=and:$V_1 \wedge V_2$,

                    $\underline{Case}$ F=or:$V_1 \vee V_2$,

                    $\underline{Case}$ F=xor:($V_1 \vee V_2$) $\wedge$ $\neg$ ($V_1 \wedge V_2$))

*

For   each Boolean value premode PRE
Let PRE_1 $\equiv$ resulting premode(PRE,PRE)
Def   apply 1 premode(not,PRE)=PRE_1

For   each static environment ENV
Def   identify apply 1 exceptions(not,PRE,ENV) = an exception map XS
         defined by
            XS=map(ENV,\{\})
For   each value V of premode PRE,
      each exception map XM

<u>Def</u>   apply 1(not,V,PRE,XM)=¬V of premode PRE₁

1.1.3 CHARACTER VALUES

(1) The base mode of a character value is written discr(char,MIN,MAX) where
    char is the ordered set defined by the CCITT alphabet n°5, and where
    {MIN:MAX} ⊆ char.

                              *

<u>For</u>   each character base mode BM
<u>Prop</u>   no holes(BM)
<u>For</u>   each value of base mode BM
<u>Def</u>   num(V,BM)=the integer number I of premode dpre(int)
           defined by the CCITT alphabet n°5

1.1.4 DECLARED SET VALUES

(1) A declared set S is specified by a list IDL of n elements which are
    either identifier texts or are occurrences of none.
    S is written set(IDL); all identifier texts in IDL are different.
(2) The set S is the set of pairs defined by S={[IDL↓i↓,i-1]|i∈{1:#IDL}} ;
    the total ordering is such that j<k ⇔ [IDL↓j↓,j-1] < [IDL↓k↓,k-1].
(3) The base mode of a value of the declared set S is written
    discr(S,MIN,MAX) where {MIN:MAX}⊆S.
(4) An element of S of the form [none,-] is called a hole for any base mode
    discr(S,-,-). An element of the form [ID,N], where ID is an identifier
    text, is not a hole, and ID denotes the corresponding value [ID,N] of S.

                              *

<u>For</u>   each base mode BM=discr(set(IDL),-,-)
<u>Prop</u>   no holes(BM) ⇔ ∀(V∈ set(BM)):V≠[none,-]
<u>For</u>   each value V of base mode BM
<u>Prop</u>   is a hole(V,BM) ⇔ V=[none,-]
<u>For</u>   each identifier text ID
          <u>such that</u> [ID,N] ∈ set(BM)
<u>Def</u>   set value(ID,BM)=[ID,N] of premode dpre(BM),
           num(V,BM)=N of premode dpre(int)

                              *

<u>For</u>   each list IDL of identifier texts,
           each list NUML of N different nonnegative numbers
<u>Let</u>   N ≡ max(NUML)
<u>Def</u>   reorder(IDL,NUML)=the list IDL₁

           defined by IDL₁=↓(<u>Case</u> i-1∈NUML: IDL↓index(i-1,NUML)↓,

                         <u>Case else</u>:↓none|i∈{1:N}↓

1.2 POWERSET VALUES

(1) The values of a powerset base mode are the subsets of an interval {L:U}
    of a totally ordered set R.
(2) A powerset base mode BM is specified by a discrete mode
    M=mode(-,discr(-,L,U)); it is written poset(M). The values with base
    mode BM are all the subsets of {L:U}.

                                    *

<u>For</u>   each base mode BM=poset(M)
<u>Def</u>   member mode(BM)=M

                                    *

<u>For</u>   each mode M=mode(-,poset(M₁)),

       each subset S of set(M₁)

<u>Def</u>   powerset tuple value(S,M)=S of premode PRE
          defined by PRE=val(vclass,nreg,stat,M)

                                    *

<u>For</u>   each pair of value premodes PRE₁,PRE₂

          <u>such that</u> base mode(PRE₁)=poset(-),

                     base mode(PRE₂)=poset(-),

                     are compatible(PRE₁,PRE₂)

<u>Let</u>   PRE₃=resulting premode(PRE₁,PRE₂)

<u>For</u>   each function F∈{or,and,xor,minus}
<u>Def</u>   apply 2 premode(F,PRE₁,PRE₂)=PRE₃

<u>For</u>   each static environment ENV
<u>Def</u>   identify apply 2 exceptions(F,PRE₁,PRE₂,ENV) = an exception map XS

          defined by
               XS=map(ENV,{})
<u>For</u>   each function F'∈{equal, non equal, greater than,
                         greater or equal, less than, less or equal}
<u>Def</u>   apply 2 premode(F',PRE₁,PRE₂)=dpre(bool)

<u>For</u>   each static environment ENV
<u>Def</u>   identify apply 2 exceptions(F',PRE₁,PRE₂,ENV) = an exception map XS

          defined by
               XS=map(ENV,{})
<u>For</u>   each value V₁ of premode PRE₁,

       each value V₂ of premode PRE₂,

       each exception map XM
<u>Def</u>   apply 2(F,V₁,PRE₁,V₂,PRE₂,XM)=V of premode PRE₃

          defined by V=(<u>Case</u> F=or:V₁ ∪ V₂,

                        <u>Case</u> F=and:V₁ ∩ V₂,

                        <u>Case</u> F=xor:(V₁ \ V₂) ∪ (V₂ \ V₁),

                        <u>Case</u> F=minus:V₁ \ V₂)

       apply 2(F',V₁,PRE₁,V₂,PRE₂,XM)=V' of premode dpre(bool)

```
defined by V'=(Case F'=equal:V₁=V₂,
```

defined by $V'=(\underline{Case}\ F'=\text{equal}:V_1=V_2,$

$\underline{Case}\ F'=\text{non equal}:V_1\neq V_2,$

$\underline{Case}\ F'=\text{greater than}:V_2\subset V_1,$

$\underline{Case}\ F'=\text{greater or equal}:V_2\subseteq V_1,$

$\underline{Case}\ F'=\text{less than}:V_1\subset V_2,$

$\underline{Case}\ F'=\text{less or equal}:V_1\subseteq V_2)$

*

For   each powerset value premode PRE_1,

       each premode PRE_2

        <u>such that</u> member mode(PRE_1)=mode(PRE_2)

Def   apply 2 premode(in,PRE_2,PRE_1)=dpre(bool)

For   each static environment ENV
Def   identify apply 2 exceptions(in,PRE_1,PRE_2,ENV) = an exception map XS

       defined by
         XS=map(ENV,{})
For   each value V_1 of premode PRE_1,

       each value V_2 of premode PRE_2,

       each exception map XM
Def   apply 2(in, V_1,PRE_1,V_2,PRE_2,XM)=T of premode dpre(bool)

       defined by $T=V_2\in V_1$

*

For   each powerset value premode PRE
Def   apply 1 premode(not,PRE)=PRE
For   each static environment ENV
Def   identify apply 1 exceptions(not,PRE,ENV) = an exception map XS
       defined by
         XS=map(ENV,{})
For   each value V of premode PRE,
       each exception map XM
Def   apply 1(not,V,PRE,XM)=V' of premode PRE
       defined by V'=set(member mode(PRE))\V
Let $PRE_1\equiv$ val(vclass,nreg,stat,member mode(PRE))

For   each function $F\in\{min,max\}$
Def   apply 1 premode(F,PRE)=PRE_1

For   each static environment ENV
Def   identify apply 1 exceptions(F,PRE,ENV) = an exception map XS
       defined by
         XS=map(ENV,{EMPTY}),
      apply 1(F,V,PRE,XM)=V_1 of premode PRE_1

       defined by
         V_1=(<u>Case</u> V={}:select exception(XM,*EMPTY*),

           <u>Case else</u> :
              (<u>Case</u> F=min:min(V),
              <u>Case</u> F=max:max(V)))

1.3 REFERENCES

(1) A reference is either a value "referring to" a location or the value
    null. For each location, there is only one reference and each reference
    except null refers to only one location. From a reference which is not
    null, the location referred to can be obtained.
(2) A reference is either
    - a "bound reference",
    - a "free reference",
    - a "row", or
    - a "location descriptor".

*

For   each pair of value reference premodes PRE_1 and PRE_2

      such that are compatible(PRE_1,PRE_2)

      each function $F \in$ {equal, non equal}
Def   apply 2 premode(F,PRE_1,PRE_2)=dpre(bool)

For   each static environment ENV
Def   identify apply 2 exceptions(F,PRE_1,PRE_2,ENV) = an exception map XS

      defined by
          XS=map(ENV,{})
For   each value R_1 of premode PRE_1,

      each value R_2 of premode PRE_2,

      each exception map XM
Def   apply 2(F,R_1,PRE_1,R_2,PRE_2,XM)=B of premode dpre(bool)

      defined by B=(Case F=equal:R_1=R_2,

                Case F=non equal:$R_1 \neq R_2$).

1.3.1 BOUND REFERENCES

(1) A bound reference, when it is not null, refers to a "static referable"
    location.
(2) The base mode BM of a bound reference is specified by a readonlyness RD
    and a mode M; it is written ref(RD,M).
(3) When the reference is not null, RD and M specify respectively the
    readonlyness and the mode of the location referred to.

*

For   each location premode PRE=loc(RG,stat,refble,RD,M)
Def   reference premode(PRE)=val(refcl,RG,stat,mode(base,ref(RD,M)))
For   each location L of premode PRE
Def   reference(L,PRE)=the value R of premode PRE_1

      defined by R=the bound reference referring to L,
              PRE_1=reference premode(PRE)

*

For   each value premode PRE

> <u>such that</u> base mode(PRE)=ref(-)
> each function F∈{succ, pred}

<u>Def</u> apply 1 premode(F,PRE)=PRE
<u>For</u> each static environment ENV
<u>Def</u> identify apply 1 exceptions(F,PRE,ENV) = an exception map XS
>   defined by
>   XS=map(ENV,{*RANGEFAIL,EMPTY*})

<u>For</u> each exception map XM,
>   each value R of premode PRE
>   <u>such that</u> R is null or refers to a location L,
>   L=A⌊i⌋,
>   A is an array location with n elements

<u>Let</u> PRE' ≡ dereference premode(PRE,none),
>   j ≡ (<u>Case</u> R=null:none,
>   <u>Case else</u>:(<u>Case</u> F=succ:i+1,
>   <u>Case</u> F=pred:i-1))

<u>Def</u> apply 1(F,R,PRE,XM)=R' of premode PRE
>   defined by R'=
>   (<u>Case</u> R=null:select exception(XM,*EMPTY*),
>   <u>Case else</u>:(<u>Case</u> j∉{1:n}:select exception(XM,*RANGEFAIL*),
>   <u>Case else</u>:reference(A⌊j⌋,PRE')))

1.3.2 FREE REFERENCES

(1) A free reference, when it is not null, refers to a "static location"
    (referable or not).
(2) The base mode of a free reference is written ptr.
(3) From a free reference which is not null, the location referred to and its
    premode can be obtained.

                                  *

<u>For</u> each free reference P referring to a location of premode PRE
<u>Def</u> pointed location premode(P)=PRE

                                  *

<u>For</u> each location premode PRE=loc(RG,-,nref,RD,M),
>   each location L of premode PRE,
<u>Def</u> reference premode(PRE)=val(dclass,RG,stat,mode(base,ptr)),
>   reference(L,PRE)=the value P of premode reference premode(PRE)
>   referring to L

1.3.3 ROWS

(1) A row R, when it is not null, refers to a "dynamic referable" location,
    hence to a location whose base mode is necessarily string(-), array(-),
    or struct(-).
(2) The base mode BM of a row is specified by a readability RD and a mode M;
    it is written row(RD,M).

(3) When the row is not null, RD and M are respectively the readonlyness and
the mode of the location referred to.

*

For   each location premode PRE=loc(-,RG,dyn,refble,RD,M)
Def   reference premode(PRE)=val(refcl,RG,stat,mode(base,row(RD,M)))
For   each location L of premode PRE
Def   reference(L,PRE)=the value R of premode PRE_1

       defined by R=the row value referring to L,
                  PRE_1=reference premode(PRE)

1.3.4. LOCATION DESCRIPTORS

(1) A location descriptor when it is not null refers to a static location; it
is used to describe result transmission of procedures.
(2) The base mode BM of a location descriptor is specified by a mode M, it is
written descr(M), where M specifies the mode of the location referred to.

*

For   each static location L of premode PRE
Let   M ≡ mode(PRE)
Def   descr(L,PRE)=D of premode PRE_1

        defined by
            D=the location descriptor describing L,
            PRE_1=val(unused,nreg,stat,mode(base,descr(M)))

*

For   each mode RM=mode(base,descr(M)),
       each location descriptor D of mode BM
Def   dedescr(D,RM)=the location L of mode M
          defined by
              L=(Case D=null:udf,
                 Case else:the location described by D)

1.4 PROCEDURES VALUES

(1) Procedure values are procedure clusters with a base mode
proc(-,-,-,general(-)), or the procedure cluster null (see 4).

*

For   each procedure premode PRE_1,

       each procedure premode PRE_2

          such that are compatible(PRE_1,PRE_2),

       each function F∈{equal,nonequal}
Def   apply 2 premode(F,PRE_1,PRE_2)=dpre(bool)

For   each static environment ENV
Def   identify apply 2 exceptions(F,PRE_1,PRE_2,ENV) = an exception map XS

       defined by
              $XS=map(ENV,\{\})$
For   each value V_1 of remode PRE_1,

       each value V_2 of premode PRE_2,

       each exception map XM
Def   apply 2(F,V_1,PRE_1,V_2,PRE_2,XM)=T of premode dpre(bool)

       defined by
              T=(Case F=equal:$V_1=V_2$,

                 Case F=nonequal:$V_1 \neq V_2$)

1.5 COMPOSITE VALUES

(1) A composite value is a list of n "components" which are values. Thus,
    two composite values are equal if they have the same components.
(2) A composite value is either
    - a "string" and it has a string base mode, or
    - an "array" and it has an array base mode, or
    - a "structure" and it has a structure base mode.
(3) Array and structure components are given a representation which is
    "unpacked", "packed" or "mapped". The representation is meant to be an
    information for the implementation:
    - an array or structure component with a packed representation should be
      implemented in such a way the number of bits it occupies in memory is
      minimized.
    - an array or structure component with an unpacked representation should
      be implemented in such a way the access time to that component when
      stored in memory is minimized.
    - an array or structure component with a mapped representation should be
      implemented according to the program defined information attached to
      the mapped representation.
(4) A mapped representation is based on a number of assumptions on hardware
    and implementation :
    - the memory of the computer is organized in words which are lists of
      bits (of length width).
    - an array or structure value V the components of which have a mapped
      representation is implemented as a bit string R in which each component
      $V \{i\}$ of V is attributed a substring $R \{a_i:b_i\}$. The interval $\{a_i:b_i\}$ is
      called the "place of $V\{i\}$".
      If $\{a_i:b_i\}$ and $\{a_j:b_j\}$ are the places of the elements $V\{i\}$ and $V\{j\}$
      ($i \neq j$) it is required that $\{a_i:b_i\} \cap \{a_j:b_j\}=\{\}$.
    - In a given implementation, each value V_1 is supposed to be represented

      by a minimum number of bits and a referable location containing that
      value by a minimum number of addressable memory units (words). These
      two numbers only depend on the base mode BM of V_1,they are called the

      "length" and the "size" of BM respectively.

1.5.1 STRINGS

(1) A string value is either
   - a "bit string" value, whose components are Boolean values called "bits"
     in this context, or
   - a "character string" value, whose components are characters.
   Its component category is bit or char accordingly.
(2) A string base mode is specified by
   - a component category C, bit or char, and
   - a length L which is a non negative integer.
   It is written string(C,L).
(3) Bit strings are ordered according to the lexical order, with false < true
   character strings are ordered according to the lexical order defined by
   the CCITT alphabet n° 5.

*

For   each premode PRE=val(CL,RG,ST,M)
       __such that__ M =mode(NV,BM),
              BM=string(CAT,L)
__Prop__ RG=nreg
__Def__   value string slice premode(PRE)=val(CL,nreg,dyn,M)
__For__   each number N∈{1:L}
__Def__   value substring premode(PRE,N)=
       val(CL,nreg,stat,mode(NV,string(CAT,N)))
__For__   each value V of premode PRE
__Prop__ ST=stat ⇒ #V=L,
       ST=dyn ⇒ #V≤L
__Def__   length(V,PRE)=#V of premode dpre(int)
__For__   each pair i,j of numbers
       __such that__ 0≤i≤j< length(V,PRE)
__Def__   value substring(V,PRE,i,j)=V_1 of premode PRE_1,

       defined by V_1=V⁅i+1:j+1⁆,

                PRE_1=value substring premode(PRE,j-i+1)

__Def__   value string slice(V,PRE,i,j)=V_2 of premode PRE_2

       defined by V_2=V⁅i+1:j+1⁆,

              PRE_2=value string slice premode(PRE)

*

__For__   each premode PRE=val(CL,-,-,mode(NV,discr(R,-,-)))
      __such that__ R∈{bool,char}
__Let__   C=(__Case__ R=bool:bit,
       __Case__ R=char:char)
__Def__   stringed premode(PRE)=val(CL,nreg,stat,
                      mode(NV,string(C,1)))

*

__For__   each premode PRE_1=val(CL_1,-,ST_1,mode(-,string(C,L_1))),

      each premode PRE_2=val(CL_2,-,ST_2,mode(-,string(C,L_2)))

       __such that__ are compatible(PRE_1,PRE_2)

__Let__   val(CL,RG,-,mode(NV,string(C,-))) ≡

                              resulting premode(PRE_1,PRE_2),

ST $\equiv$ (<u>Case</u> $ST_1=ST_2=$stat:stat,

     <u>Case else</u>:dyn),
PRE$_3$ $\equiv$ val(CL,RG,ST,mode(NV,string(C,L_1+L_2)))

<u>Def</u>   apply 2 premode(concat, PRE_1,PRE_2)=PRE_3

<u>For</u>   each static environment ENV
<u>Def</u>   identify apply 2 exceptions(concat,PRE_1,PRE_2,ENV) = an exception map XS

     defined by
       XS=map(ENV,{*RANGEFAIL*})
<u>For</u>   each value V_1 of premode PRE_1,

     each value V_2 of premode PRE_2

<u>Def</u>   apply 2(concat, V_1,PRE_1,V_2,PRE_2,-)=$V_1\|V_2$ of premode PRE_3

*

<u>For</u>   each premode PRE_1=val(-,ST_1,mode(-,string(bit,L_1))),

     each premode PRE_2=val(-,ST_2,mode(-,string(bit,L_2)))

     <u>such that</u> $ST_1=ST_2=$stat $\Rightarrow L_1=L_2$,

           are compatible(PRE_1,PRE_2)

     each function Fϵ{and,or,xor}
<u>Let</u>   PRE$_3$ $\equiv$ resulting premode(PRE_1,PRE_2)
<u>Def</u>   apply 2 premode(F,PRE_1,PRE_2)=PRE_3

<u>For</u>   each static environment ENV
<u>Def</u>   identify apply 2 exceptions(F,PRE_1,PRE_2,ENV) = an exception map XS

     defined by
       XS=map(ENV,{*RANGEFAIL*})
<u>For</u>   each value V_1 of premode PRE_1,

     each value V_2 of premode PRE_2,

     each exception map XM
<u>Let</u>   PRE$_4$ $\equiv$ dpre(bool)
<u>Def</u>   apply 2(F,V_1,PRE_1,V_2,PRE_2,XM)=V of premode PRE_3

     defined by
       (<u>Case</u> #V_1=#V_2:V={apply 2(F,V_1\{i\},PRE_4,V_2\{i\},PRE_4,XM)|iϵ{1:V}\},

       <u>Case else</u>:V=select exception(XM,*RANGEFAIL*))

*

<u>For</u>   each premode PRE=val(-,-,mode(-,string(bit,-)))
<u>Let</u>   PRE$_1$ $\equiv$ resulting premode(PRE,PRE)

<u>Def</u>   apply 1 premode(not,PRE)=PRE_1

<u>For</u>   each static environment ENV
<u>Def</u>   identify apply 1 exceptions(not,PRE,ENV)=an exception map XS
     defined by
       XS=map(ENV,{})
<u>For</u>   each value V of premode PRE,
     each exception map XM
<u>Let</u>   PRE$_2$ $\equiv$ dpre(bool)

<u>Def</u>   apply 1(not,V,PRE,XM)=a value V_1 of premode PRE_1

        defined by
            $V_1 = \{$apply 1(not,V$\{i\}$,PRE_2,XM)$|i\in\{1:\#V\}\}$

                        *

<u>For</u>   each pair of value premodes PRE_1,PRE_2

            <u>such that</u> base mode (PRE_1)=string(-)

                    ∧ are compatible (PRE_1,PRE_2)

        each function $F\in\{$equal, non equal, less than,
                            less or equal, greater than, greater or equal$\}$
<u>Def</u>   apply 2 premode(F,PRE_1,PRE_2)=dpre(bool)

<u>For</u>   each static environment ENV
<u>Def</u>   identify apply 2 exceptions(F,PRE_1,PRE_2,ENV) = an exception map XS

        defined by
            XS=map(ENV,$\{RANGEFAIL\}$)
<u>For</u>   each value V_1 of premode PRE_1,

        each value V_2 of premode PRE_2,

        each exception map XM
<u>Def</u>   apply 2$(F,V_1,PRE_1,V_2,PRE_2,XM)$=B of premode dpre(bool)

        defined by B=
          (<u>Case</u> $\#V_1=\#V_2$:

            (<u>Case</u> F=equal:$V_1=V_2$,

             <u>Case</u> F=non equal:$V_1\neq V_2$,

             <u>Case</u> F=less than:$V_1<V_2$,

             <u>Case</u> F=less or equal:$V_1\leq V_2$,

             <u>Case</u> F=greater than:$V_1>V_2$,

             <u>Case</u> F=greater or equal:$V_1\geq V_2$),

             <u>Case</u> <u>else</u>:select exception(XM,$RANGEFAIL$))

                        *

<u>For</u>   each string value premode PRE_1,

        each Boolean or character value premode PRE_2
            <u>such that</u> are compatible(PRE_1,stringed premode(PRE_2))

<u>Let</u>   PRE'$_2$ ≡ stringed premode(PRE_2)

<u>For</u>   each Boolean or character value premode PRE_3
            <u>such that</u> are compatible(PRE'$_2$, stringed premode(PRE_3))

<u>Let</u>   PRE'$_3$ ≡ stringed premode(PRE_3)

<u>Def</u>   apply 2 premode(concat,PRE_2,PRE_3)=apply 2 premode(concat,PRE'$_2$,PRE'$_3$)

<u>For</u>   each static environment ENV
<u>Def</u>   identify apply 2 exceptions(concat,PRE_2,PRE_3,ENV)

            =identify apply 2 exceptions(concat,PRE'$_2$,PRE'$_3$,ENV)

<u>For</u>   each function $F\in\{$concat, and, or, xor, equal, non equal,

less than, less or equal, greater than, greater or
equal}

__Def__   apply 2 premode(F,PRE_1,PRE_2)=apply 2 premode(F,PRE_1,PRE'_2),

apply 2 premode(F,PRE_2,PRE_1)=apply 2 premode(F,PRE'_2,PRE_1)

__Def__   identify apply 2 exceptions(F,PRE_1,PRE_2,ENV)

=identify apply 2 exceptions(F,PRE_1,PRE'_2,ENV),

identify apply 2 exceptions(F,PRE_2,PRE_1,ENV)

=identify apply 2 exceptions(F,PRE'_2,PRE_1,ENV)

__For__   each value V_1 of premode PRE_1,

each value V_2 of premode PRE_2,

each value V_3 of premode PRE_3,

each exception map XM

__Def__   apply 2$(concat,V_2,PRE_2,V_3,PRE_3,XM)$

=apply 2$(concat,\{V_2\},PRE'_2,\{V_3\},PRE'_3,XM)$,

apply 2$(F,V_1,PRE_1,V_2,PRE_2,XM)$

=apply 2$(F,V_1,PRE_1,\{V_2\},PRE'_2,XM)$,

apply 2$(F,V_2,PRE_2,V_1,PRE_1,XM)$

=apply 2$(F,\{V_2\},PRE'_2,V_1,PRE_1,XM)$

*

__For__   each non negative integer number I,
each premode PRE=val$(-,-,stat,mode(base,string(C,L)))$,
each value V of premode PRE

__Let__ $PRE_1 \equiv$ val$(dclass,nreg,stat,mode(base,string(C,L*I)))$

__Def__   repeat string(I,V,PRE)=the value V_1 of premode PRE_1

defined by
V=(__Case__ I=0:$\{\}$,
__Case__ I>0:$V_1\|$repeat string$(I-1,V,PRE)$)

1.5.2 ARRAYS

(1) The components of an array are called its "elements"; they have all the
same mode.
(2) The base mode of an array is specified by
   - a discrete mode I, the "index mode" of the array,
   - the mode E of the array elements, and
   - an array representation specification R.
   It is written array(I,E,R).
(3) An array representation specification R is either
   - unpacked, written npack, or
   - packed, written pack, or
   - mapped in which case it is specified by five numbers
      - a "word displacement" WD,
      - a "bit displacement" BD,
      - a "length" L,
      - a "step" S, and
      - a "pattern size" PZ.

It is written map(WD,BD,L,S,PZ).
(4) The bit string representing a mapped array consists of the concatenation
    of a number of patterns which are bit strings of length PZ*width, the
    head of the first pattern and the tail of the last one being not
    necessarily part of that representation.
    Each pattern consists of the representation of a number of array elements
    of which the ith one has a place $\{a_i:b_i\}$ relatively to the head of its

    pattern, such that
        with $a_i'=(WD*width)+BD+(S*(i-1))$

             $b_i'=(WD*width)+BD+(S*i)-1$

    we have $a_i \le a_i'$ and $b_i' \le b_i$.

    $\{a_i':b_i'\}$ is called the extended pattern place of the corresponding array

    element.
(5) Within the first pattern, the first array element generally occupies the
    kth extended pattern place (1≤k); k is called the first pattern position
    of the array.

                                    *

For   each premode PRE=val(-,-,ST,mode(-,array(I,-,-))),
       each value V of premode PRE
Prop   ST=stat ⇒ #V=card(I),
       ST=dyn ⇒ #V≤card(I),
       no holes(I)

                                    *

For   each pair PRE_1,PRE_2 of array value premodes

           such that are compatible(PRE_1,PRE_2),

       each function F∈{equal,nonequal}
Def   apply 2 premode(F,PRE_1,PRE_2)=dpre(bool)
For   each static environment ENV
Def   identify apply 2 exceptions(F,PRE_1,PRE_2,ENV) = an exception map XS

           defined by
                XS=map(ENV,{RANGEFAIL})
For   each value V_1 of premode PRE_1,

       each value V_2 of premode PRE_2,

       each exception map XM
Def   apply 2(F,V_1,PRE_1,V_2,PRE_2,XM)=T of premode dpre(bool)

           defined by
                T=(Case $\#V_1=\#V_2$:(Case F=equal:$V_1=V_2$,

                                Case F=nonequal:$V_1 \neq V_2$),

                Case else:select exception(XM,RANGEFAIL)

                                    *

For   each base mode BM=array(I,E,-)
Def   element mode(BM)=E,
       index mode(BM)=I
For   each value V of base mode BM
Def   upper(V,BM)=N of premode val(dclass,nreg,stat,I)

defined by N=min(I) + (#V-1)

                              *   .

For   each premode PRE=val(-,RG,ST,M)
           such that M=mode(NV,BM),
                        BM=array(I,E,R)
Let   RG₁=compose regionality(RG,E)
Def   value array element premode(PRE)=val(vclass,RG₁,stat,E),

       value array slice premode(PRE)=val(vclass,RG,dyn,M)
For   each number N∈{1:card(I)}
Let   I' ≡ range mode(min(I),min(I)+N-1,I)
Def   value subarray premode(PRE,N)
           =val(vclass,RG,stat,mode(NV,array(I',E,R)))
For   each value V of premode PRE,
       each value i₁ ∈ set(I)

           such that i₁ ≤ upper(V,PRE)

Let   k₁ ≡ index(i₁,I)

Def   value array element(V,PRE,i₁)=V₁ of premode PRE₁
           defined by PRE₁=value array element premode(PRE),
                      V₁=V⧸k₁⧸

For   each value i₂ ∈ set(I)
           such that i₁ ≤ i₂ ≤ upper(V,PRE)

Let   k₂ ≡ index(i₂,I)

Def   value array slice(V,PRE,i₁,i₂)=V₂ of premode PRE₂
           defined by PRE₂=value array slice premode(PRE),
                      V₂=V⧸k₁:k₂⧸,

Def   value subarray(V,PRE,i₁,i₂)=V₃ of premode PRE₃
           defined by PRE₃=value subarray premode(PRE,#{k₁:k₂}),
                      V₃=V⧸k₁:k₂⧸

                              *

For   each premode PRE=val(-,-,ST,mode(-,array(I,E,-)))
Let   N=card(I)
For   each list of premodes PML=⧸PREᵢ|i∈{1:N₁}⧸
           such that ST=stat ⇒ N=N₁,
                     ST=dyn ⇒ 1≤N₁≤N,
                     ∀(i∈{1:N₁}):is compatible with(E,PREᵢ),
       each list of values VL=⧸Vᵢ|i∈{1:N₁}⧸
           such that ∀(i∈{1:N₁}):
                      (the premode of Vᵢ is PREᵢ,
                      Vᵢ∈set(E))
Let   ∀(i∈{1:N}):Wᵢ=Vᵢ of mode E
Def   array tuple value(VL,PML,PRE)=VL of premode PRE
For   each list of M premodes PRL=⧸PREⱼ|j∈{1:M}⧸

such that $M \leq N$,

  $\forall(j\epsilon\{1:M\})$:is compatible with$(E,PRE_j)$,

each exception map XM,
each list of M values UL=$\{U_j | j\epsilon\{1:M\}\}$

 such that $\forall(j\epsilon\{1:M\})$:

    (the premode of U_j is PRE_j,

    $U_j\epsilon set(E)$),

each pair of lists SETLIST,PSL
 such that SETLIST=$\{S_j | j\epsilon\{1:M\}\}$,

    PSL=$\{PS_j | j\epsilon\{1:M\}\}$,

    $\forall(j\epsilon\{1:M\})$:($PS_j$ is a discrete premode

       and S_j is a set of values of that premode)

       or (PS_j and S_j are both else)

       or (PS_j and S_j are both dontcare)

Let $B_1 \equiv \forall(j\epsilon\{1:M\}):PS_j\notin\{else,dontcare\} \Rightarrow$

     (is compatible with(I,PS)
      $\wedge S_j \subseteq set(i))$,

 $\forall(j\epsilon\{1:M\}):XS_j \equiv (\underline{Case}\ S_j\epsilon\{else,dontcare\}:\{\}$,

      $\underline{Case\ else} : S_j)$,

 $CXS \equiv \cup(j\epsilon\{1:M\}):XS_j$,

 $\forall(j\epsilon\{1:M\}):SS_j \equiv (\underline{Case}\ S_j=dontcare:set(I)$,

     $\underline{Case}\ S_j=else:set(I)\backslash CXS$,

     $\underline{Case\ else}:S_j)$,

 $B_2 \equiv \forall(j,k\epsilon\{1:n\}):j\neq k \Rightarrow SS_j \cap SS_k=\{\}$,

 $LS \equiv \cup(j\epsilon\{1:M\}):SS_j$,

 $B_3 \equiv (ST=stat \Rightarrow LS=set(I)) \wedge (ST=dyn \Rightarrow LS=\{min(set(I)):max(LS)\}$

     $LS=\{min(set(I)):max(LS)\}$

Def is coherent array tuple labelling(SETLIST,PSL,PRE)
  $=(B_1 \wedge B_2 \wedge B_3)$ of premode dpre(bool)

For each integer number N
  such that $N \leq index(max(I),I)$

Def is valid number of elements(SETLIST,PSL,PRE,N)=
  =T of premode dpre(bool)
  defined by
    $T=(CXS\neq\{\} \Rightarrow N \geq index(max(CXS),I))$
      $\wedge ((ST=dyn \wedge CXS=LS) \Rightarrow N=card(LS))$

Def array labelled tuple value(UL,PRL,SETLIST,PSL,PRE,N)
  =XL of premode PRE
  defined by
    Let UP such that index(UP,I)=N,
      $VM \equiv \{[s\rightarrow v] | \exists_j:(s\epsilon XS_j \wedge v=U_j)\}$
       $\cup\{[s\rightarrow U_k] | s\epsilon\{min(I):UP\}\backslash CXS$

         $\wedge S_k\epsilon\{else,dontcare\}\}$

    $XL=\{VM[k] | k\epsilon\{min(I):UP\}\}$

        *

<u>For</u>   each value base mode BM
<u>Def</u>   length(BM)=the number which is the length of BM,
       size(BM)=the number which is the size of BM
<u>For</u>   each number S
<u>Def</u>   pat size(S)=the smallest integer PZ
          <u>such that</u> PZ*width ≥ S
<u>For</u>   each quintuple of integers Q=[WD,BD,S,L,PZ]
<u>Def</u>   is array map representation(Q,BM)=B of premode dpre(bool)
          defined by B=L ≥length(BM)
                        ∧ S ≥ L
                        ∧ (PZ*width) <u>mod</u> S ≥ (WD*width)+BD
<u>For</u>   each array representation specification
          R=map(WD,DB,L,S,PZ)
          of an array with element mode M
<u>Prop</u>   is array map representation ([WD,BD,L,S,PZ],M)

1.5.3 STRUCTURES

(1) The components of a structure are called its "fields"; they have not in
    general the same mode. Some structure values also include a
    "parameterization".

(2) The base mode of a structure is specified by a list FDL of "field
    descriptors".
    It is written struct(FDL).

(3) A field descriptor is either the descriptor of
    - a "single field",
    - the descriptor of a set of "alternatives".

(4) A field whose descriptor in FDL is a single field descriptor is called a
    "fixed field".
    A field whose descriptor is a component of the descriptor of a set of
    alternatives is a "variant field".

(5) The descriptor of a single field is written field(S,RD,M,RP), where
    - S is an identifier called the "selector" of the field,
    - RD is a readonlyness (RD∈{rdo,write}), the readonlyness of the field,
    - M is a mode, the mode of the field, and
    - RP is the "representation specification" of the field.

(6) The descriptor of a set of alternatives is written var(PL,AL,SYAL), where
    - PL is a possibly empty list of n "parameter specifiers".
      If the list PL is empty in one descriptor of FDL, then it is empty in
      all descriptors of FDL. In such a case the structure base mode is said
      to be "nonparameterizable".
    - AL is a list of k "descriptors of alternatives",
    - SYAL is a list of syntactic descriptors of alternatives (i.e. keeping
      track of else and dontcare).

(7) A parameter specifier is a triple [T,PRE,P] where
    - T is either none or a selector called a "tag selector",
    - PRE is a discrete premode called a "parameter premode",
    - P is either none or dyn or a value of premode PRE.
    When T is none in a parameter specifier, then it is none in all parameter
    specifiers of all descriptors of all set alternatives of FDL; in such a

case, the structure base mode is said to be "tagless", otherwise it is
"tagged".
Similarly, when P is none (resp. dyn) in a parameter specifier, it is
none (resp. dyn) in all parameter specifiers of all descriptors of FDL;
the structure base mode is then said to be "nonparameterized" (resp.
"dynamically parameterized"). If P is a value, the base mode is said to
be "parameterized".

(8) A tag selector T ($\neq$ none) with $[T,PRE,V]\epsilon PL$ is such that
field$(T,RD,M_1,-)\epsilon FDL$ where M_1 is mode(PRE); i.e. a tag selector is the
selector of a fixed field whose mode is M_1. Such a field is a "tag
field", its mode is a "tag mode". All tag selectors in PL are different.
If V is a value, RD is rdo. In addition, for each pair of triples
$[T,PRE_1,P]$ and $[T,PRE_1,P_1]$, where T$\neq$none, appearing in different
descriptors of set alternatives, $P=P_1$.

(9) A descriptor AD of an alternative in AL is a pair $[CS,DL]$ where
   - CS is a possibly empty set of n-tuples of values, where n is the number
     of parameter specifiers in PL; CS is the "choice set" of AD,
   - DL is a possibly empty list of descriptors of single fields, the
     "descriptor list" of AD
   CS is empty if and only if the structure base mode is nonparameterizable.

(10) The choice set CS, when nonempty, is such that for each tuple TϵCS, each
    element $T[j]\epsilon set(PRE_j)$ $(1\leq j\leq n)$, PRE_j being the parameter premode in
    PL$\{j\}$, i.e. PRE_j is such that $[-,PRE_j,-]=PL\{j\}$. The choice sets of a
    given list AL are mutually disjoint sets.

(11) A structure value V of base mode BM=struct(FDL) is constituted by a list
    V_E of components, which is the concatenation of p lists of fields with
       p=#FDL,
       $V_E=\|(i\epsilon\{1:p\}):VL_i$
    and possibly, a parameterization V_p, which only exists if BM is tagless
    and parameterized. We write V$\{i\}$ for $V_E\{i\}$.

(12) A structure value V has a "descriptor list" SDL, which is the
    concatenation of p lists of single field descriptors with
       $SDL=\|(i\epsilon\{1:p\}):SDL_i$.

(13) If FDL$\{i\}$=field(S,RD,M,RP), then VL_i has one element V_i which is a fixed
    field of selector S, readonlyness RD, mode M and representation
    specification RP; in that case, $SDL_i=\{FDL\{i\}\}$.

(14) If FDL$\{i\}$=var(PL,AL,SYAL), then VL_i is a list of q single fields (q$\geq$0)
    and SDL_i a list of q single field descriptors.
    VL_i and SDL_i are constituted as follows :
    - one alternative descriptor AD=$[CS,DL]$ is taken in AL.
    - SDL_i=DL and $VL_i=\{f_j|j\epsilon\{1:q\}\}$ where f_j is a single field value, where
      the mode M_j of f_j is such that field$(-,-,M_j,-)=DL\{j\}$.

- If the choice set CS is a nonempty set of tuples with n elements each, then PL, the list of parameter specifiers has also n elements. Let $PL=\{[S_k,PRE_k,P_k]\mid k\epsilon\{1:n\}\}$.
- To VL_i is associated a tuple $T\epsilon CS$ of n "tag values"; let $T=\{T_k\mid k\epsilon\{1:n\}\}$. If $S_k\neq none$, i.e. if S_k is a tag selector, then T_k is the value of the tag field of V with selector S_k. Moreover, if P_k is a value, $P_k=T_k$.

(15) Given a value V of base mode struct(FDL), there is, for each parameter specifier p=[S,PRE,P] within FDL, an object V_p called "the parameter of V corresponding to p", such that, if P is none, V_p is none, if P is a value, V_p=P of premode PRE, and if P is dyn, P is some value in set(PRE). Furthermore, if S is a selector and P≠none, V_p is equal to the field value of selector S in V .
- If S is none and P is dyn or is a value, the parameterization is equal to $\{\{V_p\mid p\epsilon PL\}\mid var(PL,-,-)\epsilon FDL\}$, and the components of V constitute a value of mode struct(FDL') where FDL' is FDL, where each p=[none,PRE_p,dyn] within FDL is replaced by [none,PRE_p,V_p] (i.e. the components of V obey the constraints mentioned above).

(16) Given a structure value V, the set of pairs $[S_k,TV_k]$, where S_k is a tag selector and TV_k the corresponding tag field value is called the "tagging" of V.

(17) The representation specification of a structure field is either
- unpacked, written npack, or
- packed, written pack, or
- mapped, in which case it is specified by three numbers
    - a "word displacement" WD,
    - a "bit displacement" BD, and
    - a length L.
It is written map(WD,BD,L).

(18) The place $\{a_i:b_i\}$ of a structure field with a representation specification map(WD,BD,L) is such that with
    a=(WD*width+BD)
    b=(WD*width+BD+L-1)
we have $a\leq a_i$ and $b_i\leq b$
{a:b} is called the extended place of the field.

                            *

<u>For</u>   each pair of structure value premodes PRE_1,PRE_2
      <u>such that</u> are compatible(PRE_1,PRE_2),
      each function $F\epsilon\{equal,nonequal\}$
<u>Def</u>   apply 2 premode(F,PRE_1,PRE_2)=dpre(bool)

<u>For</u>   each static environment ENV
<u>Def</u>   identify apply 2 exceptions(F,PRE_1,PRE_2,ENV)

                              = an exception map XS
          defined by
              XS=map(ENV,{*TAGFAIL*})
For   each value V_1 of premode PRE_1,

      each value V_2 of premode PRE_2,

      each exception map XM
Def   apply 2$(F,V_1,PRE_1,V_2,PRE_2,XM)=T$ of premode dpre(bool)

          defined by
              T=(Case is tagless(PRE_1) v is tagless(PRE_2):

                          implementation defined,
                  Case parameterization(V_1,PRE_1)≠parameterization(V_2,PRE_2):

                          select exception(XM,*TAGFAIL*),
                  Case else:
                      (Case F=equal:$V_1=V_2$,

                       Case F=nonequal:$V_1≠V_2$))

                              *

For   each list FDL of field descriptors,
      each triple t=[i,j,k] of positive numbers
Def   ijk descriptor(t,FDL)=the single field descriptor FD
          defined by FD=
          (Case i>#FDL:udf,
           Case i≤#FDL:
              (Case FDL↓i↓=field(-):
                  (Case j=k=1:FDL↓i↓,
                   Case else:udf),
               Case FDL↓i↓=var(-):
                  Let   var(-,AL,-) ≡ FDL↓i↓
                  (Case j>#AL:udf,
                   Case j≤#AL:
                      Let   [-,DL] ≡ AL↓j↓
                      (Case k>#DL:udf,
                       Case k≤#DL:DL↓k↓))))
Def   ijk selector(t,FDL)=the identifier T
          defined by
              T=(Case field(S,-,-,-) ≡ ijk descriptor(t,FDL):S,
                 Case else:udf)

                              *

For   each list FDL of field descriptors
Let N^3=the set of triples of positive numbers
Def   are different selectors(FDL)=B of premode dpre(bool)
          defined by
              B=∀(t,t'ϵN^3):t≠t'⇒(ijk selector(t,FDL) ≠ ijk selector(t',FDL)
                              v ijk selector(t,FDL)=udf)
Def   are tags defined before used(FDL)=B of premode dpre(bool)
          defined by B=
              ∀(iϵ{1:#FDL}):
                  ∀TL:(FDL↓i↓=var(TL,-,-)⇒
                      ∀([T,PRE,-]ϵTL):

$$T \neq none \Rightarrow (\exists(j\epsilon\{1:i-1\})):$$
$$FDL\{j\}=field(T,-,mode(PRE),-)))$$

*

<u>For</u>   each base mode BM=struct(FDL),
         each identifier S
<u>Def</u>   is field selector(S,BM)=B of premode dpre(bool)
            defined by B=(∃t:ijk selector(t,FDL)=S)

*

<u>For</u>   each structured base mode SM=struct(FDL)
<u>Def</u>   single field list(SM)=the list FFL of single field descriptors
            defined by
            <u>Let</u>   ∀(i∈{1:#FDL}):
                  FFL_i ≡ (<u>Case</u> FDL\{i\}=field(-):\{FDL\{i\}\}

                              <u>Case</u> <u>else</u>:variant field fixed field list(FDL\{i\}))
            FFL ≡ ||(i∈{1:#FDL}):FFL_i

*

<u>For</u>   each variant field descriptor F
<u>Def</u>   variant field single field list(F)
                      =the list FFL of single field descriptors
            defined by
            <u>Let</u>   var(-,AL,-) ≡ F,
                  ∀(i∈{1:#AL}):[-,FL_i] ≡ AL\{i\}

            FFL ≡ ||(i:{1:#AL}):FL_i

*

<u>For</u>   each base mode BM=struct(FDL)
<u>Prop</u>   are different selectors(FDL),
         are tags defined before used(FDL),
         are field repr compatible(FDL)
<u>For</u>   each identifier S
            <u>such that</u> is field selector(S,BM)
<u>Let</u>   t,RD,M,RP
            <u>such that</u> ijk descriptor(t,FDL)=field(S,RD,M,RP)
<u>Def</u>   field mode(S,BM)=M,
         field refy(S,BM)=
               (<u>Case</u> RP=npack:true,
                <u>Case</u> <u>else</u>:implementation defined),
         is fixed selector(S,BM)=B_1 of premode dpre(bool)

            defined by B_1=(field(S,-,-,-)∈FDL),

         is tag selector(S,BM)=B_2 of premode dpre(bool)

            defined by B_2=(var(PL,-,-)∈FDL∧[S,-,-]∈PL),

         tag selector list(BM)=the list SL
            defined by SL=\{S|FD∈FDL ∧ field(S,-,-,-)=FD
                                  ∧ is tag selector (S,BM)\},
         is variant structure mode(BM)=B_3 of premode dpre(bool)

            defined by B_3=(var(-,-,-)∈FDL)

<u>For</u>   each value V of base mode BM=struct(-)

__Def__   descriptor list(V,BM)=the descriptor list of V,
           selector list(V,BM)={S|field(S,-,-,-)∈descriptor list(V,BM)}

                                    *

__For__   each list VL of n objects which are either none or values,
           each structure base mode BM
             __such that__ ¬ is tagless(BM)
__Let__   S ≡ {V∈set(BM)|#V=n
                            ∧ ∀(i∈{1:n}):(is tag selector(selector list(V,BM){i}
                                                ⇒ VL{i}≠none)
                            ∧(VL{i}≠none ⇒ VL{i}=V{i})}
__Prop__   S≠{} ⇒ (#{descriptor list(V,BM)|V∈S}=1)
__Def__   descriptor list(VL,BM)=the list FDL of single field descriptors
              defined by
                  (__Case__ S≠{}:
                       __Let__   V'∈S
                       FDL=descriptor list(V',BM)
                  __Case else__ :
                       FDL=udf)
__Def__   selector list(VL,BM)={S|field(S,-,-,-)∈descriptor list(VL,BM)}

                                    *

__For__   each structure base mode SM=struct(FDL)
           each tag selector T of SM
__Def__   tag position(T,SM) ≡ I of premode dpre(int)
              defined by
                  I __such that__ FDL{I}=field(T,-,-,-)

                                    *

__For__   each premode PRE=val(-,RG,-,mode(-,struct(-))),
           each identifier S
             __such that__ is field selector(S,PRE)
__Let__   M ≡ field mode(S,PRE),
           RG_1 ≡ compose regionality(RG,M)
__Def__   value field premode(S,PRE)=val(vclass,RG_1,stat,M)
__For__   each value V of premode PRE,
           each identifier S_1∈selector list(V,PRE)
__Let__   k ≡ index(S_1,selector list(V,PRE))
__Def__   value field(S_1,V,PRE)=V{k} of premode PRE_1
              defined by PRE_1=value field premode(S_1,PRE)

                                    *

__For__   each base mode BM=struct(FDL)
__Def__   is parameterizable(BM)=B of premode dpre(bool)
              defined by
                  B=is variant structure mode(BM) ∧ ∀(var(PL,-,-)∈FDL):PL≠{}
__Def__   is tagless(BM)=B of premode dpre(bool)
              defined by
                  B=is variant structure mode(BM)

$$\wedge \; \forall(var(PL,-,-)\epsilon FDL):\forall([T,-,-]\epsilon PL):T=none))$$

*

<u>For</u>   each base mode BM=struct(FDL)
       <u>such that</u> is parameterizable(BM)
<u>Def</u>   is parameterized(BM)=B of premode dpre(bool)
       defined by
           $B=\forall(var(PL,-,-)\epsilon FDL):(\forall[-,-,X]\epsilon PL):X\notin\{none,dyn\}$

*

<u>For</u>   each structure base mode BM
<u>Def</u>   is dyn struct(BM)=T of premode dpre(bool)
       defined by
           $T=\exists(var(PL,-,-)\epsilon FDL):[-,-,dyn]\epsilon PL$

*

<u>For</u>   each value premode PRE
       <u>such that</u> base mode(PRE)=struct(FDL),
       each value V of premode PRE
<u>Def</u>   parameterization(V,PRE)=the list LL of lists of values V_p
                              of premode PRE_p
   defined by
       $LL=\{\{V_p$ of premode PRE_p
           $|[S,PRE_1,P]\epsilon PL$

           $\wedge \; V_p$ is the parameter of V corresponding to $[S,PRE_1,P]$
           $\wedge \; PRE_p=val(vclass,nreg,stat,mode(PRE_1))\}$
           $|var(PL,-,-)\epsilon FDL\}$
<u>Prop</u> $\forall(L\epsilon parameterization(V,PRE)):\forall(V_p\epsilon L):$
       V_p corresponds to $[S,PRE_1,P] \Rightarrow$
           $((\underline{Case}\; P=none:V_p=none,$
               $\underline{Case}\; P=dyn:V_p\epsilon set(PRE_1),$
                   $\underline{Case\; else}:V_p=P)$
       $\wedge \; (S\neq none \wedge P\neq none \Rightarrow V_p=value\; field(S,V,PRE)))$

*

<u>For</u>   each basemode BM=struct(FDL)
<u>Let</u> $PML_1 \equiv (\underline{Case}\; is\; tagless(BM):$

               $flatten(\{\{PRE|[-,PRE,-]\epsilon PL\}|var(PL,-,-)\epsilon FDL\}),$
               $\underline{Case\; else}:\{vpre(M)|field(S,-,M,-)\epsilon FDL$
                       $\wedge \; is\; tag\; selector(S,BM)\})$
<u>Def</u>   param premodes(BM)=PML_1
<u>For</u>   each list PML of premodes

<u>Def</u>   are param premodes compatible(PML,BM)=B of premode dpre(bool)
        defined by B=(#PML=#PML$_1$

                           ∧ ∀(i∈{1:#PML$_1$}):are compatible(PML⧸i⧸, PML$_1$⧸i⧸))

                                    *

<u>For</u>   each basemode BM=struct(-)
<u>Def</u>   is tagged param mode(BM)=T of premode dpre(bool)
          defined by
              T=¬ is tagless(BM)
                ∧ is parameterized(BM)

                                    *

<u>For</u>   each base mode BM=struct(FDL)
          <u>such that</u> is parameterizable(BM)
                    ∧ ¬ is parameterized(BM),
        each list PML of premodes
          <u>such that</u> are param premodes compatible(PML,BM)
        each list of values VL
          <u>such that</u> #VL=#PML,
                      ∀(i∈{1:#VL}):the premode of VL⧸i⧸ is PML⧸i⧸
<u>Let</u>   TSL ≡ tag selector list(BM)
<u>Def</u>   variant param base mode(VL,BM)=struct(FDL')
          defined by
                  FDL'=(<u>Case</u> is tagless(BM):
                            distr tagless param(VL,FDL)
                          <u>Case else</u>:
                            distr tagged param(VL,TSL,FDL))

                                    *

<u>For</u>   each structure mode M,
        each list VALL of n objects, each one being either a value or none,
        each list of field descriptors FDL
          <u>such that</u> FDL=descriptor list(VALL,M),
        each parameterization PL of some value of mode M
<u>Def</u>   are parameterization compatible(M,VALL,FDL,PL)
        =a value T of premode dpre(bool)
          defined by
          <u>Let</u>   ∀(i∈{1:n}):K$_i$ ≡ #⧸FDL⧸j⧸)|FDL⧸j⧸=field(t,-,-,-)
                                       ∧ is tag selector(T,M)
                                       ∧ 1 ≤ k ≤ i⧸
          T=∃(v∈set(M)):(descriptor list(v,M)=FDL
                    ∧ PL=parameterization(v)
                    ∧ x=#v
                    ∧ ∀(i∈{1:n}):∀s:((field(s,-,-,-)=FDL⧸i⧸
                    ∧ is tag selctor(s,M)) ⇒ (VALL⧸i⧸=PL⧸K$_i$⧸)))

                                    *

<u>For</u>   each list VL of values,
        each list FDL of field descriptors
<u>Def</u>   distr tagless param(VL,FDL)=the list FDL'
          defined by
          (<u>Case</u> VL=⧸⧸ ∨ FDL=⧸⧸:FDL'=FDL,

```
                    FDL'=⊰head(FDL)⊱
                         ‖distr tagless param(VL,tail(FDL))
              Case var(TL,AL,SYAL) ≡ head(FDL):
                   Let   n ≡ #TL,
                         m ≡ #VL,
                         TL' ≡ ⊰[S_i,PRE_i,VL⊰i⊱]
                                      |i∈{1:n} ∧ [S_i,PRE_i,-]=TL⊰i⊱⊱
                    FDL'=⊰var(TL',AL,SYAL)⊱
                         ‖distr tagless param(VL⊰n+1:m⊱,tail(FDL))))
```

For   each list of tag selectors TSL
      such that #TSL=#VL
Def   distr tagged param(VL,TSL,FDL)=the list FDL"
      defined by
      (Case FDL=⊰⊱:FDL"=⊰⊱
      Case else:

```
         (Case field(S,RD,M,RP) ≡ head(FDL):
               Let   RD' ≡ (Case S∈TSL:rdo,
                           Case else:RD),
               FDL'=field(S,RD',M,RP)
                         ‖distr tagged param(VL,TSL,tail(FDL))
            Case var(TL,AL,SYAL) ≡ head(FDL):
               Let   n ≡ #TL,
                     TL' ≡ ⊰[S_i,PRE_i,V_i]|i∈{1:n}
                                   ∧[S_i,PRE_i,-]=TL⊰i⊱
                                   ∧ V_i=VL⊰index(S_i,TSL)⊱⊱⊱
               FDL" ≡ ⊰var(TL',AL,SYAL)⊱
                         ‖distr tagged param(VL,TSL,tail(FDL))))
```

                              *

For   each base mode BM=struct(FDL)
      such that ¬ is tagless(BM) ∧ is parameterized(BM)
Def   tag value list(BM) ≡ the list TVL of tag values
      defined by
         TVL=⊰V of mode M|S∈tag selector list(BM)
                      ∧ ∃(var(TL,-)∈FDL):([S,M,V]∈TL)⊱

                              *

For   each possibly empty list SL of identifiers,
      each list FDL of single field descriptors
      such that ∀(S∈SL):∃(FD∈FDL):FD=field(S,-,-,-)
Def   tag field list(SL,FDL)=the list L of field descriptors
      defined by L=⊰FD|S∈SL ∧ FD=field(S,-,-,-)
                          ∧ FD∈FDL⊱,
      are tags fixed(SL,FDL)=the value B of premode dpre(bool)
      defined by B=∀(S∈SL):field(S,-,-,-)∈FDL

                              *

For   each quadruple of lists ALT LIST, PREL LIST, ELSE LIST,
         TAG FD LIST
      such that
      ALT LIST=⊰ALT EL_i|i∈{1:N}⊱,
      PREL LIST=⊰PREL_i|i∈{1:N}⊱,

PREL LIST=$\{$PREL$_i$ $|i\in\{1:N\}\}$,

$N \geq 1$,

$\forall(i\in\{1:N\})$:

    (ALT EL$_i$=[SL$_i$,FDL$_i$],

    SL$_i$=$\{$SET$_{ij}$$|j\in\{1:K_i\}\}$,

    PREL$_i$=$\{$PRE$_{ij}$$|j\in\{1:K_i\}\}$,

    $K_i \geq 0$,

    $\forall(j\in\{1:K_i\})$:(PRE$_{ij}$ is a discrete premode and

                      SET$_{ij}$ a set of values of that premode)

                      or (PRE$_{ij}$ and SET$_{ij}$ are both else) or

                      (PRE$_{ij}$ and SET$_{ij}$ are both dontcare),

    FDL$_i$ is a possibly empty list of single field descriptors),

ELSE LIST is either a possibly empty list of single field descriptors
or is none,

TAG FD LIST=$\{$field(TSEL$_j$,-,TMODE$_j$,-)$|j\in\{1:K\}\}$,

$K \geq 0$

__Let__ $B_1 \equiv ((\forall(i\in\{1:N\}):K_i=K_1)$

        $\wedge (K_1=0 \Rightarrow (K=0 \wedge \text{ELSE LIST=none}))$

        $\wedge (K>0 \Rightarrow K_1=K))$,

$B_2 \equiv K=0 \Rightarrow \forall(j\in\{1:K_1\}):\exists(i\in\{1:N\}):\text{PRE}_{ij}\in\{\text{else,dontcare}\})$,

$\forall(j\in\{1:K_1\}):\text{PL}_j \equiv \{\text{PRE}_{ij}|i\in\{1:N\}$

                      $\wedge$ PRE$_{ij}\notin\{\text{else,dontcare}\}\}$

TPL $\equiv$ (__Case__ K>0:$\{$vpre(TMODE$_j$)$|j\in\{1:K\}\}$,

      __Case__ K=0:$\{$resulting premode(PL$_j$)$|j\in\{1:K_1\}\}$),

$B_3 \equiv \forall(p\in\text{TPL}):p\neq\text{VAL(ALL,-,-,-)}$,

$H \equiv \#\text{TPL}$,

$B_4 \equiv \forall(i\in\{1:N\}):\forall(j\in\{1:H\})$:

    PRE$_{ij}\notin\{\text{else,dont care}\}$

        $\Rightarrow$ (K=0 $\Rightarrow$ is comptatible with(TMODE$_j$,PRE$_{ij}$))

          $\wedge$ SET$_{ij} \subseteq$ set(TPL$\{$j$\}$)),

$\forall(i\in\{1:N\})$:

    SYL$_i$ $\equiv \{$SY$_{ij}$$|j\in\{1:K_i\}$

              $\wedge$SY$_{ij}$=(__Case__ PRE$_{ij}\in\{\text{else,dontcare}\}$:PRE$_{ij}$,

                    __Case__ else:set)$\}$,

SYLL $\equiv \{$SYL$_i$$|i\in\{1:N\}\}$,

$\forall(i\in\{1:N\}):\forall(j\in\{1:H\})$:

    (XS$_{ij}$ $\equiv$ (__Case__ SET$_{ij}\in\{\text{dontcare,else}\}$:{},

           __Case__ else:SET$_{ij}$),

    CXS$_j$ $\equiv \cup(i\in\{1:N\}):XS_{ij}$,

    S$_{ij}$ $\equiv$ (__Case__ SET$_{ij}$=dontcare:set(TPL$\{$j$\}$),

        __Case__ SET$_{ij}$=else:set(TPL$\{$j$\}$)\CXS$_j$,

        __Case__ else:SET$_{ij}$)),

$\forall(i\epsilon\{1:N\}):P_i \equiv \Pi(j\epsilon\{1:H\}):S_{ij}$,

$P \equiv \Pi(j\epsilon\{1:H\}):set(TPL\{j\})$,

$P' \equiv u(i\epsilon\{1:N\}):P_i$,

$P'' \equiv P\backslash P'$,

$B_* \equiv (ELSE\ LIST=none \Rightarrow P''=\{\})$

     $\land\ (\forall(i,k\epsilon\{1:N\}):i\neq k \Rightarrow P_i \cap P_k=\{\})$,

$AL \equiv \{[P_i,FDL_i]|i\epsilon\{1:N\}\}$

Def   are coherent alternatives(ALT LIST, PREL LIST,
       ELSE LIST,TAG FD LIST)=
       $(B_1 \land B_2 \land B_3 \land B_* \land B_5)$ of premode dpre(bool)

Def   alternative list(ALT LIST,PREL LIST,
                   ELSE LIST,TAG FD LIST)=[L,SYL]
     defined by L=(<u>Case</u> ELSE LIST=none:AL,
             <u>Case else</u> AL‖{[P",ELSE LIST]\}),
         SYL=(<u>Case</u> ELSE LIST=none:SYLL,
              <u>Case else</u>:SYLL‖{else\})

Def   param spec list(TAG FD LIST,PREL LIST)
                  =the list TL of parameter specifiers
     defined ty TL=(<u>Case</u> K=0:{[none,TPL\{j\},none]|j\epsilon\{1:H\}\},
                <u>Case</u> K>0:{[TSEL$_j$,TPL\{j\},none]|j\epsilon\{1:H\}\})

*

For   each list FDL of field descriptors

Def   are field repr compatible(FDL)=B of premode dpre(bool)
     defined by

         <u>Let</u> $B_1 \equiv \exists(t\epsilon N^3):$

            (ijk descriptor(t,FDL)=field(-,-,-,map(-))

             $\Rightarrow \forall(t'\epsilon N^3):$ijk descriptor(t',FDL)
                         ϵ\{field(-,-,-,map(-)),udf\}),

           $B_2 \equiv \forall(t\epsilon N^3):$

            ((ijk descriptor(t,FDL)=field(-,M,R) $\land$ R=map(-,-,L))
              $\Rightarrow L \geq length(M))$,

         B_3=(FDL is such that in each value of

           mode struct(FDL) where P_i and P_j are

           the extended places of two different

           fields,$P_i\backslash P_j=\{\})$,

         $B=B_1 \land B_2 \land B_3$

*

For   each value premode PRE
     <u>such that</u> base mode(PRE)=struct(-)
               $\land \neg$ (is tagless(PRE) $\land$ is dyn struct(PRE))
     each single field descriptor list FDL
     <u>such that</u> $\exists(V\epsilon set(PRE)):$descriptor list(V,PRE)=FDL,

Let   n $\equiv$ #FDL,
     ML $\equiv$ \{M|field(-,M,-,-)ϵFDL\},

For   each list PML of n premodes
     <u>such that</u> $\forall(i\epsilon\{1:n\}):$is compatible with(ML\{i\},PML\{i\}),
     each list VL of n values

<u>such that</u> $\forall(i\in\{1:n\})$:the premode of VL$\{i\}$ is PML$\{i\}$,
<u>Def</u>   structure tuple value(VL,PML,FDL,PRE)=VL of premode PRE
<u>For</u>   each structure value premode PRE_1

<u>such that</u> $\exists(v\in set(PRE_1))$:descriptor list(V,PRE_1)=FDL,

each parameterization PL of some value of premode PRE_1

<u>such that</u> are parameterization compatible(M,UL,FDL,PL)
<u>Def</u>   structure labelled tuple value(UL,PML,FDL,PRE_1,PL)

=VL of premode PRE_1, including parameterization PL if PRE is

tagless and parameterized

*

<u>For</u>   each structure base mode BM=struct(FDL)
<u>Def</u>   struct staticity(BM)=ST
defined by
ST=(<u>Case</u>
($\exists$(var(TL,-) $\in$FDL):
$\exists$(t $\in$TL:t=[-,-,dyn]):dyn,
<u>Case else</u>:stat)

*

<u>For</u>   each triple of lists SETL LIST,PREL LIST,RML
<u>such that</u>
SETL LIST=$\{SETL_i | i\in\{1:N\}\}$,
PREL LIST=$\{PREL_i | i\in\{1:N\}\}$,
$N\geq1$,
$\forall(i\in\{1:N\})$:($SETL_i=\{SET_{ij} | j\in\{1:K\}\}$,
$PREL_i=\{PRE_{ij} | j\in\{1:K\}\}$,
$\forall(j\in\{1:K\})$:(PRE_{ij} is a discrete mode and
SET_{ij} a set of values of that
mode) or (PRE_{ij} and SET_{ij}
are both dontcare) or
(PRE_{ij} and SET_{ij} are
both else)),
$L\geq1$,
RML=$\{RMODE_j | j\in\{1:K\}\}$,
$\forall(j\in\{1:K\})$:$RMODE_j$ is a discrete mode
<u>Let</u> $\forall i\in\{1:N\}$:$\forall(j\in\{1:K\})$:
($XS_{ij} \equiv$ (<u>Case</u> $SET_{ij}\in\{dontcare,else\}$:$\{\}$,
<u>Case else</u>:SET_{ij},
$CXS_j \equiv \cup(i\in\{1:N\})$:$XS_{ij}$,
$S_{ij} \equiv$ (<u>Case</u> SET_{ij}=dont care:set($RMODE_j$),
<u>Case</u> SET_{ij}=else:set($RMODE_j$)\CXS_j,
<u>Case else</u>:SET_{ij})),
$\forall(i\in\{1:N\})$:$P_i \equiv \Pi(j\in\{1:K\})$:$S_{ij}$,
$P \equiv \Pi(j\in\{1:K\})$:set($RMODE_j$),

$P' \equiv \cup(i\epsilon\{1:N\}):P_i,$

$B \equiv \forall(i,k\epsilon\{1:N\}):i{\ne}k \Rightarrow P_i{\cap}P_k=\{\}$

<u>Def</u>   is coherent case selection(SETL LIST,PREL LIST,RML)=
       B of premode dpre(bool),
    case selection list(SETL LIST,PREL LIST,RML)=the list CL
      defined by CL=$\{P_i|i\epsilon\{1:N\}\}$

    case else part(SETL LIST,PREL LIST,RML)=the set S
      defined by S=P\P'

2. LOCATIONS

2.1 GENERALITIES

(1) A location is an M-object. As its dynamic property, a location
    "contains" a possibly undefined value, the "contents" of the location. A
    location has a "lifetime".
(2) The contents of a location L can be modified. This is performed by
    "storing" a value V into L; V becomes then the new contents of L. The
    action of storing a value into a location is an effect, i.e. it affects
    the computation state.
(3) The lifetime of a location characterizes the computation states in which
    the location "exists", i.e. can be operated upon. The lifetime of a
    location is the identifier of a locale.
(4) There are "permanent" and "temporary" locations. A permanent location
    exists in any computation state; it is characterized by a program node N
    and it is written perm(N); it is given an initial contents which is its
    contents at the beginning of the program elaboration. The lifetime of a
    permanent location is the identifier of the locale of the primal
    environent preenv%.
(5) A temporary location starts to exist with a specific lifetime when it is
    "created" by the elaboration of a creating function. Such a creation is
    an effect affecting the state of the computation. Each creation puts
    into existence a new location different from all other already created
    locations. The implementation, at each block entry must ensure that it
    will be able to create all locations for variables as implied by the
    elaboration of its body.
(6) Some program phrases such as <location denotation>, when elaborated,
    deliver a location, i.e., specify a location existing in the current
    environment of the elaboration. Each such phrase is given a unique
    "location premode" specifying properties of the location it may deliver.
(7) The premode of a phrase delivering a location will be called "the premode
    of the location".
(8) The premode PRE of a location is specified by
    - a regionality RG,
    - a staticity ST,
    - a "referability" RF which is either refble or nref,
    - a "readonlyness" RD which is rdo or write,
    - a mode M.
    PRE is written loc(RG,ST,RF,RD,M).
(9) Each location has a regionality, a staticity, a referability, a
    readonlyness, and a mode which are those specified by its premode.
    - The regionality RG of a location expresses whether (reg) or not (nreg)
      it may have been created during the elaboration of a critical region,
      in which case it cannot be used outside of it.
    - The staticity of a location expresses whether (stat) or not (dyn) the
      size of the location is known statically. The staticity of a
      noncomposite location is always stat.
    - The referability of a location expresses whether (refble) or not
      (nref) the location can be referred to by a reference value.
    - The readonlyness of a location expresses whether (write) or not (rdo)
      a new value can be stored in the location after it has been given an
      initial contents.
    - The mode of a location is the mode of the values that can be contained
      in it (i.e. stored into it) and that can be obtained from it by taking
      its contents.

(10) Each implementation defines for each referable location a "size" which
     is an integral value. The size of a location with premode
     PRE=loc(-,stat,refble,-,M) depends on the base mode of M only.
(11) If PRE=loc(-,-,-,RD,M), M=mode(-,BM) and DM=[RD,M] to shorten the
     description, PRE, M or DM may be written instead of BM; PRE or DM
     instead of M; PRE instead of DM.

                                    *

For   each premode PRE=loc(RG,ST,RF,-,M),
         each location L of premode PRE
Def   lifetime(L,PRE)=the lifetime of L
Let RG_1=compose regionality(RG,M)

Def   contents premode(PRE)=val(vclass,RG_1,ST,M),

         contents(L,PRE)=V of premode PRE_1

             defined by PRE_1=contents premode(PRE),

                         V is the value contained in L.
Def   alive(L,PRE)=B of premode dpre(bool)
             defined by
                      B=[lifetime(L,PRE),-]∈stack(E) for some environment E of a
                        process instance in non dead state recorded in C.S.

                                    *

For   each location premode PRE,
         each dynamic environment E
Let   LT ≡ temporary lifetime(E)
Def   create location(PRE,E)= a location L of premode PRE and an effect
             defined by
                     L is a newly created location,
                     lifetime(L,PRE)=LT,
                     is correctly initialized(L,PRE)
Def   try and create location(PRE,E)=a location L' of premode PRE,
                                              and an effect
             defined by
             (Case the implementation is able to create a new location with premode
                     PRE and lifetime LT:
                          L'=create location(PRE,E),
                 Case else:L'=udf)

                                    *

For   each location L of premode PRE
Let   C ≡ contents(L,PRE),
         CPRE ≡ contents premode(PRE)
Def   is correctly initialized(L,PRE)=B of premode dpre(bool)
             defined by
             B=(Case is synchro mode(PRE):all queues of L are empty,
                 Case base mode(PRE)=struct(-):
                   ((is tagged param mode(PE)
                         ⇒tag value list(PE)={value field(s,C,CPRE)
                                           | s∈tag selector list(CPRE)})
                     ∧ ∀(s∈selector list(C,CPRE)):
                         is correctly initialized(location field(s,L,PRE),
                             location field premode(s,PRE))),
                 Case base mode(PRE)=array(-):

                    ∀(E∈L): is correctly initialized
                            (E,location array element premode(PRE)),
         <u>Case else</u>:true)

                                    *

<u>For</u>   each location premode PRE=loc(RG,dyn,refble,RD,M)
           <u>such that</u> M=mode(NV,string(X,N)),
       each number $N_1 \in \{1:N\}$,

       each dynamic environment E
<u>Let</u> $PRE_1 \equiv$ location substring premode(PRE,N_1)

<u>Def</u>   create dyn string location(PRE,N_1,E)=a location L of

       premode PRE,and an effect
           defined by L = try and create location(PRE_1,E)

                                    *

<u>For</u>   each location premode PRE=loc(RG,dyn,refble,RD,M)
           <u>such that</u> M=mode(NV,array(I,E,R)),
       each value V∈set(I),
       each dynamic environment E
<u>Let</u> $PRE_1 \equiv$ location subarray premode(PRE,#{min(I),V})

<u>Def</u>   create dyn array location(PRE,V,E)=a location L of premode
       PRE, and an effect
           defined by L = try and create location(PRE_1,E)

                                    *

<u>For</u>   each location premode PRE=loc(RG,dyn,refble,RD,M)
           <u>such that</u> M=mode(NV,struct(FD)),
       each list VL of n values V_i of premode PM_i

           <u>such that</u>
           are param premode compatible({PM_i|i∈{1:n}},struct(FD)),

       each dynamic environment E
<u>Let</u> $BM_1 \equiv$ variant param base mode(VL,struct(FD))

       $PRE_1 \equiv$ loc(RG,stat,refble,RD,mode(N,BM_1))

<u>Def</u>   create dyn struct location(PRE,VL,E) =
           a location L of premode PRE, and an effect
           defined by L = try and create location(PRE_1,E)

                                    *

<u>For</u>   each premode PRE=loc(RG,stat,refble,-,M)
       each object V which is none or a value of premode PRE
           <u>such that</u> is compatible with(M,VPRE),
       each node N
<u>Def</u>   permanent location(V,VPRE,PRE,N)=the permanent location
       L of premode PRE
           defined by L=perm(N),
                       V≠none ⇒ the initial contents of L is V,

V=none ⇒ is correctly initialized(L,PRE)

                              *

__For__   each value premode PRE$_1$=val(CL$_1$,RG$_1$,ST$_1$,M$_1$),

           each location premode PRE$_2$=loc(RG$_2$,ST$_2$,RF$_2$,RD$_2$,M$_2$)

__Def__   is assignable(PRE$_1$,PRE$_2$)=the value B of premode dpre(bool)

           defined by
                B=is compatible with (M$_2$,PRE$_1$,ST$_2$)

                ∧ ¬ (has the synchro prop(PRE$_2$)

                    ∨ has the rdo prop(PRE$_2$))

                ∧ (RG$_1$=reg ⇒ RG$_2$=reg)

__For__   each function F∈{or, xor, and, equal, nonequal, less than, less or
                           equal, greater than, greater or equal, in, plus,
                           minus, concat, times, divide, mod, rem}
__Def__   is assign operable(F,PRE$_1$,PRE$_2$)=T of premode dpre(bool)

           defined by
                T=is operable(F,PRE$_1$,contents premode(PRE$_2$))

                ∧ F∈{or, xor, and, minus, plus, times, divide, mod, rem}

                              *

__For__   each value premode VPRE=val(-,-,VST,-),
           each location premode LPRE=loc(-,LST,-,-,-)
             __such that__ is assignable(VPRE,LPRE),
           each static environment ENV
__Let__   VBM ≡ base mode(VPRE),
           LBM ≡ base mode(LPRE)
__Def__   identify assign exceptions(VPRE,LPRE,ENV)=an exception map XM
           defined by
                XM ≡ (__Case__(LST=dyn ∨ VST=dyn) ∧ VBM∈{string(-),array(-)}:
                               map(ENV,{*RANGEFAIL*})
                      __Case__(LST=dyn ∨ VST=dyn) ∧ VBM=struct(-):
                               map(ENV,{*TAGFAIL*})
                      __Case__ VBM=discr:
                               map(ENV,{*RANGEFAIL*})
                      __Case__ __else__:map(E,{}))

                              *

__For__   each value V of premode VPRE=val(-,-,VST,-),
           each location L of premode LPRE=loc(-,LST,-,-,-)
             __such that__ is assignable(VPRE,LPRE),
           each exception map XM
__Let__   VBM ≡ base mode(VPRE),
           LBM ≡ base mode(LPRE)
__Def__   assigning exception(V,VPRE,L,LPRE,XM)=X
           defined by
                X=(__Case__ (LST=dyn ∨ VST=dyn)
                      ∧ VBM∈{string(-),array(-)} ∧ #V≠#L:
                               select exception(XM,*RANGEFAIL*),

Case (LST=dyn ∨ VST=dyn) ∧ VBM≡struct(-)
        ∧ parameterization(VPRE)
        ≠ parameterization(contents(L),
                                contents premode(LPRE)):
                select exception(XM,*TAGFAIL*),
    Case VBM=discr ∧ V∉set(LPRE):
                select exception(XM,*RANGEFAIL*),
    Case else:none)

                    *

For   each value V of premode VPRE,
      each location premode LPRE
        such that staticity(LPRE)=stat
                ∧ is assignable(VPRE,LPRE),
      each exception map XM
Let   L ≡ a location of premode LPRE
Def   in param exception(V,VPRE,LPRE,XM)=
        assigning exception(V,VPRE,L,LPRE,XM)

                    *

For   each value V of premode VPRE,
      each location L of premode LPRE,
        such that is assignable(VPRE,LPRE),
      each exception map XM
Let   VBM ≡ base mode(VPRE),
      LBM ≡ base mode(LPRE)
Def   assign(V,VPRE,L,LPRE,XM)=the object O and the effect
        defined by
        Let   EXC ≡ assigning exception(V,VPRE,L,LPRE,XM)
        (Case EXC=none:(V is stored into L, O=none),
         Case else:{# the contents of L is undefined #}
                O=EXC)

                    *

For   each premode PRE=loc(RG,stat,refble,RD,M)
      each denoted mode DM=[RD₁,M₁]

        such that is location convertible(PRE,DM)
Def   location conversion premode(PRE,DM)=the premode PRE₁

        defined by PRE₁=loc(RG,stat,refble,RD₁,M₁)

For   each location L of premode PRE
Def   location conversion(L,PRE,DM)=
      the location L of premode PRE₂

        defined by PRE₂=location conversion premode(PRE,DM)

                    *

For   each premode PRE=loc(-,ST,RF,-,-)
      each mode M
Def   is location convertible(PRE,M)=T of premode dpre(bool)
        defined by

T=(size(PRE)=size(M)) ∧ ST=stat ∧ RF=refble

*

For each premode PRE=val(-,RG,-,RM)
such that RM=mode(-,ref(RD,M))
each DM which is either none or a denotated mode [RD_1,M_1]
such that is read compatible with(DM,[RD,M])
Def dereference premode(PRE,DM)=the premode PRE_1
defined by
(Case DM=none:PRE_1 ≡ loc(RG,stat,refble,RD,M),
Case else:PRE_1 ≡ loc(RG,stat,refble,RD_1,M_1)
For each static environment ENV
Def identify deref exceptions(PRE,ENV)=an exception map XM
defined by
XM=map(ENV,{*EMPTY*})
For each value R of premode PRE,
each exception map XS
Def dereference(R,PRE,DM,XS)=the object O of premode PRE_2
defined by
PRE_2=dereference premode(PRE,DM)
(Case R≠null:O=the location
defined by
Let L_1 ≡ the location referred to by R,
L=(Case alive(L_1,PRE_2):L_1,
Case else:udf),
Case R=null:select exception(XS,*EMPTY*))

*

For each premode PRE=val(-,RG,-,M)
such that M=mode(-,ptr),
each denotated mode DM=[RD_1,M_1]
Def dereference premode(PRE,DM)=the premode PRE_1
defined by PRE_1=loc(RG,stat,refble,RD_1,M_1)
For each static environment ENV
Def identify deref exceptions(PRE,ENV) = an exception map XM
defined by
XM=map(ENV,{*MODEFAIL*,*EMPTY*})
For each value P of premode PRE,
each exception map XS
Def dereference(P,PRE,DM,XS)=the object O
defined by
(Case P≠null:
Let L ≡ the location referred to by P
PRE_1 ≡ dereference premode(PRE,DM)
PRE_2 ≡ pointed location premode(P)
(Case refy(PRE_2)≠nref ∧ alive(L,PRE_2):
(Case is read compatible with(PRE_1,PRE_2):
O=L of premode PRE_1,
Case else:

```
                    O=select exception(X,MODEFAIL)),
          Case else : O=udf),
          Case P=null:O=select exception(XS,EMPTY))
```

*

<u>For</u>   each premode PRE=val(-,RG,-,RM)
       <u>such that</u> RM=mode(-,row(RD,M)))
<u>Def</u>   derow premode(PRE)=the premode PRE$_1$

       defined by PRE$_1$=loc(RG,dyn,refble,RD,M)

<u>For</u>   each static environment ENV
<u>Def</u>   identify deref exceptions(PRE,ENV) = an exception map XM
          defined by
               XS=map(ENV,{EMPTY})
<u>For</u>   each value R of premode PRE,
       each exception map XS
<u>Def</u>   derow(R,PRE,XS)=the object O
          defined by
            (<u>Case</u> R≠null:
              <u>Let</u>   L$_1$ ≡ the location referred to by R,

                    PRE$_1$ ≡ derow premode(PRE),

                    L ≡ (<u>Case</u> alive(L$_1$,PRE$_1$):L$_1$

                              <u>Case</u> <u>else</u>:udf)
               O=L of premode PRE$_1$

            <u>Case</u> R:null:
               O=select exception(XS,EMPTY))

2.2 COMPOSITE LOCATIONS

(1) A composite location L is a list of n components L$_i$ which are locations.

(2) The components L$_i$ are created when L is created and they have the same lifetime.

(3) The contents of a composite location L with n components L$_i$ is a composite value V with n components V$_i$ such that the contents of L$_i$ is V$_i$.

(4) Thus a composite location is either
    - a string location, and contains a string, or
    - an array location, and contains an array, or
    - a structure location, and contains a structure.

*

<u>For</u>   each composite location L of premode PRE
<u>Let</u>   n ≡ #L,
       V ≡ contents(L,PRE),
       PREV ≡ contents premode(PRE),
       ∀(i∈{1:n}):(PRE$_i$ ≡ the premode of L↓i↓,

                    PREV$_i$ ≡ the premode of V↓i↓)
<u>Prop</u>   #V=n,
       ∀(i∈{1:n}):

contents premode(L⁅i⁆,PRE$_i$) ≡ PREV$_i$,

contents(L⁅i⁆,PRE$_i$)=V⁅i⁆ of premode PREV$_i$,

lifetime(L⁅i⁆,PRE$_i$)=lifetime(L,PRE)

2.2.1 STRING LOCATIONS

(1) A location L of premode PRE such that basemode(PRE) = string(C,N) is a
    string location.
(2) Each sublocation L⁅i:j⁆ of L has a referability which is implementation
    defined and which depends only on the string category C.

                                *

For   each premode PRE=loc(RG,ST,RF,RD,M)
            such that M=mode(NV,BM),
                        BM=string(C,N)
Let   RF$_1$ ≡ the referability for substrings of category C

Def   location string slice premode(PRE)=loc(RG,dyn,RF$_1$,RD,M)

For   each number K∈{1:N}
Def   location substring premode(PRE,K)=
            loc(RG,stat,RF$_1$,RD,mode(NV,string(C,K)))

For   each location L of premode PRE
Prop   ST=stat ⇒ #L=N,
         ST=dyn ⇒ #L≤N
Def   length(L,PRE)=#L of premode dpre(int)
For   each pair i,j of numbers
            such that 0≤i≤j<length(L,PRE)
Def   location substring(L,PRE,i,j)=L$_1$ of premode PRE$_1$

         defined by L$_1$=L⁅i+1:j+1⁆,

                        PRE$_1$=location substring premode(PRE,j-i+1)

Def   location string slice(L,PRE,i,j)=L$_2$ of premode PRE$_2$

         defined by L$_2$=L⁅i+1:j+1⁆,

                        PRE$_2$=location string slice premode(PRE)

2.2.2 ARRAY LOCATIONS

(1) A location L of premode PRE such that basemode(PRE) = array(-) is an
    array location.
(2) Each sublocation L⁅i⁆, respectively L⁅i:j⁆, has an "element
    referability", respectively "subarray referability", which is refble when
    PRE=array(-,-,npack) and otherwise implementation defined and depending
    on basemode(PRE) only.

                                *

For   each basemode BM=array(I,-,-),
         each location L of basemode BM

<u>Def</u>   upper(L,BM)=min(I)+(#L-1) of premode val(dclass,nreg,stat,I)

*

<u>For</u>   each premode PRE=loc(CR,ST,RF,RD,M)
        <u>such that</u> M=mode(NV,BM),
                    BM=array(I,E,R)
<u>Let</u> RF_1 ≡ the element referability of BM,

        RF_2 ≡ the subarray referability of BM

<u>Def</u>   location array element premode(PRE)
            =loc(CR,stat,RF_1,RD,E),

        location array slice premode(PRE)=loc(CR,dyn,RF_2,RD,M)

<u>For</u>   each number N∈{1:card(I)}
<u>Let</u>   I' ≡ range mode(min(I),min(I)+N-1,I)
<u>Def</u>   location subarray premode(PRE,N)=
            loc(CR,stat,RF_2,RD,mode(NV,array(I',E,R)))

<u>For</u>   each location L of premode PRE,
        each value i_1 ∈ set(I)

        <u>such that</u> i_1 ≤ upper(L,PRE)

<u>Let</u> k_1 ≡ index(i_1,I)

<u>Def</u>   location array element(L,PRE,i_1)=L_1 of premode PRE_1

            defined by L_1 = L⧸k_1⧸,

                        PRE_1=location array element premode(PRE)

<u>For</u>   each value i_2 ∈ set(I)

        <u>such that</u> i_1 ≤ i_2 ≤ upper(L,PRE)

<u>Let</u> k_2 ≡ index(i_2,I)

<u>Def</u>   location array slice(L,PRE,i_1,i_2)=L_2 of premode PRE_2

            defined by L_2=L⧸k_1:k_2⧸,

                        PRE_2=location array slice premode(PRE),

        location subarray(L,PRE,i_1,i_2)=L_3 of premode PRE_3

            defined by L_3=L⧸k_1:k_2⧸,

                        PRE_3=location subarray premode(PRE,#{k_1:k_2})

2.2.3 STRUCTURE LOCATIONS

(1) A location L of premode PRE such that basemode(PRE) = struct(-) is a
    structure location.
(2) Each element of L is called a field of L. An element of L which contains
    a tag field, a fixed field or a variant field of the contents of L is
    called respectively a tag field, a fixed field, a variant field of L.
(3) An assignment to a tag field or a variant field (in the case of a tagless
    variant structure location) of a structure location may give to that
    location a (partly) undefined contents.

*

<u>For</u>   each premode PRE=loc(RG,-,-,RD,mode(-,struct(-)))
       each identifier S
         <u>such that</u> is field selector(S,PRE)
<u>Let</u> M_1 ≡ field mode(S,PRE),

       RF_1 ≡ field refy(S,PRE)

<u>Def</u>   location field premode(S,PRE)=loc(RG,stat,RF_1,RD,M_1)

<u>For</u>   each location L of premode PRE
<u>Let</u>   PREV ≡ contents premode(PRE),
       V ≡ contents(L,PRE)
<u>Def</u>   selector list(L,PRE)=selector list(V,PREV),
       parameterization(L,PRE)=parameterization(V,PREV)
<u>For</u>   each identifier S_1∈selector list(V,PREV)

<u>Let</u>   k ≡ index(S_1,selector list(V,PREV))

<u>Def</u>   location field(S_1,L,PRE)=L⁅k⁆ of premode PRE_1

           defined by
               PRE_1=location field premode(S_1,PRE)

                              *

<u>For</u>   each value premode PRE_1

         <u>such that</u> basemode(PRE_1)=struct(-),

       each value V of premode PRE_1,

       each location premode PRE_2=loc(-,dyn,-,-,-)

         <u>such that</u> is assignable(PRE_1,PRE_2),

       each location L of premode PRE_2

<u>Def</u>   are param compatible(V,PRE_1,L,PRE_2)

             =B of premode dpre(bool)
           defined by
               B=(parameterization(V,PRE_1)=parameterization(L,PRE_2))

3. DECLARATIONS AND VISIBILITY

3.1 GENERALITIES

(1) A declaration is a program construction which at each of its elaborations
attaches an object to an identifier appearing in the declaration text and
called a "defining occurrence" of the identifier.
Any other occurrence of the identifier is an "applied occurrence" and it
is connected to one defining occurrence and thus to one declaration,
according to visibility rules. These defining occurrence and declaration
are called the defining occurrence and the declaration of the applied
occurrence, respectively. An applied occurrence, when involved in an
elaboration stands for the object connected to its defining occurrence by
one particular elaboration of its declaration.

(2) The connection between the applied occurrence and the object has two
parts : a static and a possibly dynamic one.

   (a) The static part makes the connection between the applied and the
   defining occurrences. In this description, the defining occurrence
   is uniquely characterized by its program node N, and the static
   properties of the declaration are attached to the node under the form
   of "declared attributes" N.D... ! of that node. The connection
   applied-defining occurrence is described by a "static environment",
   which is an inherited attribute (ENV↓), displaying all declarations
   visible at each node.

   (b) The dynamic part consists in connecting the defining occurrence with
   the object attached to it by one particular elaboration of the
   declaration.
   This is described by a "dynamic environment" (E%) which is a
   collection of objects passed as a parameter to the elaboration
   functions.

   It is to be noted that in some declarations (mode declarations for
   example) the object is static, and the dynamic part is not needed. The
   object is then attached to the defining occurrence under the form of a
   declared attribute.

(3) The visibility rules are based on an ALGOL-like block structure
(begin-end block, do statement, procedure, process) and on a module and
region ("modulion") structure. The latter restricts the rules of the
classical block structure; this can be roughly described as follows :
Let a "group" be a block or a modulion.

   (a) An identifier declared in a modulion, to be visible outside of it,
   must be explicitly granted, i.e. specified in a grant window of the
   modulion.

   (b) An identifier visible in a group surrounding a modulion, to be
   visible in the modulion, must be explicitly seized i.e. specified in
   a seize window of the modulion; however, identifiers with the
   "pervasive property" are automatically seized.

(4) Some cases deserve a special attention.

   (a) The field selectors of a structure mode are in general visible
   wherever an object of that mode can be used; however, the field
   selectors of a "new structure mode" have a restricted visibility when
   they are mentioned as forbidden fields in a grant window of a
   modulion.

   (b) The visibility of the set element identifiers obeys specific rules in
   the sense that it is implied automatically by the visibility of other
   identifiers.

3.2 STATIC ENVIRONMENTS AND VISIBILITY

(1) A "static environment" is a set of "definitions".
(2) There are five categories of definitions :
    - identifiers, of the form def(-),
    - forbidden fields, of the form forbid(-),
    - exceptions, of the form except(-),
    - criticalities, of the form crit proc(-),
    - ancestors, of the form ancestor(-).
(3) The implementation defines a static environment written preenv in which
    the program is supposed to be executed.

                                      *

For   each set DS of definitions
Def   id env(DS)={D∈DS|D=def(-)},
      forbid fields(DS)={D∈DS|D=forbid(-)},
      exceptions(DS)={D∈DS|D=except(-)},
      ancestors(DS)={D∈DS|D=ancestor(-)},
      criticality(DS)={D∈DS|D=crit proc(-)}

3.2.1 IDENTIFIER DEFINITIONS

(1) An identifier definition D is specified by
    - an identifier text T, and D is said to define T,
    - a program node N with declared attributes, and
    - an "origin" O.
    It is written def(T,N,O). It makes T (statically) defined by N, i.e. by
    the declared attributes of N, O being an information specifying the
    "degree of visibility" of the definition in a given set of definitions
    associated to a group.
(2) The origin O of D in a definition set DS associated to a group G is a
    pair [P₁,P₂] where

    - P₁("producer") indicates how the identifier has been made a member of

      DS. P₁ is

      - defined if D∈DS because of a declaration of G,
      - inherited if D∈DS because D belongs to a declaration set of a group
                      G' surrounding G
      - seized,
      - granted, or
      - implied
    - P₂ ("pervasiveness") is perv or nperv.

                                      *

For   each static environment E
Prop   ∀(D₁,D₂∈E):(D₁=def(T₁,-,-) ∧ D₂=def(T₂,-,-)
              ∧ T₁=T₂) ⇒ D₁=D₂

                                      *

For   each set DS of definitions
Def   is locale(DS)=B of premode dpre(bool)

defined by B=∀(D₁,D₂∈DS):

$$ (D_1=def(T_1,N_1,O_1) \land D_2=def(T_2,O_2,N_2) \land T_1=T_2) $$

$$ \Rightarrow (D_1=D_2 $$

$$ \lor \text{ is same set literal definition}(D_1,D_2)) $$

*

For   each pair D_1, D_2 of identifiers definitions
         <u>such that</u> $D_1=def(T_1,N_1,O_1)$,

              $D_2=def(T_2,N_2,O_2)$

Def   is same set literal definition(D_1,D_2)=

         B of premode dpre(bool)
       defined by
         B=($T_1=T_2$) ∧ ($O_1=O_2=$[defined,nperv])

              ∧ (N_1.DCAT!=N_2.DCAT!=lit)

              ∧ N_1.DPREMODE!=N_2.DPREMODE!=set approx(-)

*

For   each set DS of definitions
         <u>such that</u> is locale(DS)
Def   reduce(DS)=the set of definitions DS'
         defined by
       <u>Let</u> $DS_1 \equiv \{D|D\in DS \land (D=def(T,N,O)) \land (N.DCAT!=lit)$

                              ∧ N.DPREMODE!=set approx(-)\}
         $DS_2=DS \backslash DS_1$,

         $T \equiv \{t|def(t,-,-)\in DS_1\}$,

         ∀($t\in T$):($DNS_t \equiv \{N|def(t,N,-)\in DS_1\}$,

                   $N'_t \equiv$ a new dummy node

                      <u>such that</u> N'_t.DCAT! $\equiv$ lit,

                              N'_t.DIMPLIED! $\equiv$ {},

                              N'_t.DISCT! $\equiv$ lit,

                              N'_t.DEFINING NODE! $\equiv$

                                   an arbitrary element of DNS_t,

                              N'_t.DNODESET! $\equiv DNS_t$)

{# N'_t.DEFINING NODE! is used to define N'_t.DPREMODE! at a unique place
in part II. Testing that all the set definitions are similar is also
done in part II #}
         DS'=DS_2 ∪ {def(t,N'_t,[defined,nperv])|t∈T}

*

For   each node N,
         each node set NSET
Def   is recursive(N,NSET)=T of premode dpre(bool)
         defined by
           T=(<u>Case</u> N∈NSET:true,

Case else:∃(N₁∈NSET):is recursive(N,N₁.DNODESET!))

                                    *

For   each pair DS₁,DS₂ of sets of definitions
Def   DS₁ minus DS₂=({D∈DS₁|D≠def(-) ∨ (D=def(T,-,-)
                                       ∧ def(T,-,-)∉DS₂}),
         DS₁ plus DS₂=((DS₁ minus DS₂) ∪ idenv(DS₂))

                                    *

For   each static environment E,
         each identifier text T
Def   identify decla(T,E)=the identifier definition D
             defined by
                 (Case(def(T,-,-)∈E:def(T,N,O) such that def(T,N,O)∈E,
                  Case else:udf),
Def   identify node(T,E)=the node N
             defined by
                 (Case (def(T,-,-)∈E:N such that def(T,N,-)∈E,
                  Case else:udf)
Def   is register identifier(T,E)=B of premode dpre(bool)
             defined by
                 B=(identify node(T,E) is the node of an implementation
                         defined register definition)

                                    *

For   each node N with an attribute N.DCAT!,
         each identifier text T
Def   define(T,N)={def(T,N,[defined,nperv])}

                                    *

For   each identifier definition D=def(T,N,O)
Def   implied definitions(D)=the set DS of definitions
             defined by DS=(Case O=[implied,nperv]:{},
                            Case else:N.DIMPLIED!),
         imply(D)={def(T,N,[implied,nperv])}

3.2.2 FORBIDDEN FIELDS

(1) A forbidden field definition FF is specified by
    - a field selector text S, and
    - a novelty NV=new(N) of a structure mode M of which S is a selector.
    It is written forbid(S,NV). It makes S unusable as a selector of the
    mode M.

                                    *

For   each mode M=mode(new(N),struct(FDL)),
         each identifier text T such that is field selector(T,M)
Def   forbid(T,M)={forbid(T,new(N))}
For   each static environment E,

```
             each novelty NV,
             each identifier text S
Def    is allowed(S,NV,E)=B of premode dpre(bool)
             defined by B=(forbid(S,NV)∉E)
```

3.2.3 EXCEPTIONS

(1) An exception definition XD is specified by
   - a text which is either an identifier or else, and
   - a program node N of an exception handler.
   It is written except(T,N). As for identifier definitions, it makes T
   defined by N; T and N are called corresponding exception identifier text
   and exception handler node respectively.
(2) Any set {[ID→N]|-} such that ID is an exception identifier text and N the
   corresponding exception node is called an "exception map".
(3) The node errornode will stand for an implemented node whose elaboration
   is a program error; thus, the occurrence of an exception for which there
   is no handler is an error.

                                    *

```
For    each pair of definition sets DS₁,DS₂

Def    replace exceptions(DS₁,DS₂)=the definition set DS₃

             defined by DS₃=(DS₁\exceptions(DS₁)) ∪ exceptions(DS₂)

Let    XS ≡ (Case except(else,-)∈DS₂:{},

                Case else:{except(T,-)∈DS₁|except(T,-)∉DS₂}

Def    new exceptions(DS₁,DS₂)=the definition set DS₄

             defined by DS₄=replace exceptions(DS₁,DS₂) ∪ XS
```

                                    *

```
For    each static environment E,
Def    exception nodes(E)={N|except(-,N)∈E}
For    each identifier text T
Def    identify exception node(T,E)=the node N
         defined by (Case except(T,-)∈E:
                            N such that except(T,N)∈E,
                     Case else:
                        (Case except(else,-)∈E:
                                N such that exception(else,N)∈E,
                         Case else:errornode))
```

                                    *

```
For    each node N with an attribute N.DCAT!,
             each identifier text T
Def    define exception(T,N)={except(T,N)}
```

                                    *

```
For    each set XS of exception definitions
Def    is exception locale(XS)=T of mode dpre(bool)
         defined by
```

```
            T=∀(except(i,-)∈XS):
                        #{except(i',-)|i'=i}=1
```

*

For   each exception map XM,
        each exception identifier ID
Def   select exception node(XM,ID)=
                (Case [ID←-]∈XM:XM[ID]
                 Case else:errornode
Def   select exception(XM,ID)
                =exception(select exception node(XM,ID))

*

For   each static environment ENV
        each exception identifier set EXSET
Def   map(ENV,EXSET)=the exception map XM
           defined by
              XM={[ID→N]|ID∈EXSET
                 such that N=identify exception node(ID,ENV)}

3.2.4 CRITICALITY

(1) A criticality definition CD is specified by a program node N of a
    procedure declared in a critical region and granted by it. CD is written
    crit proc(N).

*

For   each identifier definition D=def(T,N,-)
Def   granted procs(D)=the set S of procedure nodes
           defined by S={crit proc(NR)|N.DCAT!=lit
                                       ∧ basemode(N.DPREMODE!)=proc(-)
                                       ∧ N.DVAL!=entry(NR,-)}

*

For   each program node NR,
        each static environment E
Def   proc regionality(NR,E)=RG
           defined by RG=(Case regionality(E)=reg ∧ critproc(NR)∉E:reg
                         Case else:nreg)

3.2.5 ANCESTOR DEFINITIONS

(1) An ancestor definition is specified by
    - a "group specification" GS, which is program, block, module(N),
      region(N), proc(N) or process(N), where N is a program node, and
    - a nesting number K ≥ 1.

It is written ancestor(GS,K).

*

For each static environment E
Let $K \equiv \max(\{j \mid \text{ancestor}(-,j) \in E\})$
Prop $\forall(i \in \{1:K\}):(\#\{D \in E \mid D=\text{ancestor}(-,i)\}=1)$,
     $\#\{D \in E \mid D=\text{ancestor}(\text{region}(-),-)\} \leq 1$,
     $\#\{D \in E \mid D=\text{ancestor}(\text{process}(-),-)\} \leq 1$,
     $\#\{D \in E \mid D=\text{ancestor}(\text{program}(-),-)\} = 1$
For each group specification GS
Def new ancestor(GS,E)=the static environment E_1

        defined by $E_1=\{\text{ancestor}(GS,1)\}$

                    $\cup \{\text{ancestor}(GS',i+1) \mid \text{ancestor}(GS',i) \in E\}$

*

For each static environment E
Def surr region(E)=the object O
        defined by
             (Case ancestor(region(-),-) $\in$ E:
                     O such that ancestor(region(O),-) $\in$ E,
               Case else:O=none)
Let $i \equiv \min(\{j \mid \text{ancestor}(GS,j) \in E$
                       $\land GS \in \{\text{proc}(-),\text{process}(-),\text{program}(-)\}\})$
Def surrounding proc(E)=the node N
        defined by ancestor(proc(N),i) $\in$ E
                    $\lor$ ancestor(process(N),i) $\in$ E,
                    $\lor$ ancestor(program(N),i) $\in$ E
Def surr process(E)=the node N
        defined by
             (Case ancestor(process(-),-) $\in$ E:
                     N such that ancestor(process(N),-) $\in$ E,
               Case else:N= such that ancestor(program(N),-) $\in$ E)
Def surr group(E)=A
        defined by ancestor(A,1) $\in$ E
Def block number(E)
        $= 1+\#\{\text{ancestor}(A,-) \in E \mid A \in \{\text{block},\text{proc}(-),\text{process}(-)\}\}$,
Def regionality(E)=RG
        defined by RG=(Case ancestor(region(-),-) $\in$ E:reg,
                       Case else:nreg)
Def is program level(E)=T of premode dpre(bool)
        defined by
             T=$\forall$(ancestor(GS,-) $\in$ E):
                     GS $\notin$ {block,proc(-),process(-)}
Def is region allowed(E)=T of premode dpre(bool)
        defined by
             T=is program level(E)
                     $\land$ ($\forall$(GS):ancestor(GS,-) $\in$ E $\Rightarrow$ GS $\neq$ region(-))
Def is process allowed(E)=is region allowed(E)

3.2.6 CONSTRUCTION OF STATIC ENVIRONMENTS

For   each identifier definition D=def(T,N,[-,PE])
Def   seize(D)={def(T,N,[seized,PE])}
For   each pervasiveness $PE_1 \in$ {perv,nperv}

Def   grant(D,PE_1)={def(T,N,[granted,PE_1])}

*

For   each static environment E,
        each set DS of definition
          such that is locale(DS),
        each set XS of exception definitions
          such that is exception locale(XS)
Let   IDD ≡ reduce(id env(DS)),
        NEW DIRECT ≡ inherit(strong part(E)) plus IDD,
        NEW IMPLIED ≡ implied(NEW DIRECT)
Def   new block env(E,DS,XS)=the static environment E_1

        defined by E_1=(NEW DIRECT ∪ NEW IMPLIED)

                    ∪ (forbid fields(DS) ∪ forbid fields(E))
                    ∪ new exceptions(exceptions(E),XS)
                    ∪ new ancestor(block,E),
    new dummy env(E)=new block env(E,{},{})

*

For   each static environment E,
        each object SG∈{module(N),region(N)}
          such that N is a program node,
        each set DS of definitions
          such that is locale(DS),
        each set XS of exception definitions
          such that is exception locale (XS)
Let   IDD ≡ reduce(id env(DS)),
        NEW DIRECT ≡ inherit(pervasive part(E)) plus IDD,
        NEW IMPLIED ≡ implied(NEW DIRECT),
        NEW CRIT ≡ (Case SG=region(-):criticality(DS),
                    Case SG=module(-):{})
Def   new modulion env(E,SG,DS,XS)=the static environment E_1

        defined by E_1=(NEW DIRECT ∪ NEW IMPLIED)

                    ∪ (forbid fields(DS) ∪ forbid fields(E))
                    ∪ new exceptions(exceptions(E),XS)
                    ∪ NEW CRIT
                    ∪ new ancestor(SG,E)

*

For   each static environment E,
        each object SG∈{proc(N),process(N),program(N)}
          such that N is a program node,
        each set DS of definitions
          such that is locale(DS),
        each pair EXS,IXS of sets of exception definitions
          such that is exception locale(EXS)
              ∧ is exception locale(IXS)

Let   IDD ≡ reduce(id env(DS)),
      NEW DIRECT ≡ inherit(strong part(E)) <u>plus</u> IDD,
      NEW IMPLIED ≡ implied(NEW DIRECT)

Def   new proc env(E,SG,DS,EXS,IXS)=the static environment E_1

      defined by E_1=(NEW DIRECT ∪ NEW IMPLIED)

                    ∪ (forbid fields(DS) ∪ forbid fields(E))
                    ∪ new exceptions(EXS,IXS)
                    ∪ new ancestor(SG,E)

                  *

For   each set DS of definitions <u>such that</u> is locale(DS),
      each object SG=program(N)

Def   program env(DS,SG)=the static environment E_1

      defined by
          E_1=new proc env(preenv,SG,DS,exception(preenv),{})

                  *

For   each static environment E,
      each set DS of definitions,
      each program node N
         <u>such that</u> N.DCAT!∈{module,region}

Let   SIE ≡ strong part(id env(E)),
      SAVED ≡ id env(E) <u>minus</u> id env(DS)

Def   grantable env(E,DS,N)=the static environment E_1

      defined by E_1=(SAVED ∪ implied from inside(SIE,N))

                    ∪ forbid fields(E)
                    ∪ exceptions(E)
                    ∪ criticality(E)
                    ∪ ancestors(E)

   seizable env(E,DS,N)=the static environment E_2

      defined by E_2=(SAVED ∪ implied from outside(SIE,N))

                    ∪ forbid fields(E)
                    ∪ exceptions(E)
                    ∪ criticality(E)
                    ∪ ancestors(E)

                  *

For   each set DS of definitions
      <u>such that</u> D∈DS ⊃ D=def(-,-,[implied,nperv])

Def   reduce implied(DS)=a set DS_1 of definitions

      defined by
          def(T,N,-)∈DS ⊃ def(T,-,-)∈DS_1,

      (def(T_1,N_1,-)∈DS_1 ∧ def(T_1,T_2,-)∈DS_1) ⊃ N_1=N_2

                *

For   each set DS of definitions
Def   strong part(DS)={D∈DS|D=def(-,-,[PR,-]) ∧ PR≠implied},
      pervasive part(DS)={D∈DS|D=def(-,-,[perv])},
      inherit(DS)={def(T,N,[inherited,PE])|def(T,N,[PR,PE])∈DS
                                   ∧ PR≠implied}

<u>Let</u> $DS_0 \equiv \cup(D\epsilon id\ env(DS))$:implied definitions(D),

      $DS_1 \equiv \{D\epsilon DS_0|D=def(T,N,-)\wedge(def(T,N_1,-)\epsilon DS_0 \Rightarrow$

                $(N=N_1 \vee are\ v\ equivalent(N.DPREMODE!,N_1.DPREMODE!)))\}$

<u>Def</u>   implied(DS)=reduce implied(DS_1)

<u>For</u>   each node N_0

      <u>such that</u> $N_0.DCAT!\epsilon\{module,region\}$

<u>Let</u> $DS_2 \equiv \{def(T,N,O)\epsilon DS_1|N\epsilon descendants(N_0)\}$,

      $DS_3 \equiv \{def(T,N,O)\epsilon DS_1|N\notin descendants(N_0)\}$

<u>Def</u>   implied from inside(DS,N_0)=reduce implied(DS_2),

      implied from outside(DS,N_0)=reduce implied(DS_3)

*

<u>For</u>   each static environment E

<u>Let</u> $DP \equiv \{def(-,-,[P,-])\epsilon E|P\epsilon\{defined,seized,granted\}\}$,

      $SD \equiv \{D\epsilon DP|is\ seizable(D,E)\}$,

      $GD \equiv \{D\epsilon DP|is\ grantable(D,E)\}$

<u>For</u>   each pervasiveness $P\epsilon\{perv,nperv\}$

<u>Def</u>   seize all(E)=$\cup(D\epsilon DP)$:seize(D),

      grant all(E,P)=$\cup(D\epsilon DP)$:grant(D,P)

*

<u>For</u>   each identifier declaration D=def(T,N,-),

      each static environment E

<u>Def</u>   is seizable(D,E)=B_1 of premode dpre(bool)

      defined by $B_1=(D\epsilon E \wedge N.DCAT!\neq with(-))$,

    is grantable(D,E)=B_2 of premode dpre(bool)

      defined by $B_2=(D\epsilon E \wedge (ancestor(region(-),1)\epsilon E$

                      $\Rightarrow$ base mode(N.DPREMODE!)=proc(-))

               $\vee$ regionality(N.DPREMODE!)=nreg)

*

<u>For</u>   each static environment E,

      each program node N with an attribute N.DWINDOW!

<u>Let</u> $DS_0 \equiv \{D\epsilon N.DWINDOW!|D=def(T,N,-)$

                   $\wedge$ identify decla(T,E)=def(T,N,O)

                   $\wedge$ $O\neq[implied,nperv]\}$

<u>Def</u>   seizable and granted(N,E)=the set DS of definitions

      defined by DS=$\cup(D\epsilon DS_0)$:seize(D)

3.2.7 DECLARED ATTRIBUTES

The declared attributes attached to a node N of a defining occurrence of
an identifier describe the static properties valid for all possible objects
attached to the identifier by means of an elaboration of the declaration.
The most used declared attributes are :

(a) N.DCAT!, which is always present and is used to classify the defining
occurrences in several categories on which depends the presence or
absence of other declared attributes.
N.DCAT! is either
- lit for set elements and procedure identifiers,
- mode(NV) where NV is syn or new,
- syn for synonym identifiers involving no dynamic object,
- loc for location identifiers (including those defined in the
parameter passing mechanism),
- based for based location identifiers,
- label(-,-) for label identifiers,
- with(PRE) for field identifiers implicitly declared in
with-statements; PRE is a structure value or location premode,
- dynsyn for synonym identifiers involving a dynamic object (as loop
counters identifiers and in receive case statements),
- signal(-,-) for signal identifiers,
- module for modules, or
- region for regions.
(b) N.DPREMODE! which specifies the premode of the object attached to the
identifier, when this object is a value or a location.
(c) N.DDENMODE! which specifies the denotated mode attached to the
identifier when this object is a mode.
(d) N.DIMPLIED! which specifies which set element identifiers are implied
by the defined identifier.
(e) N.DISCT! which is
- lit when the object is "literal"
- cst when it is "constant"
- dyn otherwise, i.e. when it is dynamic.
(f) N.DVAL! (N.DLOC!) which is the static value (location) attached to the
identifier when N.DISCT!$\epsilon\{$lit,cst$\}$, and which is none when
N.DISCT!=dyn.

*

For   each list L
      such that $C \epsilon L \Rightarrow C \epsilon\{lit,cst,dyn\}$
Def   compose isct(L)=CST
      defined by
            (Case dyn$\notin$L $\wedge$ cstϵL:CST=cst,
            Case dynϵL:CST=dyn,
            Case else:CST=lit)

3.3 DYNAMIC ENVIRONMENTS

(1) The dynamic environment of an elaboration of a phrase P in a given
process instance I is a pair written [S,D] where S is a "stack" and D a
"display". The dynamic environment in which a CHILL program is
elaborated is written preenv%; its stack and display are lists of length
one.
(2) Stacks are lists of locales. The stack S of an elaboration of a phrase P
contains one locale for each block that has been entered and not yet
exited during the elaboration of I before the elaboration of P was
started.
(3) A locale is created for each elaboration of a block. Upon creation,
locales receive a unique identification number.
(4) The locale L created when block B is entered describes the dynamic effect

of the definitions contained in B by a set of pairs of the form [N₁→O].

There is such a pair for each static definition def(T,-,N₁) corresponding

to a definition with a dynamic effect in B. The set of pairs is a
mapping. L is written [NB,M], where NB is the unique identification
number of L and M its mapping.

(5) The computation state C.S. is compatible with a dynamic environment if
and only if C.S. records the properties of each object O which is an
M-object. This description is such that environments are always used in
C.S. compatible with them. Information about location L% with lifetime
NB is needed in C.S. only when an environment with a stack containing
locale [NB,-] is used {# the description is such that no location is
accessed outside its "lifetime" #}.

(6) Displays are lists of locale identification numbers. The identification
numbers in D belong to locales in S; D contains one element for each
block statically enclosing P. (The locale of an activation of such an
enclosing block is always present in S when an elaboration of P is
started).

*

Prop   preenv%=[∤[NB,-]∤,∤NB∤]

*

For   each dynamic environment E=[S,D]
Def   stack(E)=S,
       display(E)=D,
       temporary lifetime(E)=D∤#D∤
For   each number N such that N ≤ #D
Def   trim(D,N)=D∤1:N∤,
       peel(E)=[S,D∤1:#D-1∤]

*

For   each dynamic environment E=[S,D]
Def   new(E)=an environment E₁

          defined by
              Let   NB be a number different from all the numbers that have
                    been used as locale identification number during the
                    elaboration of the program
              E₁=[S∥∤[NB,{}]∤,D∥∤NB∤],

       new process dyn env=new([S∤1:1∤,D∤1:1∤])
For   each display D₁ such that NB₃∈D₁ ⇒ [NB₃,-]∈S

Def   new call env(E,D₁)=an environment E₂

          defined by
              Let   L ≡ S∤#S∤,
                    [NB₁,-] ≡ L

              E₂=[S,D₁∥∤NB₁∤]

*

For   each dynamic environment E=[S,D]
       each dynamic environment E₁=[S₁,D₁]

          such that

$$S_1 = S \nmid 1:(\#S-1) \nmid \| LL \| -,$$

$$LL = [NB,-],$$

$$S \nmid \#S \nmid = [NB,-]$$

Def   adjust(E_1,E)=an environment E_3

defined by

$$E_3 = [S_1 \nmid 1:\#S \nmid, D]$$

*

For   each dynamic environment $E=[S,D]$

each node N

each dynamic object O

Def   declare(N,O,E)=a dynamic environment E_1

defined by

Let $[NB,M] \equiv S \nmid \#S \nmid$

$$E_1 = [S \nmid 1:\#S-1 \nmid \| \nmid [NB,M \cup \{[N \to O]\}] \nmid, D]$$

identify(N,E)=the object O_1

defined by

Let $BM \equiv \cup(NB \epsilon D): \{M | [NB,M] \epsilon S$

$$O = BM[N]$$

4. PROCEDURES

(1) A procedure is a program phrase which can be elaborated from each of its "entry points" in a "dynamic environment" and relatively to a list of "arguments". Such an elaboration is caused by a "call" of a "procedure cluster".

(2) A procedure cluster or simply a cluster is an object constituted by a triple [NP,NE,D] where
   - NP is the program node (of the *<routine>*) defining the main entry point of the procedure.
   - NE is either all in which case a call of the cluster causes the elaboration of the procedure from its main entry point, or it is the node (of the *<entry statement>*) defining a secondary entry point of the procedure, in which case a call of the cluster causes the elaboration of the procedure from that secondary entry point.
   - D is a display.

(3) The dynamic environment of a procedure elaboration caused by the call of a cluster [NP,NE,D] consists of the display D and a stack specified by the call; the list of arguments is specified by the call.

(4) The termination and result, if any, of such an elaboration are those of the elaboration of the call.

(5) A procedure P has a base mode BM which is specified by
   - a "parameter plan" PP,
   - a "result specification" RS,
   - a set XN of exception identifiers,
   - an "implementation specification" IS.
   It is written
     BM=proc(PP,RS,XN,IS).
   BM is also the base mode of the procedure clusters [NP,-,-], where NP is the node of the main entry point in P.

(6) PP is a list of formal parameters, each of them of the form [DM,AT,R], where
   - DM is a denotated mode,
   - AT is a parameter attribute, and
   - R is either a register identifier or none.

(7) The list AL of arguments (specified by the call of a cluster) has the same length as PP. Each argument $A\{i\}$ and the corresponding formal parameter $PP\{i\}=[DM_i,AT_i,R_i]$ specify an object which is transmitted from the call to the elaboration of the cluster. The premode of that object is submitted to constraints determined by DM_i.

(8) A parameter attribute AT has one of the four forms loc, in, out, or inout.
   - If AT=loc the argument is either a location which becomes denoted within the procedure by the *<formal* identifier>, or it is a value, in which case it is assigned to a location created at the call, location which becomes denoted within the procedure by the *<formal* identifier> of the parameter.
   - If AT=in, the argument is a value V. A location L_1, local to the procedure is created and becomes denoted by the *<formal* identifier> of the parameter within the procedure. The value V is assigned to L_1 at the beginning of the procedure elaboration.
   - If AT=out, the argument is a location L. A location L_1, local to the procedure is then created and becomes denoted by the *<formal* identifier> of the parameter within the procedure. At the end of the procedure elaboration, the contents of L_1 is stored into L.

- If AT=inout, the argument is a location L. A location L_1 local to the procedure is created and becomes denoted by the <_formal_ identifier> within the procedure. At the beginning of the procedure elaboration, the value V contained in L is stored into L_1; at the end of the procedure elaboration, the value V_1 contained in L_1 is stored into L.

(9) The register specification R is a hint to the implementation for using a particular register.

(10) The result specification RS is either
   - none, in which the procedure has no result, or
   - [LOC,DM,R] where
     - LOC is loc or nloc,
     - DM is a denotated mode, and
     - R is a register identifier or none.
   If LOC=loc, the result of the procedure is a static location with premode loc(-,stat,-,RD,M) where [RD,M]=DM. If LOC=nloc, the result is a value of premode val(-,-,stat,M). The register specification R is a hint to the implementation.

(11) XN is a set of exception names. If an exception with a name N∈XN is caused during the elaboration of a procedure P of mode M, and if no handler for N is found for it in the procedure static environment, the exception is "reported to the call", i.e. it is as if the exception were caused at the call.

(12) IS puts some restrictions on the use of procedures of mode M. IS has one of the forms : general(R), simple(R) or inline, where R is rec or nrec.
   - Procedure clusters for which IS=general(-) are values, others are not (and the procedure handling is therefore more static).
   - If R=nrec, no recursive call of a procedure cluster may be caused.
   - If IS is inline, the implementation is prompted to implement each call by generating inline expanded code.

                                    *

For   each procedure basemode BM=proc(PP,RS,XN,IS)
Def   result spec(BM)=RS,
      recursivity(BM)=
              (Case IS∈{general(nrec),simple(nrec),inline}:nrec,
                 Case else:rec),
      arg specs(BM)=PP
For   each procedure premode PRE ≡ val(-,RG,-,mode(-,BM))
Let   RF ≡ the implementation defined referability
Def   result premode(PRE)=the object PRE_1

          defined by
               (Case [LOC,[RD,M],-] ≡ RS:
                     PRE_1=(Case LOC=loc:val(vclass,RG,stat,M),

                           Case LOC=nloc:loc(RG,stat,RF,RD,M),
                 Case else:PRE_1=none)

                                    *

For   each procedure base mode PM
Def   is implementable(PM)=T of premode dpre(bool)
         defined by
               the implementation, and which is true if the register
               specifications of PM is implementable.

<u>For</u>   each formal parameter FP of the form [DM,AT,-],
        each regionality RG,
        each premode PRE
<u>Let</u>   [-,M] ≡ DM
<u>Def</u>   is argument(PRE,FP,RG)=the value T of premode dpre(bool)
            defined by
                T=(AT=in ⇒ (PRE=val(-)
                                ∧ is compatible with(M,PRE)
                                ∧ ¬ has the synchro prop(M)
                                ∧ (RG=nreg ⇒ regionality(PRE)=nreg)
                  ∧ AT∈{inout,out}
                     ⇒ (PRE=loc(-,stat,-,-,-)
                        ∧ is compatible with(mode(PRE),vpre(M))
                        ∧ ¬ has the synchro prop(PRE),
                        ∧ ¬ has the rdo prop(PRE)
                        ∧ (RG=nreg ⇒ regionality(PRE)=nreg)
                  ∧ AT=inout ⇒
                     is compatible with(M,vpre(contents premode(PRE)))
                  ∧ AT=loc ⇒((PRE=loc(-,stat,refble,-,-)
                                ∧ is read compatible with(DM,PRE))
                             ∨ (PRE=val(-)
                                ∧ is compatible with(M,PRE)))

                                    *

<u>For</u>   each result specification R=[AT,DM,-],
        each regionality RG,
        each premode PRE
<u>Let</u>   [RD,M]=DM
<u>Def</u>   is result(PRE,R,RG) ≡ the value B of premode dpre(bool)
            defined by
                B=(AT=loc ⇒ (PRE=loc(-,stat,-,-,-)
                                ∧ is read compatible with([DM],PRE)
                                ∧ (RG=nreg ⇒ regionality(PRE)=nreg)
                  ∧ AT=nloc ⇒ (PRE=val(-)
                                ∧ is compatible with(M,PRE)
                                ∧ RG=nreg ⇒ regionality(PRE)=nreg)

                                    *

<u>For</u>   each program node N
          <u>such that</u> N.DCAT!=procedure,
        each set D of definitions
<u>Def</u>   internal entries(N,D)=a set D₁ of definitions

          defined by D₁={def(-,N₁,-)∈D

                        |N₁.DCAT!=lit

                        ∧N₁.DVAL!=entry(N,-)},

        entries(N,D)=a set S of nodes
          defined by S={N₂|def(-,N₂,-)∈internal entries(N,D)}

                                    *

<u>For</u>   each static entry specification ES=entry(NR,NE)
          <u>such that</u> NR is a main procedure entry node,
                    NE is all or an entry node of NR,
        each dynamic environment E {# in which the procedure

                     can be called #}
Let   BN ≡ NR.DBN!,
      D ≡ trim(display(E),BN)
Def   cluster(ES,E)=the cluster [NR,NE,D]

                         *

For   each node N
        such that N.DCAT!⊂lit ∧ basemode(N.DPREMODE!)=proc(-),
      each dynamic environment E
Def   initialize recursivity test(N,E)=
               the dynamic environment E_1

      defined by
           E_1 is E such that the implementation can recognize that at most

           one call of the procedure cluster with node N has taken place
For   each dynamic environment E_2 in which the procedure is called

Def   check recursivity(N,E_2)=the element REC∈{rec,nrec}

      defined by
           (Case there is already one active call of N in E_2:rec,

           Case else:nrec).

5 LABELS

(1) A label specifies a point in the program, from which the elaboration can
be resumed in a dynamic environment; this can be caused by the
elaboration of a *<break statement>*.

(2) All labels can be used in *<goto statements>*, some can also be used in
<exit statements>, and moreover, module label identifiers can be used in
<visibility statements> as shorthand notations. Labels are given a
category (the same label may be given a different category in different
program parts). The category of a label is written label(TYPE,SPP).

(3) TYPE is either exitposs, noexit, module(N) or region(N)
   - exitposs means that the label can be used in *<exit statement>*s,
   - noexit means that it cannot,
   - module(N) or region(N) means that it cannot be used in an exit
     statement, but that it can be used in a *<visibility statement>*.

(4) SPP is the process or procedure node directly surrounding the label
definition; it allows to control that no jump is made out of a procedure
or a process.

$$*$$

For   each set D of definitions
Def   labels(D)={N|def(-,N,-)ϵD $\wedge$ N.DCAT!=label(-)}.

6. PARALLEL PROCESSING

6.1. PROCESSES AND PROCESS INSTANCES

(1) A "process" P is an object characterized by a program node N called the "process node".

(2) A process P has the "category" written process and a parameter plan PP. This parameter plan has the same form as that of procedures, but with parameter attributes of formal parameters restricted to be in or loc.

(3) A "process instance" I is an M-object with two dynamic properties called its "state", and its "regions".

(4) The creation of a process instance specifies a process P (with process node N), a dynamic environment E and a list AL of arguments; the process instance is said to be created for P (or N), E and AL. The elaboration function N.ELAB(E,AL) specifies the "sequence of actions of I".

(5) The list of arguments has the form $AL=AL_1 \| AL_2$, where $\#AL_1=\#PP$. The correspondence $PP\{i\}$, $AL_1\{i\}$ ($1 \leq i \leq \#PP$) is the same as the one defined between formal and actual parameters of procedures. AL_2 is a possibly empty argument list submitted to implementation defined constraints.

(6) The state of a process instance I is either
 - active in which case actions in the action sequence of I may be executed.
 - delayed(QDSET), where QDSET is a set of queue descriptors; in this case, no action in the action sequence of I may be executed, and I is said to be "waiting on" each queue described in QDSET.
 - reactivated(D,O) where O is a value, a triple, or unused and D is a descriptor of the process instance which has "reactivated" the process instance I.

A process instance ceases to exist when all the actions specified by its elaboration function have been executed.

When a process instance I (in active state) executes a sequence of actions, the notation **myself** in the specification of these actions stands for the process instance I itself.

(7) A process instance I in active state may change its state into delayed(-) by executing an action of its action sequence, and it may also change the state delayed(-) of a process instance $I_1(I_1 \neq I)$ into reactivated(-,D), where D is a descriptor of I.

(8) A process instance in a state reactivated(-) puts itself in state active as its first action (reactivated(-) is a transient state).

(9) The "regions" of a process instance I is a possibly empty list of program nodes. For an active process, each such node is the node of a region that the process has locked (possibly by calling a critical procedure) and not yet released. For a delayed process, the first element of the list, if any, is the node of a region the process has released when it was delayed; the other nodes (if any) are those of (preceedingly entered) regions still locked by the delayed process.

(10) A "process instance descriptor" is either nil or a value describing a process instance. The basemode of a process instance descriptor is written instance.

(11) The "main process instance" is the instance created by the
implementation for the node <*program*>, an implementation defined actual
parameter list, and the dynamic environment preenv%.

                                    *

For   each parameter plan P
Def   is process plan(P)=the value T of premode dpre(bool)
           defined by
                T=([,-,AT,-]∈P ⇒ AT∉{out,inout})

                                    *

For   each process P with process node N
Let   PLAN ≡ the parameter plan of P
For   each argument list A={A_i|i∈{1:n}}

        such that the premode of A_i is P_i,

                   #PLAN≤n,
                   ∀(i∈{1:#PLAN}):
                     is argument(P_i,PLAN{i},nreg),

                   ∀(i∈{#PLAN:n}):
                     A_i conforms implemented constraints,

        each dynamic environment E
Let   PRE=val(dclass,nreg,stat,mode(base,instance))
Def   create and start(N,A,E)=V of premode PRE, and an effect
           defined by
                The process instance I for N, A and E, is created in state active
                with regions = {}, and the elaboration of the action sequence
                specified by N.ELAB(E,A) is started in parallel with the present
                elaboration),
                V=descr(I)

                                    *

For   each process instance PI of a process P with node N
Def   descr(PI)=the descriptor of the process instance PI,
        state(PI)=the state of PI,
        regions(PI)=the regions of PI,
        process node(PI)=N
For   each process state ST
Def   change state(PI,ST)=the effect
           defined by
                state(PI) becomes ST

                                    *

For   each process instance descriptor PD which is not nil
Def   instance(PD)=the process instance described by PD,
        is dead(PD)=T of premode dpre(bool)
           defined by
                T=(instance(PD) has ceased to exist)

                                    *

For   each node N of a region
Def   enter region(N)=the effect
           defined by

```
                    regions(myself) becomes ⁅N⁆‖regions(myself)
Def   leave region(N)=the effect
          defined by
                Case regions(myself) ≠ ⁅⁆:
                       regions(myself) becomes tail(regions(myself))
For   each queue descriptor QD,
      each priority P,
      each value V
Def   delay 1(QD,P,V)=the effect
          defined by
                change state(myself,delayed({QD})),
                change queue value(QD,queue value(QD)
                relax region(),
                                  ‖⁅[descr(myself),P,V]⁆)


                            *


For   each list QDL of queue descriptors,
      each list of priorities PL
          such that #QDL=#PL
Let   n ≡ #QDL
Def   delay(QDL,PL)=the effect
          defined by
          change state(myself,delayed({q|q∈QDL})),
          relax region(),
          ∀(i∈{1:n}):
                change queue value(QDL⁅i⁆,
                                  queue value(QDL⁅i⁆)
                                      ‖⁅[descr(myself),PL⁅i⁆,i]⁆)


                            *


For   each process instance descriptor D,
      each queue element object O
Def   reactivate(D,O)=the effect
          defined by
                change state(instance(D),
                       reactivated(descr(myself),O)


                            *


Def   restart=the object O and the effect
          defined by
                (Case reactivated(I,j) ≡ state(myself):
                       (change state(myself,active),Reenter and lock(),
                       O=[I,j]),
                   Case else:udf)
Def   end()=the effect
          defined by
                making myself cease to exist


                            *


For   the main process instance
Def   program end()=the effect
```

defined by
> when all other process instances have ceased to exist, the main
> process instance ceases to exist.

6.2 QUEUES

(1) A "queue" is an M-object with a dynamic property which is a "queue value".
(2) Queues are sublocations of event and buffer locations, they can also be obtained from signals. They are created together with the event and buffer locations in the first case, they are permanent objects as the signals in the second case.
(3) A queue value is a list of triples $[D,p,0]$ where
  - D is a process instance descriptor,
  - p is a "priority", i.e. an integer value in an implementation defined range, and
  - 0 is a value or a pair $[D_1,VL]$ where D_1 is a process instance

  descriptor and VL a value list. 0 is called a queue element object. The basemode of a queue value is written queueval.
(4) A "queue descriptor" is a value describing a queue, its basemode is written descr(queue).
(5) A queue Q is called a "waiting queue" if for all $[D,-,-]$ in its queue value, the state of the process described by D is always delayed(QDSET), and QDSET contains a descriptor of Q itself.
(6) The program is in error if a waiting queue ceases to exist when its queue value is not empty.

*

For   each queue Q,
Def   queue value(Q)=the queue value of Q of basemode queueval,
      descriptor(Q)=the queue descriptor describing Q

*

For   each queue descriptor QD
Def   queue(QD)=the queue described by QD,
      queue value(QD)=queue value(queue(QD))
For   each queue value QV
Def   change queue value(QD,QV)=the effect
         defined by
              queue value(QD) becomes QV
      choose in(QV)=a triple $[D,p,j]$
         defined by
              $[D,p,j] \in QV \land \forall([-,p_1,-] \in QV):p \geq p_1$

*

For   each set QDS of queue descriptors,
      each process instance descriptor D
Def   extract(D,QDS)=the effect
         defined by

$\forall(d \in QDS)$:change queue value($\{t \mid t \in$queue value(d) $\land t \neq [D,-,-]\}$)

*

<u>For</u>   each queue Q,
       each triple T
<u>Def</u>   insert in queue(Q,T)=the effect
           defined by
               change queue value descriptor(Q,queue value(Q)$\|\{T\}$)

6.3 EVENTS

(1) An event E is a value of basemode event(N), where N is none or a positive
    integer; an event location is a location containing an event value, and
    thus also of basemode event(-).
(2) Let EL be an event location of basemode event(N); there is a sublocation
    QL of EL which is a waiting queue. QL (which is created when EL is
    created) is called the "consumer queue" of EL.
    The queue value QV of QL is such that #QV≤N if N≠none. The triples
    belonging to QV have the form [-,-,j] where j is a positive integer.

*

<u>For</u>   each event location EL of base mode BM=event(N)
<u>Def</u>   cqueue(EL,BM)=the consumer queue of EL,
       cqueue value(EL,BM)=queue value(cqueue(EL,BM))
<u>Prop</u>   N#none $\Rightarrow$ $\neq$cqueue value(EL,BM)≤N

*

<u>For</u>   each list BML of n base modes
           <u>such that</u> BML=$\{$event(N_i)$\mid i \in\{1:n\}\}$,

       each list EL of n event locations
           <u>such that</u> $\forall(i \in\{1:n\})$:
               (the basemode of EL$\{i\}$ is BML$\{i\}$,
                $N_i \neq$none $\Rightarrow$ #cqueue value(EL$\{i\}$,BML$\{i\}$)$<N_i$),

       each list PL of n priorities
<u>Let</u>   QDL $\equiv \{$descriptor(cqueue(EL$\{i\}$,BML$\{i\}$))$\mid i \in\{1:n\}\}$
<u>Def</u>   waitev(EL,BML,PL)=V and the effect
           defined by
               <u>Action</u> 1 : delay(QDL,PL)
               <u>Action</u> 2 :
               {# when reactivated by a process instance described by D #}
               [D,j] $\leftarrow$ restart
               V=[D,j]

*

<u>For</u>   each location L of basemode BM=event(-)
<u>Let</u>   QV $\equiv$ cqueue value(L,BM)
<u>Def</u>   wake up(L,BM)=the effect
           defined by
               <u>Action</u>:(<u>Case</u> QV=$\{\}$:<u>skip</u>,
                       <u>Case</u> <u>else</u>:
                       (<u>Let</u>   [D,-,j] $\equiv$ choose in (QV),
                               delayed(QS) $\equiv$ state instance(D),

                    <u>Step</u> 1 : extract(D,QS)
                    <u>Step</u> 2 : reactivate(D,j)))

                                    *

<u>For</u>   each list BML of n base modes
          <u>such that</u> BML=≠event(N_i)|i∈{1:n}≠,

        each list ELL of n event locations
          <u>such that</u> ∀(i∈{1:n}):
                        the basemode of ELL≠i≠ is BML≠i≠,
        each list PL of n priorities,
        each object L which is either none or a location of basemode instance
<u>Let</u>   PREL ≡ loc(nreg,stat,refble,write,mode(base,instance)),
        PREV ≡ contents premode(PREL)
<u>Def</u>   delay until event(ELL,BML,PL,L)=V and the effect
          defined by
              (<u>Case</u>(∃(i∈{1:n}):N_i=none ∧ #cqueue value(ELL≠i≠,BML≠i≠)=N_i:

                        V=exception(*DELAYFAIL*),

              <u>Case</u> <u>else</u> :
                  (<u>Let</u>   PREV ≡ dpre(instance)
                  <u>Step</u> 1 : [I,j] ← waitev(ELL,BML,PL)
                  <u>Step</u> 2 : <u>Case</u> L ≠none:
                              assign(I,PREV,L,PREL,{})
                  V=j)

6.4 BUFFERS

(1) A buffer is a value of base mode buffer(N,DM) where N is none or a
    nonnegative integer and DM is a denoted mode; a buffer location is a
    location containing a buffer value.
(2) Let BL be a buffer location of base mode buffer(N,DM); there are three
    sublocations of BL which are queues, respectively :
    - the message queue MQ,
    - the overflow queue OQ, and
    - the consumer queue CQ.
(3) The queue value MQV of MQ has no more than N elements if N≠none.
(4) OQ is a waiting queue; its queue value OQV is always empty when N=none or
    when #MQV≤N. When not empty, OQV is a set of triples [-,-,V] where V is
    a value of mode M, with [-,M] = DM.
(5) CQ is a waiting queue; its value CQV is a set of triples of the form
    [-,-,j], where j is a positive integer. If CQV is not empty, then MQV is
    empty and conversely.

                                    *

<u>For</u>   each basemode BM=buffer(N,DM)
<u>Prop</u>   ¬ has the synchro prop(DM)
<u>For</u>   each buffer location BL of basemode BM
<u>Def</u>   msg queue(BL,BM)=the message queue of BL,
        ov queue(BL,BM)=the overflow queue of BL,
        cqueue(BL,BM)=the consumer queue of BL,
        msg queue value(BL,BM)=queue value(msg queue(BL,BM)),
        ov queue value(BL,BM)=queue value(ov queue(BL,BM)),
        cqueue value(BL,BM)=queue value(cqueue(BL,BM))
<u>Prop</u>   #msg queue value(BL,BM)>0 ⇒ #cqueue value(BL,BM)=0,
        #cqueue value(BL,BM)>0 ⇒ #msg queue value(BL,BM)=0,

```
            #ov queue value(BL,BM)>0 ∧ N≠none
                      ⇒ # msg queue value(BL,BM)=N,
            N=none ⇒ # ov queue value(BL,BM)=0
```

*

For   each list BML of n basemodes
            such that BML=≬buffer(L_i,M_i)|i∈{1:n}≬,

        each list BL of n buffer locations
            such that ∀(i∈{1:n}):(the basemode of BL≬i≬ is BML≬i≬,
                              #msg queue value(BL≬i≬,BML≬i≬)=0),
        each list PL of n priorities
Let   QDL ≡ ≬descriptor(cqueue(BL≬i≬,BML≬i≬))|i∈{1:n}≬
Def   wait msg(BL,BML,PL)=V and the effect
            defined by
                Action 1 : delay(QDL,PL)
                Action 2 :
                {#when reactivated by process instance described by I #}
        [I,j] ← restart
                V=[I,j]

*

For   each base mode BM=buffer(N,[-,M])
            such that N≠none,
        each buffer location BL of basemode BM
            such that # msg queue value(BL,BM)=N,
        each value V of premode PRE
            such that is comptatible with(M,PRE),
        each priority P
Let   QD ≡ descriptor(ov queue(BL,BM))
Def   wait room(BL,BM,V,PRE,P)=the effect
            defined by
                Action 1 : delay 1(QD,P,V)
                Action 2 :
                  {#when reactivated#}
                  ← restart

*

For   each basemode BM=buffer(N,[-,M]),
        each buffer location BL of basemode BM,
        each value V of premode PRE,
            such that is compatible with(M,PRE),
        each priority P
Let   CQ ≡ cqueue value(BL,BM),
        MQ ≡ msg queue value(BL,BM)
Def   Try to put msg in buffer(BL,BM,V,PRE,P)=the effect
            defined by
                Action :
                  (Case #CQ>0:
                        (Let   [D,-,j] ≡ choose in(CQ),
                                delayed(QS) ≡ state(instance(D))
                         Step 1 : extract(D,QS)
                         Step 2 : reactivate(D,[j,V])),
                   Case #CQ=0 ∧ N≠none ⇒ #MQ<none)
                     insert in queue(msg queue(BL,BM),
                                     [descr(myself),P,V]),
```
```

    <u>Case</u> #MQ=N:
       wait room(BL,BM,V,PRE,P))

          *

<u>For</u>   each list BML of n basemodes
     <u>such that</u> BML=⧴buffer(N_i,DM_i)|i∈{1:n}⧵,

    each list BLL of n buffer locations
     <u>such that</u> ∀(i∈{1:n}):(the basemode of BLL⧴i⧵ is BML⧴i⧵),
    each list PL of n priorities,
    each object L which is either none or a location of
        premode PREL <u>such that</u> basemode(PREL)=instance
<u>Let</u> ∀(i∈{1:n}):(MSQ_i ≡ msg queue value(BLL⧴i⧵,BML⧴i⧵),

           OVQ_i ≡ ov queue value(BLL⧴i⧵,BML⧴i⧵),

           CQ_i ≡ cqueue value(BLL⧴i⧵,BML⧴i⧵)),

   PREV ≡ contents premode(PREL)
<u>Def</u> get msg from buflist(BLL,BML,PL,L,PREL)=M and the effect
    defined by
<u>Action</u> (<u>Case</u> (∀(i∈{1:n}):#MSQ_i=0):

     M=[none,nomsg],
       <u>Case else</u> :
        <u>Let</u> BQ ≡ ‖(i∈{1:n}):(MSQ_i ‖ OVQ_i),

           [D,K,V] ≡ choose in(BQ),
           j <u>such that</u> ([D,K,V]∈MSQ_j

                  ∨ [D,K,V]∈OVQ_j

      <u>Step</u> 1 :
       (<u>Case</u> [D,K,V]∈OVQ_j:

        <u>Let</u>   delayed(QDS) ≡ state(instance(D)
        extract(D,QDS),
        reactivate(D,unused)
       <u>Case</u> [D,K,V]∈MSQ_j ∧ #OVQ_j≠0:

        (<u>Let</u>   [D_1,K_1,V_1] ≡ choose in(OVQ_j),

             delayed(QS) ≡ state(instance(D_1))

       <u>Step</u> 1.1:extract(D_1,QS)

       <u>Step</u> 1.2:reactivate(D_1,unused)

       <u>Step</u> 1.3:change queue value
          (descriptor(msg queue(BLL⧴j⧵,BML⧴j⧵))),
          take out ([D,K,V],MSQ_j)‖⧴D_1,K_1,V_1⧵)

      <u>Case</u> [D,K,V]∈MSQ_j ∧ #OVQ_j=0 :

        change queue value
          (descriptor(msg queue(BLL⧴j⧵,BML⧴j⧵))),
        take out([D,K,V],MSQ_j)

      <u>Step</u> 2:(<u>Case</u> L≠none:assign(D,PREV,L,PREL,{})),
      M=[V,j])
<u>Def</u> try to get msg from buflist(BLL,BML,PL,L,PREL)=V and the effect
    defined by
<u>Step</u> 1 : [V_1,K_1]← get msg from buflist(BLL,BML,PL,L,PREL)

<u>Step</u> 2:(<u>Case</u> K_1≠nomsg:V=[V_1,K_1]

    <u>Case</u> K_1=nomsg:

                    Step 2.1:[I,[j,V]] ← wait msg(BL,BML,PL)
                    Step 2.2:Case L≠none:assign(D,PREV,L,PREL,{}),
         M=[V,j]

6.5 SIGNALS

(1) A signal S is an M-object associated with a program node N, with category
    signal(ML,R) where ML is a possibly empty list of modes, and R a process
    node or any. {# If R≠any, only process instances with node R may receive
    a signal from S #}. S is written signal(N).
(2) Signals are permanent M-objects; thus they need not be created. From a
    signal S, two queues can be obtained, the "signal queue" SQ and the
    "consumer queue" CQ of S; SQ and CQ are permanent objects with the same
    category as S.
    The dynamic properties of S are the two queue values SQV and CQV of SQ
    and CQ respectively : they are called the "signal queue value" and the
    "consumer queue value" of S. These queues are initially empty.
(3) The signal queue value SQV of S is a list of triples of the form
    $[-,-,[D_1,VL]]$ where D_1 is either any or the descriptor of a process

    instance, and VL is a list of values such that #VL=#ML and the mode of
    VL↓i↓ is ML↓i↓. {# If D_1≠any, only the process instance described by D_1

    may "consume" the triple $[-,-,[D_1,-]]$. #}
(4) The consumer queue CQ of S is a waiting queue; its queue value CQV is a
    list of triples of the form [-,-,j] where j is a positive integer.

                                  *

For   each signal S of category C=signal(ML,R)
Prop   ∀(i∈{1:n}):¬ has the synchro prop(ML↓i↓)
Def   sgn queue(S,C)=the signal queue of S,
       cqueue(S,C)=the consumer queue of S,
       sgn queue value(S,C)=queue value(sgn queue(S,C)),
       cqueue value(S,C)=queue value(cqueue(S,C))
For   each triple T=[-,-,[D,VL]] ∈ sgn queue value(S,C)
Prop   R≠any ∧ D≠any ⇒ process node(instance(D))=R

                                  *

For   each signal queue value SQV,
       each process node R
Def   is signal available(R,SQV)=B of premode dpre(bool)
          defined by
              B=#SQV≠0
                ∧ ∃([-,-,[D_1,-]]∈SQV):D_1∈{any,descr(myself)}

              ∧ R≠any ⇒ process node(myself)=R

                                  *

For   each consumer queue value QV of a signal S,
       each object D which is any or a process instance descriptor
          such that D=any ∨ ∃([D_1,-,-]∈QV):D=D_1

Def   choose signal consumer(D,QV)=T
          defined by
              Let   [D_1,p_1,j_1] such that

$$(D \neq any \Rightarrow D=D_1$$
$$\wedge [D_1,p_1,j_1] \epsilon QV$$
$$\wedge \forall([D_1,p_2,-]\epsilon QV):p_1 \geq p_2)$$
$$T=[D_1,p_1,j_1]$$

*

__For__   each list SQVL of n queue values SQV_i,
        each list CL of n signal categories $C_i=signal(-,R_i)$
            __such that__ $(\forall(i\epsilon\{1:n\}):$the category of $SQV_i=C_i$,
                    $\exists(i\epsilon\{1:n\}):$is signal available$(R_i,SQV_i))$
__Def__   choose signal(SQVL,CL)=T
          defined by
              __Let__   BSQ $\equiv \|(i\epsilon\{1:n\}):SQV_i$,
                    $[D_s,p,[D_r,VL]]$ __such that__
                        $([D_s,p,[D_r,VL]]\epsilon BSQ$
                        $\wedge (D_r=any \vee D_r=descr(\underline{myself}))$
                        $\wedge \forall(-,p_1,[D_1,-]]\epsilon BSQ):$
                            $((D_1=any \vee D_1=descr(\underline{myself}))$
                                    $\Rightarrow p \geq p_1$
            $T=[D_s,p,[D_r,VL]]$

*

__For__   each list SL of n signals S_i of category $C_i=signal(ML_i,R_i)$
          __such that__
              $\forall(i\epsilon\{1:n\}):\neg$ is signal available$(R_i,$ sgn queue value$(S_i,C_i)))$,
          each list PL of n priorities
__Let__   QDL $\equiv \{descriptor(cqueue(S_i,C_i))|i\epsilon\{1:n\}\}$
          CL $\equiv \{C_i|i\epsilon\{1:n\}\}$
__Def__   wait sgn(SL,CL,PL)=V and the effect
          defined by
              (__Action__ 1 : delay(QDL,PL),
              __Action__ 2 :
              {# When reactivated by process I #}
              [I,O] ← restart),
              V=[I,O]

*

__For__   each signal S of category C=signal(ML,R),
        each list PREL of n premodes,
        each list VL of values
          __such that__ n=#ML,
                      $\forall(i\epsilon\{1:n\}):$
                          (the premode of VL$\{i\}$ is PREL$\{i\}$
                          $\wedge$ is compatible with(ML$\{i\}$,PREL$\{i\}$)
        each object D which is either the descriptor of a process instance or
                      any

<u>such that</u> D≠any ∧ R≠any ⇒ process node(instance(D))=R,
      each priority P
<u>Def</u>   send msg to signal(S,C,VL,PREL,D,P)=the effect
          defined by
                Action
              (<u>Case</u> # cqueue value(S,C)>0
                    ∧ D≠any ⇒ [D,-,-]∈cqueue value(S,C)):
                      (<u>Let</u>   [D₁,-,j] ≡ choose signal consumer
                                              (D,cqueue value(S,C))),
                            delayed(QDS) ≡ state(instance(D₁))
                        reactivate(D₁,[VL,j])
                        extract(D₁,QDS)),
              <u>Case</u> <u>else</u> :
                  insert in queue(sgn queue(S,C),
                                    {[descr(<u>myself</u>),P,[D,VL]]})

                              *

<u>For</u>   each list SL of n signals S_i of category C_i=signal(ML_i,R_i),
      each list PL of n priorities,
      each object L which is either none or a location of premode PREL
         <u>such that</u> basemode(PREL)=instance
<u>Let</u>   CL ≡ {C_i|i∈{1:n}}
      ∀(i∈{1:n}):(SQ_i ≡ sgn queue value(S_i,C_i),
                  CQ_i ≡ cqueue value(S_i,C_i)),
      PREV ≡ contents premode(PREL)
<u>Def</u>   get msg from sgn list(SL,CL,PL,L,PREL)=T and the effect
          defined by
                Action
              (<u>Case</u> (∀(i∈{1:n}):¬ is signal available(R_i,SQ_i):
                      T=[none,nomsg]
                  <u>Case</u> <u>else</u> :
                      <u>Let</u>   S ≡ choose signal({SQ_i|i∈{1:n}},CL),
                              [D_s,-,[-,VL]-] ≡ S,
                              j <u>such that</u> S∈SQ_j,
                      <u>Step</u> 1 : change queue value
                                      (descriptor(signal queue(S_j,C_j))),
                              take out(S,SQ_j)
                          <u>Step</u> 2 : (<u>Case</u> L≠none: assign(D_s,PREV),L,PREL,{})
                      T=[VL,j])
<u>Def</u>   try to get msg from sgn list(SL,CL,PL,L,PREL)=V and the effect
          defined by
      <u>Step</u> 1 : [VL_1,K_1] ← get msg from sgn list(SL,CL,PL,L,PREL)
      <u>Step</u> 2 :
          <u>Case</u> K_1≠nomsg:
                  V=[VL_1,K_1]
          <u>Case</u> K_1=nomsg:
                  <u>Step</u> 2.1:[I,[VL_2,ML_2,K_2]] ← wait sgn(SL,CL,PL)
                  <u>Step</u> 2.2:<u>Case</u> L≠none:assign(D,PREV,L,PREL,{})

$$V=[VL_2,K_2]$$

6.6 REGIONS

(1) A region is a program node with the category region; this node is the node of a modulion. Procedures granted by such a modulion are "critical procedures".
(2) A region ensures mutual exclusion between executions of critical procedures, and also between the execution of its body and one of its critical procedures. In this description, this is modelled by associating with the node N of each region a permanent M-object called a lock, written lock(N)
(3) The dynamic property of a lock is its "state", wich is open or closed. When the execution of the program starts all locks are open.
(4) Waiting for a lock to open is described here as "busy waiting" but the implementation may use other suitable methods.

                                      *

<u>For</u>   each region node N
<u>Def</u>   state(N)=the state of lock(N),
       Enter and lock(N)=the effect
          defined by
              Action : (<u>Case</u> state(N)=open:(state(N) <u>becomes</u> closed,
                                              enter region(N)),
                        <u>Case else</u>:enter and lock(N)),
       Exit(N)=the effect
          defined by
              Action : (state(N) becomes open,
                        enter region (N)),
       Reenter and lock()=the effect
          defined by
              Action(<u>Case</u> region(<u>myself</u>)≠⧸⧹:
                        <u>Let</u>   N ≡ region(<u>myself</u>)⧸1⧹
                        <u>Step</u> 1 : leave region()
                        <u>Step</u> 2 : Enter and lock(N))
       Relax region()=the effect
          defined by
              <u>Case</u> region(<u>myself</u>)≠⧸⧹:
                        <u>Let</u>   N ≡ region(<u>myself</u>⧸1⧹
                        <u>Action</u> : state(N) <u>becomes</u> open

7. MODE HANDLING

(1) Premodes, modes and basemodes are attributes of values and locations {#
    see sections 1 and 2 #}.
(2) Writing a recursive mode would be infinite; in this description, it is
    given a finite notation by writing "node(N)" at some places,where N is
    the node of the defining occurrence of a mode identifier. The explicit
    notation (possibly infinite) for the mode could be obtained step by step
    by applying to "node(N)" the function develop; for recursive modes the
    complete process is endless, but it is never needed.
(3) In this description, the replacements of node(N), are left implicit.

                                    *

For   each mode M=mode(-,BM),
        each premode PRE_1=val(CL_1,RG,ST_1,M_1),

        each premode PRE_2=loc(RG,ST_2,RF_2,RD_2,M_2),

        each denotated mode DM_3=[-,M_3]

Def   basemode(M)=BM,
        mode(PRE_1)=M_1,

        mode(PRE_2)=M_2,

        mode(DM_3)=M_3,

        staticity(PRE_1)=ST_1,

        staticity(PRE_2)=ST_2,

        denmode(PRE_1)=[write,M_1],

        denmode(PRE_2)=[RD_2,M_2],

        regionality(PRE_1)=CR_1,

        regionality(PRE_2)=CR_2,

        class(PRE_1)=CL_1,

        refy(PRE_2)=RF_2

                                    *

For   each root R of a discrete base mode
Let   {MIN:MAX} ≡ R
Def   dpre(R)=
            val(dclass,nreg,stat,mode(base,discr(R,MIN,MAX)))

                                    *

For   each mode M
Def   vpre(M)=
            val(vclass,nreg,stat,M)

                                    *

For   each mode M
Def   develop(M)=the mode M_1

            defined by
                M_1=(Case M=node(N):mode(N.DDENMODE!),

```
                  Case else∈M)
           {# the use of this function is often implicit. #}


                              *


For    each mode M,
       each proram node N
Def    is wellformed(N,M)=T of premode dpre(bool)
          defined by
              T=
                 (Case M=node(N₁):

                     (Case N=N₁:false,

                      Case else is wellformed(N,develop(M))),
                  Case basemode(M)=struct(-):
                     Let    FFL=single field list(basemode(M))
                     ∀(i∈{1:#FFL}):
                         (Let    field(-,-,Mᵢ,-) ≡ FFL↓i↓

                          is wellformed(N,Mᵢ)),
                  Case array(I,E,R) ≡ basemode(M):
                              is wellformed(N,E),
                  Case else:true)


                         *


For    each list RGL of regionalities
Def    compose regionality(RGL)=a regionality RG
          defined by
                RG=(Case reg∈RGL:reg,
                    Case else:nreg)


                              *


For    each regionality RG∈{reg,nreg},
       each base mode BM
Def    compose regionality(RG,BM)=a regionality RG₁

          defined by
                RG₁=(Case RG=nreg:nreg,

                     Case RG=reg ∧ has the ref prop(BM):reg,
                     Case else:nreg)


                         *


For    each pair of readonlynesses RD₁,RD₂

Def    most restrictive(RD₁,RD₂)=a readonlyness

          defined by
                Case RD₁=rdo:RD=rdo,

                Case else:RD=RD₂)


                         *


For    each pair of base modes BM₁ and BM₂,

       each staticity ST
Def    are similar(BM₁,BM₂,ST)=T of premode dpre(bool)
```

defined by T=
  ($\underline{Case}$ discr($K_1,-,-$) $\equiv BM_1$

    $\land$ discr($K_2,-,-$) $\equiv BM_2:K_1=K_2$,

  $\underline{Case}$ discr($S_1,-,-$) $\equiv BM_1$

    $\land$ string(K_2,L) $\equiv BM_2:(S_1=bool \Leftrightarrow K_2=bit \lor S_1=char \Leftrightarrow K_2=char)$

                          $\land$ ST=stat $\Rightarrow L=1$,

  $\underline{Case}$ string(K_1,L) $\equiv BM_1$

    $\land$ discr($S_2,-,-$) $\equiv BM_2:(K_1=bit \Leftrightarrow S_2=bool \lor K_1=char \Leftrightarrow S_2=char)$

                          $\land$ ST=stat $\Rightarrow L=1$,

  $\underline{Case}$ poset(M_1) $\equiv BM_1$

    $\land$ poset(M_2) $\equiv BM_2$:are equivalent(M_1,M_2,stat),

  $\underline{Case}$ ref($-,M_1$) $\equiv BM_1$

    $\land$ ref($-,M_2$) $\equiv BM_2$:are equivalent(M_1,M_2,stat),

  $\underline{Case}$ $BM_1 \equiv$ ptr

    $\land BM_2 \equiv$ ptr:true,

  $\underline{Case}$ row($-,M_1$) $\equiv BM_1$

    $\land$ row($-,M_2$) $\equiv BM_2$:are equivalent(M_1,M_2,dyn),

  $\underline{Case}$ proc(PP_1,RS_1,XN_1,general(RC_1)) $\equiv BM_1$

    $\land$ proc(PP_2,RS_2,XN_2,general(RC_2)) $\equiv BM_2$:

      ($\#PP_1=\#PP_2$

      $\land \forall(i\in\{1:\#PP_1\})$:

        ($\underline{Let}$ ([[RD_{i_1},M_{i_1}],AT_{i_1},R_{i_1}] $\equiv PP_1\{i\}$,

               [[RD_{i_2},M_{i_2}],AT_{i_2},R_{i_2}] $\equiv PP_2\{i\}$)

        $RD_{i_1}=RD_{i_2}$

        $\land$ are 1-equivalent([RD_{i_1},M_{i_1}],[RD_{i_2},M_{i_2}],stat)

        $\land AT_{i_1}=AT_{i_2}$,

        $\land R_{i_1}=R_{i_2}$)

      $\land$ ($RS_1=$none $\Leftrightarrow RS_2=$none

        $\lor$ ($\underline{Let}$ ([LOC_1,[RD_1,M_1],R_1] $\equiv RS_1$,

             [LOC_2,[RD_2,M_2],R_2] $\equiv RS_2$)

        $LOC_1=LOC_2$

        $\land RD_1=RD_2$

        $\land$ are 1-equivalent([RD_1,M_1],[RD_2,M_2],stat)

        $\land R_1=R_2$))

      $\land XN_1=XN_2$

      $\land RC_1=RC_2$),

  $\underline{Case}$ $BM_1=$instance $\land BM_2=$instance:true,

<u>Case</u> event(N$_1$)=BM$_1$

$\land$ event(N$_2$)=BM$_2$:N$_1$=N$_2$,

<u>Case</u> buffer(N$_1$,[RD$_1$,E$_1$]) $\equiv$ BM$_1$

$\land$ buffer(N$_2$,[RD$_2$,E$_2$]) $\equiv$ BM$_2$:(N$_1$=N$_2$

$\land$ RD$_1$=RD$_2$

$\land$ are 1-equivalent([RD$_1$,E$_1$],

[RD$_2$,E$_2$])),

<u>Case</u> string(K$_1$,L$_1$) $\equiv$ BM$_1$

$\land$ string(K$_2$,L$_2$) $\equiv$ BM$_2$:(K$_1$=K$_2$

$\land$ (ST=stat $\Rightarrow$ L$_1$=L$_2$)),

<u>Case</u> array(I$_1$,E$_1$,R$_1$) $\equiv$ BM$_1$

$\land$ array(I$_2$,E$_2$,R$_2$) $\equiv$ BM$_2$:(are v-equivalent(I$_1$,I$_2$)

$\land$ are equivalent(E$_1$,E$_2$)

$\land$ R$_1$=R$_2$

$\land$ ST=stat $\Rightarrow$ card(I$_1$)=card(I$_2$)),

<u>Case</u> struct(FDL$_1$) $\equiv$ BM$_1$

$\land$ struct(FDL$_2$) $\equiv$ BM$_2$:(# FDL$_1$=#FDL$_2$

$\land$ $\forall$(i$\in${1:#FDL$_1$}:

are field equivalent
(FDL$_1$[i],BM$_1$,FDL$_2$[i],BM$_2$)),

<u>Case</u> <u>else</u>:false)

*

<u>For</u>   each pair of modes M$_1$ and M$_2$,

each staticity ST
<u>Let</u>   mode(NV$_1$,BM$_1$) $\equiv$ M$_2$

mode(NV$_2$,BM$_2$) $\equiv$ M$_2$

<u>Def</u>   are v-equivalent(M$_1$,M$_2$,ST)=T of premode dpre(bool)

defined by T=
(NV$_1$=NV$_2$

$\land$ are similar(BM$_1$,BM$_2$,ST)),

are equivalent(M$_1$,M$_2$,ST)=T of premode dpre(bool)

defined by T=
(are v-equivalent(M$_1$,M$_2$,ST)

$\land$ (BM$_1$=discr(-) $\Rightarrow$ BM$_1$=BM$_2$))

*

<u>For</u>   each pair of denotated modes DM$_1$,DM$_2$,

each staticity ST
<u>Let</u>   [RD$_1$,M$_1$] $\equiv$ DM$_1$,

[RD$_2$,M$_2$] $\equiv$ DM$_2$,

```
        mode(NV₁,BM₁) ≡ M₁,
        mode(NV₂,BM₂) ≡ M₂
```

Def   are 1-equivalent(DM_1,DM_2,ST)=T of premode dpre(bool)

```
        defined by T=
            (are equivalent(M₁,M₂,ST)
         ∧ has the rdo prop(DM₁) ⊶ has the rdo prop(DM₂)
         ∧ (Case ref(RD₃,M₃) ≡ BM₁
                ∧ ref(RD₄,M₄) ≡ BM₂:
                    are 1-equivalent([RD₃,M₃],[RD₄,M₄],stat),
            Case row(RD₃,M₃) ≡ BM₁
                ∧ row(RD₄,M₄) ≡ BM₂:
                    are 1-equivalent([RD₃,M₃],[RD₄,M₄],dyn),
            Case array(I₁,E₁,R₁) ≡ BM₁
                ∧ array(I₂,E₂,R₂) ≡ BM₂:
                    are 1-equivalent([RD₁,E₁],[RD₂,E₂],stat),
            Case struct(FDL₁) ≡ BM₁
                ∧ struct(FDL₂) ≡ BM₂:
                    (#FDL₁ ≡ #FDL₂,
                    ∀(i∈{1:#FDL₁}:
                        are field 1-equivalent(FDL₁⌽i⌽,FDL₂⌽i⌽)))
```

                                    *

For   each pair of field descriptors F_1,F_2,

        each pair of structure base modes SM_1,SM_2

Def   are field equivalent(F_1,SM_1,F_2,SM_2)=T of premode dpre(bool)

```
        defined by
            T=(Case F₁=field(-) ∧ F₂=field(-):
                    are fixed field equivalent(F₁,F₂),
                Case F₁=var(-) ∧ F₂=var(-):
                    are variant field equivalent(F₁,SM₁,F₂,SM₂),
                Case else:false)
```

Def   are field 1-equivalent(F_1,F_2)=T of premode dpre(bool):

```
        defined by
            T=(Case F₁=field(-) ∧ F₂=field(-):
                    are fixed field 1-equivalent(F₁,F₂),
                Case F₁=var(-) ∧ F₂=var(-):
                    are variant field 1-equivalent(F₁,SM₁,F₂,SM₂),
                Case else:false)
```

                                    *

For   each pair of fixed field descriptors F_1,F_2

<u>Let</u> $field(S_1,RD_1,M_1,RP_1)=F_1$,
      $field(S_2,RD_2,M_2,RP_2)=F_2$

<u>Def</u>   are fixed field equivalent$(F_1,F_2)=T$ of premode dpre(bool)
        defined by
            T=are equivalent$(M_1,M_2,stat)$

            $\wedge\ RP_1=RP_2$

<u>Def</u>   are fixed field 1-equivalent$(F_1,F_2)=T$ of premode dpre(bool)
        defined by
            T=are 1-equivalent$(M_1,M_2,stat)$

            $\wedge\ RP_1=RP_2$

                              *

<u>For</u>   each pair of base modes SM_1=struct(FDL_1),SM_2=struct(FDL_2),
      each $F_1\epsilon FDL_1$ <u>such that</u> D_1=var(-),
      each $F_2\epsilon FDL_2$ <u>such that</u> D_2=var(-)

<u>Let</u>   var$(PL_1,AL_1,SYAL_1) \equiv D_1$,
      var$(PL_2,AL_2,SYAL_2) \equiv D_2$
      $\forall(i\epsilon\{1:\#PL_1\}):[T_{1_i},PRE_{1_i},P_{1_i}] \equiv PL_1\{i\}$,
      $\forall(i\epsilon\{1:\#AL_1\}):[CS_{1_i},DL_{1_i}] \equiv AL_1\{i\}$,
      $\forall(i\epsilon\{1:\#PL_2\}):[T_{2_i},PRE_{2_i},P_{2_i}] \equiv PL_2\{i\}$,
      $\forall(i\epsilon\{1:\#AL_2\}):[CS_{2_i},DL_{2_i}] \equiv AL_2\{i\}$,

<u>Def</u>   are variant field equivalent(F_1,SM_1,F_2,SM_2)
                    $=T$ of premode dpre(bool)
        defined by
            T=($\#PL_1=\#PL_2$

              $\wedge\ \#PL_1\neq0 \Rightarrow$

                  ($\forall(i\epsilon\{1:\#PL_1\})$:

                    (T_{1_i}=none $\Leftrightarrow T_{2_i}$=none

                    $\wedge\ T_{1_i}\neq$none $\Rightarrow$ tag position(T_{1_i},SM_1)

                                    =tag position(T_{2_i},SM_2)

                    $\wedge$ are compatible(PRE_{1_i},PRE_{2_i})

                    $\wedge\ P_{1_i}$=none $\Leftrightarrow P_{2_i}$=none

                    $\wedge\ (P_{1_i}=P_{2_i} \vee P_{1_i}$=dyn $\vee P_{2_i}$=dyn)))

              $\wedge\ \#AL_1=\#AL_2$

              $\wedge\ \forall(i\epsilon\{1:\#AL_1\})$:

                    are variant alternative equivalent(AL_{1_i},AL_{2_i})

              $\wedge\ SYAL_1=SYAL_2$)

<u>Def</u>   are variant field 1-equivalent(F_1,SM_1,F_2,SM_2)
                    $=T_1$ of premode dpre(bool)

        defined by
            T=are variant field equivalent(F_1,SM_1,F_2,SM_2)

$\wedge \ \forall(i\epsilon\{1:\#AL_1\}:$

$\qquad$ are variant alternative 1-equivalent$(AL_{1_i},AL_{2_i}))$

$\qquad\qquad\qquad *$

For each pair of variant alternative AL_1,AL_2

$\qquad$ <u>such that</u> $\# \ AL_1=\# \ AL_2$

Let $\forall(i\epsilon\{1:\#AL_1\}):[CS_{1_i},FL_{1_i}] \equiv AL_1,$

$\qquad\qquad\qquad [CS_{2_i},FL_{2_i}] \equiv AL_2$

Def are variant alternative equivalent(AL_1,AL_2)

$\qquad\qquad\qquad$ =T of premode dpre(bool)

$\qquad$ defined by

$\qquad\qquad T=\forall(i\epsilon\{1:\#AL_1\}):CS_{1_i}=CS_{2_i} \ \wedge$

$\qquad\qquad\qquad\qquad \#FL_{1_i}=\#FL_{2_i} \ \wedge$

$\qquad\qquad\qquad\qquad \forall(j\epsilon\{1:\#FL_{1_i}\}):$

$\qquad\qquad\qquad\qquad\qquad$ are fixed field equivalent$(FL_{1_i}\{j\},FL_{2_i}\{j\})$

Def are variant alternative 1-equivalent(AL_1,AL_2)

$\qquad\qquad\qquad$ =T_1 of premode dpre(bool)

$\qquad$ defined by

$\qquad\qquad T_1=\forall(i\epsilon\{1:\#AL_1\}):CS_{1_i}=CS_{2_i} \ \wedge$

$\qquad\qquad\qquad\qquad \#FL_{1_i}=\#FL_{2_i} \ \wedge$

$\qquad\qquad\qquad\qquad \forall(j\epsilon\{1:\#FL_{1_i}\}):$

$\qquad\qquad\qquad\qquad\qquad$ are fixed field 1-equivalent$(FL_{1_i}\{j\},FL_{2_i}\{j\})$

$\qquad\qquad\qquad *$

For each mode $M_1,$

$\qquad$ each value premode PRE=val$(CL,RG,ST,M_2),$

$\qquad$ each staticity ST'

Let mode$(NV_1,BM_1) \equiv M_1,$

$\qquad$ mode$(NV_2,BM_2) \equiv M_2,$

$\qquad ST_1 \equiv$ (<u>Case</u> ST=stat $\wedge$ ST'=stat:stat,

$\qquad\qquad$ <u>Case else</u>:dyn)

Def is compatible with(M_1,PRE,ST')=T of premode dpre(bool)

$\qquad$ defined by T=

$\qquad\qquad$ (<u>Case</u> CL=all:true,

$\qquad\qquad$ <u>Case</u> CL=null

$\qquad\qquad\qquad \wedge \ BM_1\epsilon\{ref(-),ptr,row(-),proc(-),instance\}$

$\qquad\qquad\qquad\qquad$:true,

$\qquad\qquad$ <u>Case</u> CL=refcl $\wedge$ ref$(RD_3,M_3) \equiv BM_1$

$\qquad\qquad\qquad\qquad \wedge$ ref$(RD_4,M_4) \equiv BM_2$

$\qquad\qquad\qquad\qquad$:is read compatible with$([RD_3,M_3],$

$\qquad\qquad\qquad\qquad\qquad\qquad\qquad\qquad [RD_4,M_4],stat),$

$\qquad\qquad$ <u>Case</u> CL=refcl $\wedge BM_1 \equiv$ ptr

$$\wedge \ BM_2 \equiv ref(-)$$

:true

Case CL≡refcl ∧ row(RD_3,M_3) ≡ BM_1

$\wedge$ (ref(RD_4,M_4) ≡ BM_2

$\vee$ row(RD_4,M_4) ≡ BM_2)

:is read compatible with([RD_3,M_3],

[RD_4,M_4],dyn),

Case CL=dclass

: are similar(M_1,M_2,ST_1),

Case CL=vclass

: ¬ has the ref prop(M_1)

⇒ are v-equivalent(M_1,M_2,ST)

∨ has the ref prop(M_1)

⇒ is restrictable to (M_2,M_1,ST)

Case else false)

*

For   each pair of denotated modes DM_1,DM_2

Let   [RD_1,M_1] ≡ DM_1,

[RD_2,M_2] ≡ DM_2,

BM_1 ≡ basemode(M_1),

BM_2 ≡ basemode(M_2)

Def   is read compatible with(DM_1,DM_2,ST)=T of premode dpre(bool)

defined by

T=are equivalent(DM_1,DM_2,ST)

∧ is read only(DM_2) ⇒ is read only(DM_1)

∧ (Case ref(RD_3,M_3) ≡ BM_1 ∧

ref(RD_4,M_4) ≡ BM_2:

is read compatible with([RD_3,M_3],[RD_4,M_4],stat),

Case row(RD_3,M_3) ≡ BM_1 ∧

row(RD_4,M_4) ≡ BM_2:

is read compatible with([RD_3,M_3],[RD_4,M_4],dyn),

Case array(-,E_1,-) ≡ BM_1 ∧

array(-,E_2,-) ≡ BM_2:

is read compatible with([RD_1,E_1],[RD_2,E_2],stat),

Case struct(FDL_1) ≡ BM_1 ∧

struct(FDL_2) ≡ BM_2:

Let FFL_1 ≡ single field list(BM_1),

FFL_2 ≡ single field list(BM_2)

$\forall(i\in\{1:\#FFL_1\})$:

are field read compatible with($FFL_1\{i\}$,$FFL_2\{i\}$)

<u>Case</u> <u>else</u>:true)

*

<u>For</u>   each pair of fixed field descriptors F_1, F_2

<u>Let</u>   field$(-, RD_1, M_1, -) \equiv F_1$,

field$(-, RD_2, M_2, -) \equiv F_2$

<u>Def</u>   are field read compatible with$(F_1, F_2) = T$ of premode dpre(bool)

defined by
T=is read compatible with$([RD_1, M_1], [RD_2, M_2], stat)$

*

<u>For</u>   each pair of modes M_1, M_2,

each staticity ST

<u>Let</u> $BM_1 \equiv$ basemode(M_1),

$BM_2 \equiv$ basemode(M_2)

<u>Def</u>   is restrictable to$(M_1, M_2, ST) = T$ of premode dpre(bool)

defined by
T=(<u>Case</u> $\neg$ has the ref prop(BM_1):

are equivalent(M_1, M_2, ST),

<u>Case</u> ref$(RD_3, M_3) \equiv BM_1 \wedge$

ref$(RD_4, M_4) \equiv BM_2$:

is read compatible with$([RD_4, M_4], [RD_3, M_3], stat)$,

<u>Case</u> BM_1=ptr $\wedge BM_2$=ptr:

are equivalent$(M_1, M_2, stat)$,

<u>Case</u> row$(RD_3, M_3) \equiv BM_1 \wedge$

row$(RD_4, M_4) \equiv BM_2$:

is read compatible with$([RD_4, M_4], [RD_3, M_3], dyn)$,

<u>Case</u> array$(-, E_1, -) \equiv BM_1 \wedge$

array$(-, E_2, -) \equiv BM_2$:

is restrictable to$(E_1, E_2, stat)$,

<u>Case</u> struct$(FDL_1) \equiv BM_1 \wedge$ struct$(FDL_2) \equiv BM_2$:

$\#FDL_1 = \#FDL_2$

$\wedge$ (<u>Let</u> FFL_1=single field list(BM_1),

FFL_2=single field list(BM_2)

$\Psi(i \epsilon\{1 : \#FFL_1\}$:is field restrictable to

$(FFL_1\{i\}, FFL_2\{i\})$,

<u>Case</u> <u>else</u>:false)

*

<u>For</u>   each pair of field descriptors F_1, F_2

<u>Let</u>   field$(-, -, M_1, -) \equiv F_1$,

```
        field(-,-,M₂,-) ≡ F₂
```
$$\text{field}(-,-,M_2,-) \equiv F_2$$

<u>Def</u>   is field restrictable to(F_1,F_2)=is restrictable to(M_1,M_2,stat)

*

<u>For</u>   each pair of value premodes PRE_1 and PRE_2

<u>Let</u>   val(CL_1,RG_1,ST_1,M_1) ≡ PRE_1,

val(CL_2,RG_2,ST_2,M_2) ≡ PRE_2,

mode(NV_1,BM_1) ≡ M_1,

mode(NV_2,BM_2) ≡ M_2,

ST ≡ (<u>Case</u> ST_1=stat ∧ ST_2=stat:stat,

      <u>Case else</u> : dyn)

<u>Def</u>   are compatible(PRE_1,PRE_2)=T of premode dpre(bool)

   defined by T=

      (<u>Case</u> PRE_1=PRE_2:true,

       <u>Case</u> CL_1=all:true,

       <u>Case</u> CL_1=null:CL_2:refcl,

           ∨ (CL_2ϵ{dclass,vclass}

               ∧ BM_2 ϵ {ref(-),ptr,row(-),proc(-),instance})

       <u>Case</u> CL_1=refcl:

          (<u>Case</u> CL_2=refcl:<u>Let</u> K_1(-,M_3) ≡ BM_1

                      K_2(-,M_4) ≡ BM_4:

                  (<u>Case</u> K_1=row ∨ K_2=row:

                     are equivalent(M_3,M_4,dyn)

                  <u>Case else</u>

                     are equivalent(M_3,M_4,stat)),

        <u>Case</u> CL_2ϵ{dclass,vclass}:

          (BM_2ϵ{ref(-),ptr,row(-)}

         ∧((ref(RD_3,M_3) ≡ BM_1

           ∧ ref(RD_4,M_4) ≡ BM_2

           ∧ are equivalent(M_4,M_3,stat))

          ∨(ref(-) ≡ BM_1

           ∧ BM_2=ptr)

          ∨(row(RD_4,M_4) ≡ BM_2

           ∧ K(RD_3,M_3) ≡ BM_1

           ∧ Kϵ{ref,row}

           ∧ are equivalent(M_4,M_3,dyn))),

     <u>Case</u> CL_1 ≡ dclass ∧ CL_2 ϵ{dclass,vclass}:

         are similar(BM_1,BM_2,ST),

     <u>Case</u> CL_1=vclass ∧ CL_2=vclass:

         are v-equivalent(M_1,M_2,ST),

     <u>Case</u> are compatible(PRE_2,PRE_1):true,

        Case else:false)

*

For   each list of value premodes PREL
Def   are compatible(PREL)=T of premode dpre(bool)
        defined by
            $T=\forall(i,j\in\{1:\#PREL\})$:are compatible($PRE_i,PRE_j$)

*

For   each denotated mode DM
Let   [RD,-] ≡ DM,
        BM ≡ basemode(DM)
Def   is readonly(DM)=T of premode dpre(bool)
        defined by T=(RD=rdo),
Def   has the rdo prop(DM)=T of premode dpre(bool)
        defined by T=
            is readonly(DM)
            v(Case array(-,E,-) ≡ BM:
                has the rdo prop([RD,E]),
             Case struct(FDL) ≡ BM:
                (Let   FFL ≡ single field list(BM)
                  $\exists(i\in\{1:\#FFL\})$:has field the rdo prop(FFL↓i↓)),
             Case else:false)

*

For   each fixed field descriptor F=field(-,RD,M,-)
Def   has field the rdo prop(F)=T of premode dpre(bool)
        defined by
            T=has the rdo prop([RD,M])

*

For   each base mode BM
Def   is reference mode(BM)=T of premode dpre(bool)
        defined by
            $T=(BM\in\{ref(-),ptr,row(-)\})$
Def   has the ref prop(BM)=T of premode dpre(bool)
        defined by T=
             is reference mode(BM)
             v(Case array(-,E,-) ≡ BM:
                has the ref prop(E),
             Case struct(FDL) ≡ BM:
                (Let   FFL ≡ single field list(BM)
                    $\exists(i\in\{1:\#FFL\})$:has field the ref prop(FFL↓i↓)),
             Case else:false)

*

For   each fixed field descriptor F=field(-,-,M,-)
Def   has field the ref prop(F)=has the ref prop(M)

*

For   each base mode BM
Def   is synchro mode(BM)=T of premode dpre(bool)

```
          defined by
              T=(BMε{event(-),buffer(-)})
Def    has the synchro prop(BM)=T of premode dpre(bool)
          defined by T=
              is synchro mode(BM)
              v(Case array(-,E,-) ≡ BM:
                     has the synchro prop(E),
                  Case struct(FDL) ≡ BM:
                     (Let    FFL ≡ single field list(BM)
                      ∃(iε{1:#FFL}):has field the synchro prop(FFL⦃i⦄)),
                  Case else:false)
```

                                       *

For   each fixed field descriptor F=field(-,-,M,-)
Def   has field the synchro prop(F)=has the synchro prop(M)

                                       *

For   each pair of value premodes PRE₁,PRE₂
$$\underline{such\ that}\ are\ compatible(PRE_1,PRE_2),$$
$$class(PRE_1),class(PRE_2)$$
$$\varepsilon\{all,vclass,dclass\},$$
$$base\ mode(PRE_1),base\ mode(PRE_2)$$
$$\varepsilon\{discr(-),poset(-),string(-)\}$$

```
Let    val(CL₁,RG₁,ST₁,M₁) ≡ PRE₁,
       val(CL₂,RG₂,ST₂,M₂) ≡ PRE₂,
       mode(NV₁,BM₁) ≡ M₁,
       mode(NV₂,BM₂) ≡ M₂
Def    resulting premode(PRE₁,PRE₂)=the premode PRE
          defined by
          PRE ≡ (Case CL₁=dclass ∧ CL₂=dclass:PRE₁,
                 Case CL₁=vclass ∧ CL₂ε{vclass,dclass}
                     (Case M₁≠discr(-):PRE₁,
                      Case discr(R,-,-) ≡ PRE₁:
                           Let    {MIN:MAX} ≡ R
                           val(vclass,RG₁,ST₁,
                               mode(NV₁,discr(R,MIN,MAX))))),
                 Case CL₁=all:PRE₂,
                 Case else:resulting premode(PRE₂,PRE₁))
```

                                       *

```
For    each list PREL of premodes
          such that ∀(i,jε{1:#PREL}):
              val(CLᵢ,RGᵢ,STᵢ,Mᵢ)=PREL⦃i⦄
              mode(NVᵢ,BMᵢ)=Mᵢ
              are compatible(PREL⦃i⦄,PREL⦃j⦄),
              CLᵢε{all,vclass,dclass},
```

$$BM_i \epsilon \{discr(-),poset(-),string(-)\}$$

<u>Def</u>   resulting premode(PREL)=the premode PRE
           defined by
                  PRE=(<u>Case</u> #PREL=1:resulting premode(PREL↯1↯,PREL↯1↯)
                        <u>Case</u> #PREL=2:resulting premode(PREL↯1↯,PREL↯2↯)
                        <u>Case</u> <u>else</u>:resulting premode(PREL↯1↯,
                                         resulting premode(PREL↯2:#PREL↯)

*

<u>For</u>   each pair of premodes PRE_1,PRE_2
<u>Let</u> $ST_1 \equiv staticity(PRE_1)$,

      $ST_2 \equiv staticity(PRE_2)$,

      $BM_1 \equiv basemode(PRE_1)$,

      $BM_2 \equiv basemode(PRE_2)$,

      $ST \equiv$ (<u>Case</u> $(ST_1=stat) \wedge (ST_2=stat)$:stat,

          <u>Case</u> <u>else</u>:dyn)
<u>For</u>   each pair of modes M_3,M_4
<u>Let</u> $BM_3 \equiv basemode(M_3)$,

      $BM_4 \equiv basemode(M_4)$
<u>Def</u>   are similar(PRE_1,PRE_2)=are similar(BM_1,BM_2,ST),

      are similar(PRE_1,BM_3)=are similar(BM_1,BM_3,ST_1),

      are similar(BM_3,PRE_1)=are similar(BM_3,BM_1,ST_1),

      are similar(BM_3,BM_4)=are similar$(BM_3,BM_4,stat)$

<u>For</u>   each function Fϵ\{are v-equivalent, are equivalent, is restrictable to\},
<u>Let</u> $M_1 \equiv mode(PRE_1)$,

      $M_2 \equiv mode(PRE_2)$
<u>Def</u> $F(PRE_1,PRE_2)=F(M_1,M_2,ST)$,

      $F(PRE_1,M_3)=F(M_1,M_3,ST_1)$,

      $F(M_3,PRE_1)=F(M_3,M_1,ST_1)$,

      $F(M_3,M_4)=F(M_3,M_4,stat)$

<u>For</u>   each function $F_1 \epsilon$\{are 1-equivalent, is read compatible with\}

      each pair of denotated modes DM_5,DM_6
<u>Let</u> $DM_1 \equiv denmode(PRE_1)$,

      $DM_2 \equiv denmode(PRE_2)$
<u>Def</u> $F_1(PRE_1,PRE_2)=F_1(DM_1,DM_2,ST)$,

      $F_1(PRE_1,DM_5)=F_1(DM_1,DM_5,ST_1)$,

      $F_1(DM_5,PRE_1)=F(DM_5,DM_1,ST_1)$,

      $F_1(DM_5,DM_6)=F_1(DM_5,DM_6,stat)$

*

<u>For</u>   each value premode VPRE,
      each mode M
<u>Def</u>   is compatible with$(M_1,VPRE)$=is compatible with(M,VPRE,stat)

PART II : SYNTAX AND SEMANTICS

1. MODE DENOTATIONS

Syntax

(a) *<mode denotation>*
    (1) → *<non composite mode denotation>*
    (2) | *<composite mode denotation>*
(b) *<non composite mode denotation>*
    (1) → *<discrete mode denotation>*
    (2) | *<powerset mode denotation>*
    (3) | *<reference mode denotation>*
    (4) | *<procedure mode denotation>*
    (5) | *<concurrent mode denotation>*

Semantics

<u>Pass</u> ENV↓,
      DENMODE↑,
      DECLA↑,
      IMPLIED↓,
      NODESET↑

1.1 DISCRETE MODE DENOTATIONS

Syntax

(a) *<discrete mode denotation>*
    (1) → *<integer mode denotation>*
    (2) | *<boolean mode denotation>*
    (3) | *<character mode denotation>*
    (4) | *<set mode denotation>*
    (5) | *<range mode denotation>*

Semantics

<u>Pass</u> ENV↓,
      DENMODE↑,
      DECLA↑,
      IMPLIED↓,
      NODESET↑

1.1.1 INTEGER MODE DENOTATIONS

Syntax

(a) *<integer mode denotation>*
    (1) → *<read>* INT
    (2) | *<read>* BIN
    (3) | *<<u>integer</u> derived mode denotation>*
(b) *<read>*
    (1) → *<empty>*
    (2) | *READ*

Semantics

(a1,a2) *<integer mode denotation>*
<u>With</u> RD ≡ *<read>*.READↂ
<u>Let</u>   DM ≡ [RD,mode(base,discr(int,minint,maxint))]
<u>Def</u>   DENMODEↂ ≡ DM,
        DECLAↂ ≡ {},
        IMPLIEDↂ ≡ {},
        NODESETↂ ≡ {}

(a3) *<integer mode denotation>*
              → *<<u>integer</u> derived mode denotation>*
<u>Pass</u> ENVↂ,
        DENMODEↂ,
        IMPLIEDↂ,
        NODE SETↂ
<u>When</u> base mode(DENMODEↂ)=discr(int,minint,maxint)
<u>Def</u>   DECLAↂ ≡ {}

(b1) *<read>* → *<empty>*
<u>Def</u>   READↂ ≡ write

(b2) *<read>* → *READ*
<u>Def</u>   READↂ ≡ rdo

1.1.2 BOOLEAN MODE DENOTATIONS

Syntax

(a) *<boolean mode denotation>*
    (1) → *<read> BOOL*
    (2) | *<<u>boolean</u> derived mode denotation>*

Semantics

(a1) *<boolean mode denotation>* → *<read> BOOL*
<u>With</u> RD ≡ *<read>*.READↂ
<u>Let</u>   DM ≡ [RD,mode(base,discr(bool,false,true))]
<u>Def</u>   DENMODEↂ ≡ DM,
        DECLAↂ ≡ {},
        IMPLIEDↂ ≡ {},
        NODESETↂ ≡ {}

(a2) *<boolean mode denotation>*
              → *<<u>boolean</u> derived mode denotation>*
<u>Pass</u> ENVↂ,
        DENMODEↂ,
        IMPLIEDↂ,
        NODESETↂ
<u>When</u> base mode(DENMODEↂ)=discr(bool,false,true)
<u>Def</u>   DECLAↂ ≡ {}

1.1.3 CHARACTER MODE DENOTATIONS

Syntax

(a) *<character mode denotation>*
    (1) → *<read> CHAR*
    (2) | *<u>character</u> derived mode denotation>*

Semantics

(a1) *<character mode denotation>* → *<read> CHAR*
<u>With</u> RD ≡ *<read>*.READ↑
<u>Let</u>   DM ≡ [RD,mode(base,discr(char,minchar,maxchar))]
<u>Def</u>   DENMODE↑ ≡ DM,
     DECLA↑ ≡ {},
     IMPLIED↑ ≡ {},
     NODESET↑ ≡ {}

(a2) *<character mode denotation>*
      → *<u>character</u> derived mode denotation>*
<u>Pass</u> ENV↓,
     DENMODE↑,
     IMPLIED↑,
     NODESET↑
<u>When</u> base mode(DENMODE↑)=discr(char,minchar,maxchar)
<u>Def</u>   DECLA↑ ≡ {}

1.1.4 SET MODE DENOTATIONS

Syntax

(a) *<set mode denotation>*
    (1) → *<read> SET (L(,)<set element>)*
    (2) | *<read> SET (L(,)<numbered set element>)*
    (3) | *<u>set</u> derived mode denotation>*
(b) *<set element>*
    (1) → *<identifier>*
    (2) | *∗*
(c) *<numbered set element>*
     → *<identifier>=<u>integer</u> literal expression>*

Semantics

(a1) *<set mode denotation>* → *<read> SET (L(,)<set element>)*
<u>With</u> RD ≡ *<read>*.READ↑,
    ∀(i∈L):(IDEN$_i$ ≡ *<set element>*$_i$.IDEN↑,
          D$_i$ ≡   "   .DECLA↑,
          NS$_i$ ≡   "   .NODESET↑)
<u>Test</u> ∀(i,j∈L):i≠j∧IDEN$_i$≠none∧IDEN$_j$≠none ⇒ IDEN$_i$≠IDEN$_j$,
    ∃(i∈L):IDEN$_i$≠none
<u>Let</u>   IDEN LIST ≡ {IDEN$_i$|i∈L},
    SET ≡ set(IDENLIST),
    MIN ≡ min(SET),

```
        MAX ≡ max(SET),
        MODE ≡ mode(base,discr(SET,MIN,MAX)),
        DM ≡ [RD,MODE]
```
Def $\forall(i\epsilon L):(\langle set\ element\rangle_i.\text{SMODE}↓ ≡ \text{MODE},$
                         " $.\text{AMODE}↓ ≡ \{i|i\epsilon\text{IDENLIST}\}),$
```
        DENMODE↑ ≡ DM,
        DECLA↑ ≡ ∪(iεL):D_i,

        IMPLIED↑ ≡ ∪(iεL):imply(D_i),

        NODESET↑ ≡ ∪(iεL):NS_i
```

(a2) *<set mode denotation>*
         → *<read> SET (L(,)<numbered set element>)*
Pass ENV↓
With RD ≡ *<read>*.READ↑,
      $\forall(i\epsilon L):(\text{IDEN}_i ≡ \langle numbered\ set\ element\rangle_i.\text{IDEN}↑,$
```
            NUM_i   ≡         "            .NUM↑,

            D_i     ≡         "            .DECLA↑,

            NS_i    ≡         "            .NODESET↑)
```
Test $\forall(i,j\epsilon L):(i≠j ⇒ \text{IDEN}_i≠\text{IDEN}_j,$
                  $i≠j ⇒ \text{NUM}_i≠\text{NUM}_j)$
Let   IDEN LIST$_1$ ≡ $\{\text{IDEN}_i|i\epsilon L\}$,

      NUM LIST$_1$ ≡ $\{\text{NUM}_i|i\epsilon L\}$,

      IDEN LIST ≡ reorder(IDEN LIST$_1$,NUM LIST$_1$),
```
        SET ≡ set(IDENLIST),
        MIN ≡ min(SET),
        MAX ≡ max(SET),
        MODE ≡ mode(base,discr(SET,MIN,MAX)),
        DM ≡ [RD,MODE]
```
Def $\forall(i\epsilon L):(\langle numbered\ set\ element\rangle_i.\text{SMODE}↓ ≡ \text{MODE},$
                         " $.\text{AMODE}↓ ≡ \{i|i\epsilon\text{IDENLIST}\})$
```
        DENMODE↑ ≡ DM,
        DECLA↑ ≡ ∪(iεL):D_i,

        IMPLIED↑ ≡ ∪(iεL):imply(D_i),

        NODESET↑ ≡ ∪(iεL):NS_i
```

(a3) *<set mode denotation>* → *<set derived mode denotation>*
Pass ENV↓,
```
        DENMODE↑,
        IMPLIED↑,
        NODESET↑
```
When base mode(DENMODE↑)=discr(set(-),-,-)
Let   discr(SET,MIN,MAX) ≡ base mode(DENMODE↑),
      set(IDL) ≡ SET
When MIN=min(SET),
      MAX=max(SET)
Def   DECLA↑ ≡ {}

(b1) *<set element>* → *<identifier>*
With SMODE↓,
      AMODE↓

<u>Let</u>   N ≡ node(<identifier>),
       T ≡ text(<identifier>),
       D ≡ define(T,N),
       N_1 ≡ identify node(T,ENV↓)

<u>Test</u> basemode(N_1.DPREMODE!)=SMODE↓

<u>Def</u>   IDEN↑ ≡ T,
       DECLA↑ ≡ D,
       NODESET↑ ≡ {},
       N.DCAT! ≡ lit,
       N.DPREMODE! ≡ setapprox(AMODE↓),
       N.DIMPLIED! ≡ {},
       N.DISCT! ≡ lit,
       N.DVAL! ≡ set value(T,SMODE↓),
       N.DNODESET! ≡ {},
       <u>Case</u> N_1.DEFINING NODE!=N:

             N_1.DPREMODE! ≡ val(dclass,nreg,stat,SMODE↓)

(b2) <i>\<set element\></i> → *
<u>Def</u>   IDEN↑ ≡ none,
       DECLA↑ ≡ {},
       NODESET↑ ≡ {}

(c) <i>\<numbered set element\></i>
         → <identifier> = <i>\<integer literal expression\></i>
<u>Pass</u> ENV↓
<u>With</u> SMODE↓,
       AMODE↓,
       PRE ≡ <i>\<integer literal expression\></i>.PREMODE↑,
       VAL ≡   "   .VAL↑,
       NS   ≡   "   .NODESET↑
<u>Test</u> base mode(PRE)=discr(int,-,-),
       VAL≥0
<u>Let</u>   T ≡ text(<identifier>),
       N ≡ node(<identifier>),
       D ≡ define(T,N),
       N_1 ≡ identify node(T,ENV↓)

<u>Test</u> ¬ is recursive(N_1,NS),

       base mode(N_1.DPREMODE!)=SMODE↓

<u>Def</u>   IDEN↑ ≡ T,
       NUM↑ ≡ VAL,
       DECLA↑ ≡ D,
       NODESET↑ ≡ NS,
       N.DCAT! ≡ lit,
       N.DPREMODE! ≡ setapprox(AMODE↓),
       N.DIMPLIED! ≡ {},
       N.DVAL! ≡ set value(T,SMODE↓),
       N.DISCT! ≡ lit,
       N.DNODESET! ≡ NS,
       <u>Case</u> N=N_1.DEFINING NODE!:

             N_1.DPREMODE! ≡ val(dclass,nreg,stat,SMODE↓)

1.1.5 RANGE MODE DENOTATIONS

Syntax

(a) *<range mode denotation>*
    (1) → *<<u>discrete</u> derived mode denotation>*
                    (<literal range>)
    (2) | *<read> RANGE (<literal range>)*
    (3) | *<read> BIN (<<u>integer</u> literal expression>)*
    (4) | *<<u>range</u> derived mode denotation>*
(b) *<literal range>*
        → *<literal expression <u>1</u>> : <literal expression <u>2</u>>*

Semantics

(a1) *<range mode denotation>*
            → *<<u>discrete</u> derived mode denotation>*
                (<literal range>)

<u>Pass</u>   ENV↓
<u>With</u>   DM ≡ *<<u>discrete</u> derived mode denotation>*.DENMODE↑,
        IMP ≡   "   .IMPLIED↑,
        NS$_1$ ≡   "   .NODESET↑,

        MIN ≡ *<literal range>*.MIN↑,
        MAX ≡   "   .MAX↑,
        PRE ≡   "   .PREMODE↑,
        NS$_2$ ≡   "   .NODESET↑

<u>Test</u>   is compatible with(DM,PRE),
        base mode(DM)=discr(-)
<u>Let</u>   [RD,mode(NV,discr(ROOT,MIN$_1$,MAX$_1$))] ≡ DM,

        DM$_1$ ≡ [RD,mode(NV,discr(ROOT,MIN,MAX))]

<u>Test</u>   MIN$_1$≤MIN≤MAX≤MAX$_1$

<u>Def</u>   DENMODE↑ ≡ DM$_1$,

        DECLA↑ ≡ {},
        IMPLIED↑ ≡ IMP,
        NODESET↑ ≡ NS$_1$∪NS$_2$

(a2) *<range mode denotation>*
            → *<read> RANGE (<literal range>)*

<u>Pass</u>   ENV↓
<u>With</u>   RD ≡ *<read>*.READ↑,
        MIN ≡ *<literal range>*.MIN↑,
        MAX ≡   "   .MAX↑,
        PRE ≡   "   .PREMODE↑,
        NS ≡   "   .NODESET↑
<u>Let</u>   val(-,-,-,mode(NV,discr(ROOT,MIN$_1$,MAX$_1$)) ≡ PRE,

        DM ≡ [RD,mode(NV,discr(ROOT,MIN,MAX))]
<u>Def</u>   DENMODE↑ ≡ DM,
        DECLA↑ ≡ {},
        IMPLIED↑ ≡ {},
        NODESET↑ ≡ NS

(a3) *<range mode denotation>*
            → *<read> BIN (<<u>integer</u> literal expression>)*
<u>Pass</u>   ENV↓

<u>With</u> RD ≡ <read>.READ↑,
      PRE ≡ <u><integer literal expression></u>.PREMODE↑,
      VAL ≡   "   .VAL↑,
      NS ≡   "   .NODESET↑
<u>Test</u> base mode(PRE)=discr(int,-,-),
      0≤VAL
<u>Let</u>   MAX ≡ 2**VAL-1,
      DM ≡ [RD,mode(base,discr(int,0,MAX))]
<u>Def</u>   DENMODE↑ ≡ DM,
      DECLA↑ ≡ {},
      IMPLIED↑ ≡ {},
      NODESET↑ ≡ NS

(a4) <range mode denotation>
        → <u><range</u> derived mode denotation>
<u>Pass</u> ENV↓,
      DENMODE↑,
      IMPLIED↑,
      NODESET↑
<u>Test</u> base mode(DENMODE↑)=discr(-)
<u>Let</u>   discr(SET,MIN,MAX) ≡ base mode(DENMODE↑)
<u>When</u> {MIN:MAX} ≠ {min(SET):max(SET)}
<u>Def</u>   DECLA↑ ≡ {}

(b) <literal range>
        → <literal expression <u>1</u>> : <literal expression <u>2</u>>
<u>Pass</u> ENV↓
<u>With</u> PRE₁ ≡ <literal expression <u>1</u>>.PREMODE↑,

      VAL ≡   "   .VAL↑,
      NS₁ ≡   "   .NODESET↑,

      PRE₂ ≡ <literal expression <u>2</u>>.PREMODE↑,

      VAL₂ ≡   "   .VAL↑,

      NS₂ ≡   "   .NODESET↑

<u>Test</u> are compatible(PRE₁,PRE₂),

      VAL₁≤VAL₂

<u>Def</u>   PREMODE↑ ≡ resulting premode(PRE₁,PRE₂),

      MIN↑ ≡ VAL₁,

      MAX↑ ≡ VAL₂,

      NODESET↑ ≡ NS₁ ∪ NS₂

1.2 POWERSET MODE DENOTATIONS

Syntax

(a) <powerset mode denotation>
    (1) → <read> POWERSET <discrete mode denotation>
    (2) | <u>powerset</u> derived mode denotation>

Semantics

(a1) *<powerset mode denotation>*
        → *<read>* POWERSET *<discrete mode denotation>*
<u>Pass</u> ENV↓
<u>With</u> RD ≡ *<read>*.READ↑,
        DM ≡ *<discrete mode denotation>*.DENMODE↑,
        D   ≡   "   .DECLA↑,
        IMP ≡   "   .IMPLIED↑,
        NS ≡   "   .NODESET↑
<u>Let</u>   [-,MODE] ≡ DM,
        DM₁ ≡ [RD,mode(base,poset(MODE))]

<u>Def</u>   DENMODE↑ ≡ DM₁,

        DECLA↑ ≡ D,
        IMPLIED↑ ≡ IMP,
        NODESET↑ ≡ NS

(a2) *<powerset mode denotation>*
            → *<<u>powerset</u> derived mode denotation>*
<u>Pass</u> ENV↓,
        DENMODE↑,
        IMPLIED↑,
        NODESET↑
<u>When</u> base mode(DENMODE↑)=poset(-)
<u>Def</u>   DECLA↑ ≡ {}

1.3 REFERENCE MODE DENOTATIONS

Syntax

(a) *<reference mode denotation>*
        (1) → *<bound reference mode denotation>*
        (2) | *<free reference mode denotation>*
        (3) | *<row mode denotation>*

Semantics

(a) *<reference mode denotation>*
<u>Pass</u> ENV↓,
        DENMODE↑,
        DECLA↑,
        IMPLIED↑,
        NODESET↑

1.3.1 BOUND REFERENCE MODE DENOTATIONS

Syntax

(a) *<bound reference mode denotation>*
        (1) → *<read>* REF *<mode denotation>*
        (2) | *<<u>bound reference</u> derived mode denotation>*

Semantics

(a1) *<bound reference mode denotation>*
           → *<read> REF <mode denotation>*
<u>Pass</u> ENV↓
<u>With</u> RD ≡ *<read>*.READ↑,
      DM ≡ *<mode denotation>*.DENMODE↑,
      D   ≡   "   .DECLA↑,
      IMP ≡   "   .IMPLIED↑,
      NS ≡   "   .NODESET↑
<u>Let</u> [RD₁,MODE] ≡ DM,

      DM₁ ≡ [RD,mode(base,ref(RD₁,MODE))],

<u>Def</u> DENMODE↑ ≡ DM₁,

      DECLA↑ ≡ D,
      IMPLIED↑ ≡ IMP,
      NODESET↑ ≡ NS

(a2) *<bound reference mode denotation>*
          → *<<u>bound reference</u> derived mode denotation>*
<u>Pass</u> ENV↓,
     DENMODE↑,
     IMPLIED↑,
     NODESET↑
<u>When</u> base mode(DENMODE↑)=ref(-)
<u>Def</u> DECLA↑ ≡ {}

1.3.2 FREE REFERENCE MODE DENOTATIONS

Syntax

(a) *<free reference mode denotation>*
      (1) → *<read> PTR*
      (2) | *<<u>free reference</u> derived mode denotation>*

Semantics

(a1) *<free reference mode denotation>* → *<read> PTR*
<u>With</u> RD ≡ *<read>*.READ↑
<u>Let</u> DM ≡ [RD,mode(base,ptr)]
<u>Def</u> DENMODE↑ ≡ DM,
      DECLA↑ ≡ {},
      IMPLIED↑ ≡ {},
      NODESET↑ ≡ {}

(a2) *<free reference mode>*
          → *<<u>free reference</u> derived mode denotation>*
<u>Pass</u> ENV↓,
     DENMODE↑,
     IMPLIED↑,
     NODESET↑
<u>When</u> basemode(DENMODE↑)=ptr
<u>Def</u> DECLA↑ ≡ {}

1.3.3 ROW MODE DENOTATIONS

Syntax

(a) *<row mode denotation>*
  (1) → *<read> ROW <string mode denotation>*
  (2) | *<read> ROW <array mode denotation>*
  (3) | *<read> ROW <u>variant structure</u> mode identifier>*
  (4) | *<u>row</u> derived mode denotation>*

Semantics

(a1) *<row mode denotation>*
   → *<read> ROW <string mode denotation>*

<u>Pass</u> ENV↓
<u>With</u> RD ≡ *<read>*.READ↑,
   SDM ≡ *<string mode denotation>*.DENMODE↑,
   D ≡   "   .DECLA↑,
   IMP ≡   "   .IMPLIED↑,
   NS ≡   "   .NODESET↑
<u>Let</u> [RD$_1$,STRINGMODE] ≡ SDM,

   DM ≡ [RD,mode(base,row(RD$_1$,STRINGMODE)),

<u>Def</u> DENMODE↑ ≡ DM,
   DECLA↑ ≡ D,
   IMPLIED↑ ≡ IMP,
   NODESET↑ ≡ NS

(a2) *<row mode denotation>*
   → *<read> ROW <array mode denotation>*

<u>Pass</u> ENV↓
<u>With</u> RD ≡ *<read>*.READ↑,
   ADM ≡ *<array mode denotation>*.DENMODE↑,
   D ≡   "   .DECLA↑,
   IMP ≡   "   .IMPLIED↑,
<u>Let</u> [RD$_1$,ARRAY MODE] ≡ ADM,

   DM ≡ [RD,mode(base,row(RD$_1$,ARRAY MODE))]

<u>Def</u> DENMODE↑ ≡ DM,
   DECLA↑ ≡ D,
   IMPLIED↑ ≡ IMP,
   NODESET↑ ≡ NS

(a3) *<row mode denotation>*
   → *<read> ROW <u>variant structure</u> mode identifier>*

<u>Pass</u> ENV↓
<u>With</u> RD ≡ *<read>*.READ↑,
   VDM ≡ *<u>variant structure</u> mode identifier>*.DENMODE↑,
   IMP ≡   "   .IMPLIED↑,
   NS ≡   "   .NODESET↑
<u>Let</u> [RD$_1$,STRUCT MODE] ≡ VDM,

   DM ≡ [RD,mode(base,row(RD$_1$,STRUCT MODE))]

<u>Test</u> is variant structure mode(STRUCT MODE)
<u>Def</u> DENMODE↑ ≡ DM,
   DECLA↑ ≡ {},
   IMPLIED↑ ≡ IMP,
   NODESET↑ ≡ NS

(a4) <row mode denotation>
         → <<u>row</u> derived mode denotation>
<u>Pass</u> ENV↓,
      DENMODE↑,
      IMPLIED↑,
      NODESET↑
<u>When</u> base mode(DENMODE↑)=row(-)
<u>Def</u>   DECLA↑ ≡ {}

1.4 PROCEDURE MODE DENOTATIONS

Syntax

(a) <procedure mode denotation>
      (1) → <read> PROC (<formal parameter plan>)
                <result> <exceptions> <recursive>
      (2) | <<u>procedure</u> derived mode denotation>
(b) <formal parameter plan>
      (1) → <empty>
      (2) | L(,) {<mode denotation>
                <register specification>}
(c) <result>
      (1) → <empty>
      (2) | <return> (<mode denotation> <loc>
                      <register specification>)
(d) <register specification>
      (1) → <empty>
      (2) | <<u>register</u> identifier>
(e) <loc>
      (1) → <empty>
      (2) | LOC
(f) <return>
      (1) → <empty>
      (2) | RETURNS
(g)
      (1) → <empty>
      (2) | LOC
      (3) | IN
      (4) | OUT
      (5) | INOUT
(h) <exceptions>
      (1) → <empty>
      (2) | EXCEPTIONS (L(,) <<u>exception</u> identifier>)
(i) <recursive>
      (1) → <empty>
      (2) | RECURSIVE

Semantics

(a1) <procedure mode denotation>
         → <read> PROC (<formal parameter plan>)
             <result> <exceptions> <recursive>
<u>Pass</u> ENV↓
<u>With</u> RD ≡ <read>.READ↑,
      PLAN ≡ <formal parameter plan>.PLAN↑,
      D₁   ≡   "   .DECLA↑,

NS_1 ≡   "   .NODESET↑,

RESULT ≡ <result>.RESULT↑,
D_2 ≡   "   .DECLA↑,

IMP   ≡   "   .IMPLIED↑,
NS_2 ≡   "   .NODESET↑,

X ≡ <exceptions>.EXCEPT↑,
REC ≡ <recursive>.REC↑

<u>Let</u> XN ≡ {T|[T,-]∈X},
PROCMODE ≡ mode(base,proc(PLAN,RESULT,XN,general(REC))),
DM ≡ [RD,PROCMODE]
<u>Test</u> is implementable(PROCMODE)
<u>Def</u> DENMODE↑ ≡ DM,
DECLA↑ ≡ D_1 ∪ D_2,

IMPLIED↑ ≡ IMP,
NODESET↑ ≡ NS_1 ∪ NS_2

(a2) <procedure mode denotation>
        → <<u>procedure</u> derived mode denotation>
<u>Pass</u> ENV↓,
DENMODE↑,
IMPLIED↑,
NODESET↑
<u>When</u> base mode(DENMODE↑)=proc(-)
<u>Def</u> DECLA↑ ≡ {}

(b1) <formal parameter plan> → <empty>
<u>Def</u> PLAN↑ ≡ ∤∤,
DECLA↑ ≡ {},
NODESET↑ ≡ {}

(b2) <formal parameter plan>
        → L(,) {<mode denotation>
              <register specification>}
<u>Pass</u> ENV↓
<u>With</u> ∀(i∈L):(DM_i ≡ <mode denotation>$_i$.DENMODE↑,
                D_i ≡   "   .DECLA↑,
                NS_i ≡   "   .NODESET↑,
                AT_i ≡ <parameter attribute>$_i$.AT↑,
                R_i ≡ <register specification>$_i$.REG↑)
<u>Test</u> ∀(i,j∈L):i≠j ⟺ (R_i≠R_j ∨ R_i=none),
     ∀(i∈L):has the synchro prop(DM_i) ⇒ AT_i=loc
<u>Def</u> PLAN↑ ≡ ∤[DM_i,AT_i,R_i]|i∈L∤,
DECLA↑ ≡ ∪(i∈L):D_i,
NODESET↑ ≡ ∪(i∈L):NS_i

(c1) <result> → <empty>
<u>Def</u> RESULT↑ ≡ none,
DECLA↑ ≡ {},
IMPLIED↑ ≡ {},
NODESET↑ ≡ {}

(c2) *<result>* → *<return>*(*<mode denotation>* *<loc>*
                    <register specification>)
<u>Pass</u>   ENV↓
<u>With</u>   DM ≡ *<mode denotation>*.DENMODE↑,
       D   ≡   "   .DECLA↑,
       IMP ≡   "   .IMPLIED↑,
       NS ≡   "   .NODESET↑,
       LOC ≡ *<loc>*.LOC↑,
       REG ≡ *<register specification>*.REG↑
<u>Test</u>   has the synchro prop(DM) ⇒ LOC=loc
<u>Def</u>   RESULT↑ ≡ [LOC,DM,REG],
       DECLA↑ ≡ D,
       IMPLIED↑ ≡ IMP,
       NODESET↑ ≡ NS

(d1) *<register specification>* → *<empty>*
<u>Def</u>   REG↑ ≡ none

(d2) *<register specification>* → *<<u>register</u> identifier>*
<u>With</u>   ENV↓
<u>Let</u>   T ≡ text(*<<u>register</u> identifier>*)
<u>Test</u>   is register identifier(T,ENV↓)
<u>Def</u>   REG↑ ≡ T

(e1) *<loc>* → *<empty>*
<u>Def</u>   LOC↑ ≡ nloc

(e2) *<loc>* → *LOC*
<u>Def</u>   LOC↑ ≡ loc

(g1) *<parameter attribute>* → *<empty>*
<u>Def</u>   AT↑ ≡ in

(g2) *<parameter attribute>* → *LOC*
<u>Def</u>   AT↑ ≡ loc

(g3) *<parameter attribute>* → *IN*
<u>Def</u>   AT↑ ≡ in

(g4) *<parameter attribute>* → *OUT*
<u>Def</u>   AT↑ ≡ out

(g5) *<parameter attribute>* → *INOUT*
<u>Def</u>   AT↑ ≡ inout

(h1) *<exceptions>* → *<empty>*
<u>Def</u>   EXCEPT↑ ≡ {}

(h2) *<exceptions>*
          → *EXCEPTIONS (*L(,) *<<u>exception</u> identifier>)*
<u>With</u>   ENV↓
<u>Let</u>   ∀(i∈L):(T$_i$ ≡ text(*<<u>exception</u> identifier>*$_i$),
            N$_i$ ≡ node(*<<u>exception</u> identifier>*$_i$))
<u>Test</u>   ∀(i,j∈L):i≠j ⇒ T$_i$≠T$_j$
<u>Def</u>   EXCEPT↑ ≡ ∪(i∈L):define exception(T$_i$,N$_i$)

(i1) *<recursive>* → *<empty>*
Def   REC↑ ≡ nrec

(i2) *<recursive>* → *RECURSIVE*
Def   REC↑ ≡ rec

1.5 COMPOSITE MODE DENOTATIONS

Syntax

(a) *<composite mode denotation>*
    (1) → *<string mode denotation>*
    (2) | *<array mode denotation>*
    (3) | *<structure mode denotation>*

Semantics

Pass   ENV↓,
       DENMODE↑,
       DECLA↑,
       IMPLIED↑,
       NODESET↑

1.5.1. STRING MODE DENOTATIONS

Syntax

(a) *<string mode denotation>*
    (1) → *<read>* *<string element mode>*(*<string length>*)
    (2) | *<string derived mode denotation>*
    (3) | *<string derived mode denotation>*(*<string length>*)
(b) *<string element mode>*
    (1) → *CHAR*
    (2) | *BIT*
(c) *<string length>*
       → *<integer literal expression>*

Semantics

(a1) *<string mode denotation>*
       → *<read>* *<string element mode>*(*<string length>*)
Pass ENV↓
With RD ≡ *<read>*.READ↑,
      M ≡ *<string element mode>*.STRINGM↑,
      L ≡ *<string length>*.VAL↑,
      NS ≡   "   .NODESET↑
Let   DM ≡ [RD,mode(base,string(M,L))]
Def   DENMODE↑ ≡ DM,
       DECLA↑ ≡ {},
       IMPLIED↑ ≡ {},
       NODESET↑ ≡ NS

(a2) *<string mode denotation>*
       → *<string derived mode denotation>*
Pass   ENV↓,

```
        DENMODE↑,
        IMPLIED↑,
        NODESET↑
When  base mode(DENMODE↑)=string(-)
Def   DECLA↑ ≡ {}
```

(a3) *<string mode denotation>*
          → *<string derived mode denotation>*(*<string length>*)

```
Pass  ENV↓
With  DM  ≡ <string derived mode denotation>.DENMODE↑,
      D   ≡            "                .DECLA↑,
      IMP ≡            "                .IMPLIED↑,
      NS₁ ≡            "                .NODESET↑,

      V   ≡ <string length>.VAL↑,
      NS₂ ≡          "       .NODESET↑

Test  base mode(DM)=string(-)
Let   [RD,mode(NV,string(M,L))] ≡ DM,
      DM₁ ≡ [RD,mode(NV,string(M,V))]

Test  0≤V≤L
Def   DENMODE↑ ≡ DM₁,

      DECLA↑ ≡ D,
      IMPLIED↑ ≡ IMP,
      NODESET↑ ≡ NS₁∪NS₂
```

(b1) *<string element mode>* → *CHAR*
```
Def   STRINGM↑ ≡ char
```

(b2) *<string element mode>* → *BIT*
```
Def   STRINGM↑ ≡ bit
```

(c) *<string length>* → *<integer literal expression>*
```
Pass  ENV↓
With  PRE ≡ <integer literal expression>.PREMODE↑,
      V   ≡            "               .VAL↑
      NS  ≡            "               .NODESET↑
Test  base mode(PRE)=discr(int,-,-)
Def   VAL↑ ≡ V
      NODESET↑ ≡ NS
```

1.5.2. ARRAY MODE DENOTATIONS

Syntax

(a) *<array mode denotation>*
    (1) → *<read><array>*(*<index mode>*)
       <mode denotation><element layout attribute>
    (2) | *<array derived mode denotation>*
    (3) | *<array derived mode denotation>*
            (*<discrete literal expression>*)
(b) *<array>*
    (1) → *<empty>*
    (2) | *ARRAY*
(c) *<index mode>*
    (1) → *<discrete mode denotation>*
    (2) | *<discrete literal range>*

(d) *<element layout attribute>*
    (1) → *NOPACK*
    (2) | *PACK*
    (3) | <empty>
    (4) | *<step attribute>*
(e) *<step attribute>*
       → *STEP (<pos attribute><comma><sizes>)*
(f) *<pos attribute>*
       → *POS(<u>word number</u> literal expression><comma>*
                  <bit displacement and length>)
(g) *<comma>*
    (1) → <empty>
    (2) | ,
(h) *<sizes>*
    (1) → <empty>
    (2) | *<u>step size</u> literal expression><comma><pattern size>*
(i) *<bit displacement and length>*
    (1) → <empty>
    (2) | *<u>start</u> literal expression><comma><length>*
    (3) | *<u>start</u> literal expression> : <u>end</u> literal expression>*
(j) *<pattern size>*
    (1) → <empty>
    (2) | *<u>integer</u> literal expression>*
(k) *<length>*
    (1) → <empty>
    (2) | *<u>integer</u> literal expression>*

Semantics

(a1) *<array mode denotation>*
       → *<read><array> (<index mode>) <mode denotation>*
              <element layout attribute>

<u>Pass</u> ENV↓
            *   *
<u>When</u> (*<read>* ⇒ <empty> ∧ *<array>* ⇒ <empty>)
           ⇒ predecessor(*<array mode denotation>*) ≠ *BUFFER*
<u>With</u> RD ≡ *<read>*.READ↓,
     IDM ≡ *<index mode>*.DENMODE↓,
     D_1 ≡   "   .DECLA↓,

     IMP_1 ≡   "   .IMPLIED↓,

     NS_1 ≡   "   .NODESET↓,

     EDM ≡ *<mode denotation>*.DENMODE↓,
     D_2 ≡   "   .DECLA↓,

     IMP_2 ≡   "   .IMPLIED↓,

     NS_2 ≡   "   .NODESET↓,

     REPR ≡ *<element layout attribute>*.REPR↓,
     NS_3 ≡   "   .NODESET↓

<u>Test</u> no holes(IDM)
<u>Let</u>   [-,IM] ≡ IDM,
     [RD₁,EM₁] ≡ EDM,

     RD_2 ≡ most restrictive(RD,RD_1),

     ADM ≡ [RD_2,mode(base,array(IM,EM,REPR))]

<u>Def</u> *<element layout attribute>*.COMP MODE↓ ≡ EM_1,

```
        DENMODE↑ ≡ ADM,
        DECLA↑ ≡ D₁∪D₂,

        IMPLIED↑ ≡ IMP₁ ∪ IMP₂,

        NODESET↑ ≡ NS₁∪NS₂∪NS₃
```

(a2) *<array mode denotation>*
        → *<array derived mode denotation>*
Pass ENV↓,
        UMODE↑,
        DENMODE↑,
        IMPLIED↑,
        NODESET↑
When base mode(DENMODE↑)=array(-)
Def DECLA↑ ≡ {}

(a3) *<array mode denotation>*
            → *<array derived mode denotation>*
                  (*<discrete literal expression>*)
Pass ENV↓
With ADM ≡ *<array derived mode denotation>*.DEN MODE↑,
        IMP ≡   "   .IMPLIED↑,
        NS₁ ≡   "   .NODESET↑,

        IPM ≡ *<discrete literal expression>*.PREMODE↑,
        V   ≡   "   .VAL↑
        NS₂ ≡   "   .NODESET↑
Let [RD,mode(NV,array(I,E,R))] ≡ ADM,
        mode(NV₁,discr(ROOT,L,U)) ≡ I

Test is compatible with(I,IPM),
        L≤V≤U
Let I₁ ≡ mode(NV₁,discr(ROOT,L,V)),

        DM ≡ [RD,mode(NV,array(I₁,E,R))]

Def DENMODE↑ ≡ DM,
        DECLA↑ ≡ {},
        IMPLIED↑ ≡ IMP,
        NODESET↑ ≡ NS₁∪NS₂

(c1) *<index mode>* → *<discrete mode denotation>*
Pass ENV↓,
        DENMODE↑,
        DECLA↑,
        IMPLIED↑,
        NODESET↑

(c2) *<index mode>* → *<discrete literal range>*
Pass ENV↓,
        NODESET↑
With PRE ≡ *<discrete literal range>*.PREMODE↑,
        L   ≡   "   .MIN↑,
        U   ≡   "   .MAX↑
Let M ≡ mode(PRE),
        mode(NV,discr(ROOT,-,-)) ≡ M,
        DM ≡ [unused,mode(NV,discr(ROOT,L,U))]
Def DENMODE↑ ≡ DM,
        DECLA↑ ≡ {},
```
```

```
        IMPLIED↑ ≡ {}
```

(d1) <element layout attribute> → NOPACK
<u>Def</u>   REPR↑ ≡ npack,
        NODESET↑ ≡ {}

(d2) <element layout attribute> → PACK
<u>Def</u>   REPR↑ ≡ pack,
        NODESET↑ ≡ {}

(d3) <element layout attribute> → <empty>
<u>Def</u>   REPR↑ ≡ npack or pack according to implementation,
        NODESET↑ ≡ {}

(d4) <element layout attribute> → <step attribute>
<u>Pass</u> ENV↓,
        COMP MODE↓,
        REPR↑,
        NODESET↑

(e) <step attribute>
            → STEP (<pos attribute> <comma> <sizes>)
<u>Pass</u> ENV↓
<u>When</u> empty(<comma>) ⟺ empty(<sizes>)
<u>With</u> CM ≡ COMP MODE↓,
        [WDISPL,BDISPL,LENGTH] ≡ <pos attribute>.POS↑,
        NS₁   ≡   "   .NODESET↑,

        [STEP,PATSZ] ≡ <sizes>.SIZES↑,
        NS₂   ≡   "   .NODESET↑

<u>Let</u>   STEP₁ ≡ (<u>Case</u> STEP=none:LENGTH,

                 <u>Case else</u>:STEP),
        PATSZ₁ ≡ (<u>Case</u> PATSZ=none:pat size(STEP₁),

                 <u>Case else</u>:PATSZ)
<u>Test</u> is array map repr([WDISPL,BDISPL,LENGTH,
                          STEP₁,PATSZ₁],CM)

<u>Def</u>   REPR↑ ≡ map(WDISPL,BDISPL,LENGTH,STEP₁,PATSZ₁),

        NODESET↑ ≡ NS₁∪NS₂

(f) <pos attribute>
            → POS (<u>word number</u> literal expression>
                  <comma> <bit displacement and length>)
<u>Pass</u> ENV↓
<u>When</u> empty(<comma>) ⟺ empty(<bit displacement and length>)
<u>With</u> CM ≡ COMPMODE↓,
        PRE   ≡ <u>word number</u> literal expression>.PREMODE↑,
        WDISPL ≡   "   .VAL↑,
        NS₁   ≡   "   .NODESET↑,

        BDISPL ≡ <bit displacement and length>.BDISPL↑,
        LENGTH ≡   "   .LENGTH↑,
        NS₂   ≡   "   .NODESET↑

<u>Test</u> base mode(PRE)=discr(int,-,-),
        0≤WDISPL
<u>Let</u>   BDISPL₁ ≡ (<u>Case</u> BDISPL=none:0,

                 <u>Case else</u>:BDISPL),

```
       LENGTH₁ ≡ (Case BDISPL=none,

                     ∧ LENGTH=none:size(CM),
                  Case BDISPL ≠ none
                     ∧ LENGTH=none:length(CM),
                  Case else:LENGTH),
```

Def   POS↑ ≡ [WDISPL,BDISPL₁,LENGTH₁],

       NODESET↑ ≡ NS₁∪NS₂

(h1) *<sizes>* → *<empty>*
Def   SIZES↑ ≡ [none,none],
       NODESET↑ ≡ {}
(h2) *<sizes>* → *<step size literal expression>*
                        <comma><pattern size>

Pass ENV↓
When empty(*<comma>*) ⇔ empty(*<pattern size>*)
With PRE ≡ *<step size literal expression>*.PREMODE↑,
       STEP ≡   "   .VAL↑,
       NS₁ ≡   "   .NODESET↑

       PATSZ ≡ *<pattern size>*.PATSZ↑,
       NS₁   ≡   "   .NODESET↑

Test base mode(PRE)=discr(int,-,-),
       0≤STEP
Def   SIZES↑ ≡ [STEP,PATSZ],
       NODESET↑ ≡ NS₁∪NS₂

(i1) *<bit displacement and length>* → *<empty>*
Def   BDISPL↑ ≡ none,
       LENGTH↑ ≡ none,
       NODESET↑ ≡ {}

(i2) *<bit displacement and length>*
         → *<start literal expression><comma><length>*
Pass ENV↓
When empty(*<comma>*) ⇔ empty(*<length>*)
With PRE ≡ *<start literal expression>*.PREMODE↑,
       BDISPL ≡   "   .VAL↑,
       NS₁   ≡   "   .NODESET↑,

       LENGTH ≡ *<length>*.LENGTH↑,
       NS₂   ≡   "   .NODESET↑

Test base mode(PRE) ≡ discr(int,-,-),
       0≤BDISPL
Def   BDISPL↑ ≡ BDISPL,
       LENGTH↑ ≡ LENGTH
       NODESET↑ ≡ NS₁∪NS₂

(i3) *<bit displacement and length>*
         → *<start literal expression>:<end literal expression>*
Pass ENV↓
With PRE₁ ≡ *<start literal expression>*.PREMODE↑,

       VAL₁ ≡   "   .VAL↑,

       NS₁ ≡   "   .NODESET↑,

       PRE₂ ≡ *<end literal expression>*.PREMODE↑,
```
```

$$VAL_2 \equiv \qquad\qquad " \qquad\qquad .VAL\!\uparrow,$$
$$NS_2 \equiv \qquad\qquad " \qquad\qquad .NODESET\!\uparrow$$

<u>Test</u> base mode(PRE_1)=discr(int,-,-),

base mode(PRE_2)=discr(int,-,-),

$0{\leq}VAL_1{\leq}VAL_2$

<u>Def</u>   BDISPL↑ $\equiv VAL_1,$

LENGTH↑ $\equiv VAL_2-VAL_1+1,$

NODESET↑ $\equiv NS_1{\cup}NS_2$

(j1) *<pattern size>* → *<empty>*
<u>Def</u>   PATSZ↑ $\equiv$ none,
      NODESET↑ $\equiv$ {}

(j2) *<pattern size>* → *<u>integer</u> literal expression>*
<u>Pass</u> ENV↓
<u>With</u> PRE $\equiv$ *<u>integer</u> literal expression>*.PREMODE↑,
      VAL $\equiv$ \qquad\qquad " \qquad\qquad .VAL↑,
      NS $\equiv$ \qquad\qquad " \qquad\qquad .NODESET↑
<u>Test</u> base mode(PRE) $\equiv$ discr(int,-,-),
      $0{\leq}VAL$
<u>Def</u>   PATSZ↑ $\equiv$ VAL,
      NODESET↑ $\equiv$ NS

(k1) *<length>* → *<empty>*
<u>Def</u>   LENGTH↑ $\equiv$ none,
      NODESET↑ $\equiv$ {}

(k2) *<length>* → *<u>integer</u> literal expression>*
<u>Pass</u> ENV↓,
      NODESET↑
<u>With</u> PRE $\equiv$ *<u>integer</u> literal expression>*.PREMODE↑,
      VAL $\equiv$ \qquad\qquad " \qquad\qquad .VAL↑
<u>Test</u> base mode(PRE) $\equiv$ discr(int,-,-),
      $0{\leq}VAL$
<u>Def</u>   LENGTH↑ $\equiv$ VAL

1.5.3. STRUCTURE MODE DENOTATIONS

Syntax

(a) *<structure mode denotation>*
     (1)→ *<read>* STRUCT (L(,)*<fields>*)
     (2) | *<u>structure</u> derived mode denotation>*
     (3) | *<u>variant</u> derived mode denotation>*
             (L(,)*<literal expression>*)
(b) *<fields>*
     (1) → *<fixed fields>*
     (2) | *<varying fields>*
(c) *<fixed fields>*
          → L(,)*<identifier>* *<mode denotation>*
          <field layout attribute>
(d) *<varying fields>*
          → CASE *<tags>* OF L(,)*<variant alternative><else fields>* ESAC

(e) *<tags>*
    (1) → <empty>
    (2) | L(,)*<tag field* identifier>
(f) *<variant alternative>*
       → *<decision table selector>*:*<fixed field list>*
(g) *<decision table selector>*
    (1) → <empty>
    (2) | L(,)*<tag label subset>*
(h) *<label subset>*
    (1) → (L(,)*<label interval>*)
    (2) | (*)
    (3) | (ELSE)
(i) *<label interval>*
    (1) → *<discrete* literal expression>
    (2) | *<literal range>*
    (3) | *<discrete* mode identifier>
(j) *<else fields>*
    (1) → <empty>
    (2) | ELSE *<fixed field list>*
(k) *<fixed field list>*
    (1) → <empty>
    (2) | L(,)*<fixed fields>*
(l) *<field layout attribute>*
    (1) → <empty>
    (2) | PACK
    (3) | NOPACK
    (4) | *<pos attribute>*

Semantics

(a1) *<structure mode denotation>*
      → *<read>* STRUCT (L(,)*<fields>*)

Pass ENV↓
With RD ≡ *<read>*.READ↑,
    ∀(i∈L):(F_i ≡ *<fields>*.FIELDS↑,
           FF_i ≡   "   .FFIELDS↑,
           D_i ≡   "   .DECLA↑,
           $IMPL_i$ ≡   "   .IMPLIED↑,
           NS_i ≡   "   .NODESET↑)

Let FDL ≡ ‖(i∈L):F_i,
    BM ≡ struct(FDL),
    DM ≡ [RD,mode(base,BM)]
Test are different selectors(FDL),
    are tags defined before used(FDL),
    are field repr compatible(FDL)
Def DENMODE↑ ≡ DM,
    DECLA↑ ≡ ∪(i∈L):D_i,
    IMPLIED↑ ≡ ∪(i∈L):$IMPL_i$,
    NODESET↑ ≡ ∪(i∈L):NS_i,
    ∀(i∈L):*<fields>*$_i$.FIXED FIELDS↓ ≡ ‖(j∈L):FF_j

(a2) *<structure mode denotation>*
      → *<structure derived mode denotation>*

<u>Pass</u> ENV↓,
       DENMODE↑,
       DECLA↑,
       IMPLIED↑,
       NODESET↑
<u>When</u> basemode(DENMODE↑)=struct(-)

(a3) *<structure mode denotation>*
         → *<<u>variant</u> derived mode denotation>*
           (L(,)<literal expression>)
<u>Pass</u> ENV↓
<u>With</u> DM ≡ *<<u>variant</u> derived mode denotation>*.DENMODE↑,
       IMPL ≡   "   .IMPLIED↑,
       NS   ≡   "   .NODESET↑,
       ∀(i∈L):(PREM$_i$ ≡ *<literal expression>*$_i$.PREMODE↑,

                 VAL$_i$ ≡   "   .VAL↑,

                 NS$_i$ ≡   "   .NODESET↑)

<u>Let</u>   PML ≡ ⦃PREM$_i$|i∈L⦄,

       VL ≡ ⦃VAL$_i$|i∈L⦄,

       [RD,mode(NV,BM)] ≡ DM,
       BM$_1$ ≡ variant param base mode(VL,BM),

       VPM ≡ [RD,mode(NV,BM$_1$)]

<u>Test</u> BM=struct(-),
       are param premodes compatible(PML,BM),
       is parameterizable(BM) ∧ ¬ is parameterized(BM)
<u>Def</u>   DENMODE↑ ≡ VPM,
       DECLA↑ ≡ ∪(i∈L):D$_i$,

       IMPLIED↑ ≡ IMPL,
       NODESET↑ ≡ NS∪(∪(i∈L):NS$_i$)

(b1) *<fields>* → *<fixed fields>*
<u>Pass</u> ENV↓,
       FIELDS↑,
       DECLA↑,
       IMPLIED↑,
       NODESET↑
<u>Def</u>   FFIELDS↑ ≡ FIELDS↑

(b2) *<fields>* → *<varying fields>*
<u>Pass</u> ENV↓,
       FIXED FIELDS↑,
       FIELDS↑,
       DECLA↑,
       IMPLIED↑,
       NODESET↑
<u>Def</u>   FFIELDS↑ ≡ ⦃⦄

(c) *<fixed fields>*
         → L(,)*<identifier> <mode denotation>*
             <field layout attribute>
<u>Pass</u> ENV↓
<u>With</u> DM ≡ *<mode denotation>*.DENMODE↑,
       D   ≡   "   .DECLA↑,
       IMPL ≡   "   .IMPLIED↑,

```
        NS₁  ≡              "         .NODESET↓,

        REPR ≡ <field layout attribute>.REPR↓,
        NS₂  ≡              "              .NODESET↓
Test    REPR=map(-) ⇒ #L=1
Let     ∀(i∈L):(Tᵢ ≡ text(<identifier>ᵢ),
                 Nᵢ ≡ node(<identifier>ᵢ)),
        [RD,M] ≡ DM,
        FIELDS ≡ ≰field(Tᵢ,RD,M,REPR)|i∈L≱
Def     FIELDS↓ ≡ FIELDS,
        DECLA↓ ≡ D,
        IMPLIED↓ ≡ IMPL,
        NODESET↓ ≡ NS₁∪NS₂
```

(d) *<varying fields>*
        → *CASE* <tags> *OF* L(,)*<variant alternative>*
                  <else fields> ESAC

```
Pass    ENV↓
With    FIXED FIELDS↓,
        TAGL ≡ <tags>.TAG IDEN LIST↓,
        ∀(i∈L):(ALT ELᵢ ≡ <variant alternative>ᵢ.ALT EL↓,

               PRELᵢ   ≡              "              .PRE LIST↓,

               Dᵢ      ≡              "              .DECLA↓,

               IMPLᵢ   ≡              "              .IMPLIED↓,

               NSᵢ     ≡              "              .NODESET↓),

        ELSE LIST ≡ <else fields>.ELSE FIELDS↓,
        D        ≡         "     .DECLA↓,
        IMPL     ≡         "     .IMPLIED↓,
        NS       ≡         "     .NODESET↓
Let     ALT LIST ≡ ≰ALT ELᵢ|i∈L≱

        PREL LIST ≡ ≰MODELᵢ|i∈L≱,

        TFDL ≡ tag field list(TAGL,FIXED FIELDS↓),
        TL   ≡ param spec list(TFDL,PREL LIST),
        [AL,SYAL] ≡ alternative list(ALT LIST,PREL LIST,ELSE LIST,TFDL)
Test    are coherent alternatives(ALT LIST,PREL LIST,ELSE LIST,TFDL),
        are tags fixed(TAGL,FIXED FIELS↓)
Def     FIELDS↓ ≡ ≰var(TL,AL,SYAL)≱,
        DECLA↓ ≡ (∪(i∈L):Dᵢ)∪D,

        IMPLIED↓ ≡ (∪(i∈L):IMPLᵢ)∪IMPL,

        NODESET↓ ≡ NS∪(∪(i∈L):NSᵢ)
```

(e1) *<tags> → <empty>*
Def   TAG IDEN LIST↓ ≡ ≰≱

(e2) *<tags> → L(,)<tags field identifier>*
Let   ∀(i∈L):(Tᵢ ≡ text(<tag field identifier>ᵢ)

Def   TAG IDEN LIST↓ ≡ ≰Tᵢ|i∈L≱

(f) *<variant alternative>*
        → *<decision table selector>:<fixed fields list>*
Pass   ENV↓

<u>With</u>   SET LIST ≡ *<decision table selector>*.SET LIS T↑,
       PRE LIST ≡   "   .PRE LIST↑,
       NS$_1$ ≡   "   .NODESET↑,

       FFL ≡ *<fixed field list>*.FIELDS↑,
       D   ≡   "   .DECLA↑,
       IMPL ≡   "   .IMPLIED↑,
       NS$_2$ ≡   "   .NODESET↑

<u>Def</u>   ALT EL↑ ≡ [SET LIST,FFL],
       PRE LIST↑ ≡ PRE LIST,
       DECLA↑ ≡ D,
       IMPLIED↑ ≡ IMPL,
       NODESET↑ ≡ NS$_1$∪NS$_2$

(g1) *<decision table selector>* → *<empty>*
<u>Def</u>   SET LIST↑ ≡ |≠|,
       PRE LIST↑ ≡ |≠|,
       NODESET↑ ≡ {}

(g2) *<decision table selector>* → L(,)*<<u>tag</u> label subset>*
<u>Pass</u> ENV↓
<u>With</u> ∀(i∈L):(S$_i$ ≡ *<<u>tag</u> label subset>*$_i$.SET↑,
                PRE$_i$ ≡   "   .PRE MODE↑,
                NS$_i$ ≡   "   .NODESET↑)
<u>Def</u>   SET LIST↑ ≡ |S$_i$|i∈L|,
       PRE LIST↑ ≡ |PRE$_i$|i∈L|,
       NODESET↑ ≡ ∪(i∈L):NS$_i$

(h1) *<label subset>* → (L(,) *<label interval>*)
<u>Pass</u> ENV↓
<u>With</u> ∀(i∈L):(INTERV$_i$ ≡ *<label interval>*$_i$.INTERV↑,
                PRE$_i$ ≡   "   .PRE MODE↑,
                NS$_i$ ≡   "   .NODESET↑)
<u>Test</u> ∀(i,j∈L):are compatible(PRE$_i$,PRE$_j$)
<u>Let</u>   PRE ≡ resulting premode(|PRE$_i$|i∈L|)
<u>Def</u>   SET↑ ≡ ∪(i∈L):INTERV$_i$,
       PRE MODE↑ ≡ PRE,
       NODESET↑ ≡ ∪(i∈L):NS$_i$

(h2) *<label subset>* → (*)
<u>Def</u>   SET↑ ≡ dontcare,
       PRE MODE↑ ≡ dontcare,
       NODESET↑ ≡ {}

(h3) *<label subset>* → (ELSE)
<u>Def</u>   SET↑ ≡ else,
       PRE MODE↑ ≡ else,
       NODESET↑ ≡ {}

(i1) *<label interval>* → *<<u>discrete</u> literal expression>*
<u>Pass</u> ENV↓,
       NODESET↑

<u>With</u> PRE ≡ <*discrete literal expression*>.PREMODE↑,
      V   ≡   "   .VAL↑
<u>Test</u> base mode(PRE)=discr(-)
<u>Def</u>   PREMODE↑ ≡ PRE,
      INTERV↑ ≡ {V}

(12) <*label interval*> → <*literal range*>
<u>Pass</u> ENV↓,
      NODESET↑
<u>With</u> PRE ≡ <*literal range*>.PREMODE↑,
      MIN ≡   "   .MIN↑,
      MAX ≡   "   .MAX↑
<u>Def</u>   PREMODE↑ ≡ PRE,
      INTERV↑ ≡ {MIN:MAX}

(13)<*label interval*> → <*discrete mode identifier*>
<u>Pass</u> ENV↓,
      NODESET↑
<u>With</u> DM ≡ <*mode identifier*>.DENMODE↑
<u>Test</u> base mode(DM)=discr(-)
<u>Let</u>   M ≡ mode(DM)
<u>Def</u>   PREMODE↑ ≡ resulting premode(≮vpre(M)≯),
      INTERV↑ ≡ set(M)

(j1) <*else fields*> → <empty>
<u>Def</u>   ELSE FIELDS↑ ≡ none,
      DECLA↑ ≡ {},
      IMPLIED↑ ≡ {},
      NODESET↑ ≡ {}

(j2) <*else fields*> → ELSE <*fixed field list*>
<u>Pass</u> ENV↓,
      DECLA↑,
      IMPLIED↑,
      NODESET↑
<u>With</u> FF ≡ <*fixed field list*>.FIXED FIELDS↑
<u>Def</u>   ELSE FIELDS↑ ≡ FF

(k1) <*fixed field list*> → <empty>
<u>Def</u>   FIXED FIELDS↑ ≡ ≮≯,
      DECLA↑ ≡ {},
      IMPLIED↑ ≡ {},
      NODESET↑ ≡ {}

(k2) <*fixed field list*> → L(,) <*fixed fields*>
<u>Pass</u> ENV↓,
<u>With</u> ∀(i∈L):(FF$_i$ ≡ <*fixed fields*>.FIELDS↑,
                D$_i$ ≡   "   .DECLA↑,
                IMPL$_i$ ≡   "   .IMPLIED↑,
                NS$_i$ ≡   "   .NODESET↑)
<u>Def</u>   FIXED FIELDS↑ ≡ ∥(i∈L):FF$_i$,
      DECLA↑ ≡ ∪(i∈L):D$_i$,
      IMPLIED↑ ≡ ∪(i∈L):IMPL$_i$,
      NODESET↑ ≡ ∪(i∈L):NS$_i$

(11) *<field layout attribute>* → \<empty>
<u>Def</u>   REPR↑ ≡ pack or npack according to implementation,
         NODESET↑ ≡ {}

(12) *<field layout attribute>* → *PACK*
<u>Def</u>   REPR↑ ≡ pack,
         NODESET↑ ≡ {}

(13) *<field layout attribute>* → *NOPACK*
<u>Def</u>   REPR↑ ≡ npack,
         NODESET↑ ≡ {}

(14) *<field layout attribute>* → *<pos attribute>*
<u>Pass</u> ENV↓,
         NODESET↑
<u>With</u> [WD,BD,L] ≡ *<pos attribute>*.POS↑
<u>Def</u>   REPR↑ ≡ map(WD,BD,L)

1.6 DERIVED MODE DENOTATIONS

Syntax

(a) *<derived mode denotation>*
            → *<read><mode identifier>*
(b) *<mode identifier>*
          → \<identifier>

Semantics

(a) *<derived mode denotation>* → *<read><mode identifier>*
<u>With</u> ENV↓,

      RD ≡ *<read>*.READ↑,
      DM ≡ *<mode identifier>*.DENMODE↑,
      IMP ≡   "   .IMPLIED,
      NS ≡   "   .NODESET↑
<u>Let</u>   [RD₁,M] ≡ DM,

      RD₂ ≡ most restrictive (RD,RD₁)

<u>Def</u>   DENMODE↑ ≡ [RD₂,M],

      DECLA↑ ≡ {},
      IMPLIED↑ ≡ IMP,
      NODESET↑ ≡ NS

(b) *<mode identifier>* → \<identifier>
<u>With</u> ENV↓
<u>Let</u>   T ≡ text(\<identifier>),
      N ≡ identify node(T,ENV↓)
<u>Test</u> N≠udf,
      N.DCAT!=mode(-)
<u>Def</u>   NODE↑ ≡ N,
      DENMODE↑ ≡ node(N),
      IMPLIED↑ ≡ N.DIMPLIED!,
      NODESET↑ ≡ {N}

2. DATA STATEMENTS

Syntax

(a) *<data statement list>*
    (1) → <empty>
    (2) | L*<data statement>*
(b) *<data statement>*
    (1) → *<definition statement>;*
    (2) | *<declaration statement>;*
    (3) | *<critical region>;*
(c) *<definition statement>*
    (1) → <empty>
    (2) | *<mode definition statement>*
    (3) | *<synonym definition statement>*
    (4) | *<procedure definition statement>*
    (5) | *<concurrent definition statement>*

Semantics

(a1) *<data statement>* → <empty>
__Def__   DECLA↑ ≡ {}
__Dyn__   PREELAB(PE%):
     <u>Step</u> ←PE%
     ELAB(E%):
     <u>Step</u> ←E%
(a2) *<data statement list>* → L*<data statement>*
__Pass__ ENV↓
__With__ D ≡ υ(i∈L):*<data statement>*$_i$.DECLA↑

__Def__   DECLA↑ ≡ D
__Dyn__   PREELAB=(PE%$_0$):

     <u>Step</u>:S(i∈L):(PE%$_i$←*<data statement>*$_i$.PREELAB(PE%$_{i-1}$))

     ELAB=(E%$_0$):

     <u>Step</u>:S(i∈L):(E%$_i$←*<data statement>*$_i$.ELAB(E%$_{i-1}$))

(b) *<data statement>*
__Pass__ ENV↓,
      DECLA↑
__Dyn__   PREELAB=(PE%)
     ELAB=(E%)

(c1) *<definition statement>* → <empty>
__Def__   DECLA↑ ≡ {}
__Dyn__   PREELAB=(PE%):
     <u>Step</u> : ← PE%
     ELAB=(E%):
     <u>Step</u> : ← E%

(c2,c3,c5) *<definition statement>* → *<mode definition statement>*
__Pass__ ENV↓,
      DECLA↑
__Dyn__   PREELAB=(PE%):
     <u>Step</u> : ← PE%
     ELAB=(E%):
     <u>Step</u> : ← E%

(c4) *<definition statement>*
__Pass__ ENV↓,
          DECLA↑
__Dyn__   PREELAB=(PE%)
          ELAB=(E%):
          __Step__ : ← E%

2.1 MODE DEFINITION STATEMENTS

Syntax

(a) *<mode definition statement>*
    (1) → *<newmode definition>*
    (2) | *<synmode definition>*
(b) *<newmode definition>*
      → NEWMODE L(,)*<mode definition>*
(c) *<synmode definition>*
      → SYNMODE L(,)*<mode definition>*
(d) *<mode definition>*
      → L(,)<identifier> = <u>*defining* mode denotation</u>*

Semantics

(a) *<mode definition statement>*
__Pass__ ENV↓,
          DECLA↑

(b) *<newmode definition>*
      → NEWMODE L(,)*<mode definition>*
__Pass__ ENV↓
__With__ $\forall(i \in L):D_i$ ≡ *<mode definition>*$_i$.DECLA↑

__Def__ $\forall(i \in L):$*<mode definition>*$_i$.NOVTY↓ ≡ new,

      DECLA↑ ≡ $\cup(i \in L):D_i$

(c) *<synmode definition>*
      → SYNMODE L(,)*<mode definition>*
__Pass__ ENV↓
__With__ $\forall(i \in L):D_i$ ≡ *<mode definition>*$_i$.DECLA↑

__Def__ $\forall(i \in L):$*<mode definition>*$_i$.NOVTY↓ ≡ syn,

      DECLA↑ ≡ $\cup(i \in L):D_i$

(d) *<mode definition>*
      → L(,)<identifier>=<u>*defining* mode denotation</u>*
__Pass__ ENV↓
__With__ NOVTY↓,
      DM ≡ <u>*defining* mode denotation</u>*.DENMODE↓,
      D   ≡   "   .DECLA↓,
      IMP ≡   "   .IMPLIED↓,
      NS ≡   "   .NODESET↓
__Let__   [RD,mode(-,BM)] ≡ DM,
      $\forall(i \in L):(T_i$ ≡ text(<identifier>$_i$),

              N_i ≡ node(<identifier>$_i$),

              D_i ≡ define(T_i,N_i)),

$$DM_i \equiv (\underline{Case}\ NOVTY\!\!\downarrow=syn:DM,$$
$$\underline{Case}\ \underline{else}\ :\ [RD,mode(new(N_i),BM]),$$

<u>Test</u> $\forall(i\epsilon L):is\ wellformed(N_i,DM)$

<u>Def</u> $\forall(i\epsilon L):(N_i.DCAT!\ \equiv\ mode(NOVTY\!\!\downarrow),$

$\qquad\qquad N_i.DDENMODE!\ \equiv\ DM_i,$

$\qquad\qquad N_i.DSURR\ GROUP\ \equiv\ surr\ group(ENV\!\!\downarrow),$

$\qquad\qquad N_i.DIMPLIED!\ \equiv\ IMP,$

$\qquad\qquad N_i.DNODESET!\ \equiv\ NS)$

$\qquad DECLA\!\!\uparrow\ \equiv\ (\cup(i\epsilon L):D_i)\cup D$

2.2. SYNONYM DEFINITION STATEMENTS

Syntax

(a) *<synonym definition statement>*
$\qquad$ → *SYN* L(,)*<synonym definition>*
(b) *<synonym definition>*
$\qquad$ → L(,)*<identifier><mode denotation option>*
$\qquad\qquad$ = *<constant expression>*
(c) *<mode denotation option>*
$\qquad$ (1) → *<empty>*
$\qquad$ (2) | *<mode denotation>*

Semantics

(a) *<synonym definition statement>*
$\qquad$ → SYN L(,) *<synonym definition>*
<u>Pass</u> ENV↓
<u>With</u> $\forall(i\epsilon L):D_i\ \equiv$ *<synonym definition>*$_i$.DECLA↑
<u>Def</u> $DECLA\!\!\uparrow\ \equiv\ \cup(i\epsilon L):D_i$

(b) *<synonym definition>*
$\qquad$ → L(,)*<identifier><mode denotation option>*
$\qquad\qquad$ = *<constant expression>*
<u>Pass</u> ENV↓
<u>With</u> DM $\quad\equiv$ *<mode denotation option>*.DENMODE↓,
$\qquad\ D_1\quad\equiv$ $\qquad\quad$ " $\qquad\qquad$ .DECLA↓,

$\qquad\ NS_1\ \equiv$ $\qquad\qquad$ " $\qquad\qquad$ .NODESET↓,

$\qquad\ PRE\ \equiv$ *<constant expression>*.PREMODE↓,
$\qquad\ VAL\ \equiv$ $\qquad$ " $\qquad\quad$ .VAL↓,
$\qquad\ ISCT\ \equiv$ $\qquad$ " $\qquad\quad$ .ISCT↓,
$\qquad\ NS_2\ \equiv$ $\qquad$ " $\qquad\quad$ .NODESET↓

<u>Test</u> DM≠none ⇒ (is compatible with(DM,PRE)
$\qquad\qquad\qquad$ ∧ VAL∊set(DM))
<u>Let</u> $\forall(i\epsilon L):(T_i\ \equiv\ text(<identifier>_i),$

$\qquad\qquad N_i\ \equiv\ node(<identifier>_i),$

$\qquad\qquad D_i\ \equiv\ define(T_i,N_i)),$

$\qquad\ PRE_1\ \equiv\ (\underline{Case}\ DM=none:PRE,$

                    Case else:val(vclass,nreg,stat,mode(DM))

Test $\forall(i\epsilon L):\neg$ is recursive$(N_i,NS_1\cup NS_2)$

Def   *<constant expression>*.POSTMODE↓
                    $\equiv$ (Case DM≠none:mode(DM),
                        Case else:none),

        DECLA↑ $\equiv$ $(\cup(i\epsilon L):D_i)\cup D_1$,

        $\forall(i\epsilon L):(N_i$.DCAT! $\equiv$ syn,

                N_i.DPREMODE! $\equiv$ PRE$_1$,

                N_i.DIMPLIED! $\equiv$ {},

                N_i.DISCT! $\equiv$ ISCT,

                N_i.DVAL! $\equiv$ VAL,

                N_i.DNODESET! $\equiv$ NS$_1\cup$NS$_2$

(c1) *<mode denotation option>* → *<empty>*

Def   DECLA↑ $\equiv$ {},
        DENMODE↑ $\equiv$ none,
        NODESET↑ $\equiv$ {}

(c2) *<mode denotation option>* → *<mode denotation>*

Pass ENV↓,
        DECLA↑,
        DENMODE↑,
        NODESET↑

2.3. DECLARATION STATEMENTS

Syntax

(a) *<declaration statement>*
        → DCL L(,) *<declaration>*

(b) *<declaration>*
        (1) → *<location declaration>*
        (2) | *<loc identity declaration>*
        (3) | *<based declaration>*

Semantics

(a) *<declaration statement>* → DCL L(,) *<declaration>*

Pass ENV↓
With $\forall(i\epsilon L):D_i \equiv$ *<declaration>*$_i$.DECLA↑

Def   DECLA↑ $\equiv$ $\cup(i\epsilon L):D_i$

Dyn   PREELAB=(PE%$_0$):

        Step:S$(i\epsilon L)$:PE%$_i$ ← *<declaration>*$_i$.PREELAB(PE%$_{i-1}$)

        ELAB=(E%$_0$):

        Step:S$(i\epsilon L)$:E%$_i$ ← *<declaration>*$_i$.ELAB(E%$_{i-1}$)

(b) *<declaration>*

Pass ENV↓,
        DECLA↑

<u>Dyn</u>   PREELAB=(PE%)
        ELAB=(E%)

2.3.1. LOCATION DECLARATIONS

Syntax

(a) *<location declaration>*
         → L(,) <identifier><mode denotation> <static><initialization>
(b) *<static>*
    (1) → <empty>
    (2) | *STATIC*
(c) *<initialization>*
    (1) → <empty>
    (2) | *<init> <assignment symbol><value denotation><handler>*
(d) *<init>*
    (1) → <empty>
    (2) | *INIT*
(e) *<assignment symbol>*
    (1) → :=
    (2) | =

Semantics

(a) *<location declaration>*
         → L(,) <identifier><mode denotation>
                  <static><initialization>
<u>With</u> ENV↓,
        DM   ≡ *<mode denotation>*.DENMODE↓,
        D₁   ≡   "   .DECLA↓,
        IMP ≡   "   .IMPLIED↓,
        STATIC ≡ *<static>*.STATIC↓,
        INIT ≡ *<initialization>*.INIT↓,
        ISCT ≡   "   .ISCT↓,
        V   ≡   "   .VAL↓,
        PRE ≡   "   .PREMODE↓,
        HD   ≡   "   .HDECLA↓
<u>Let</u>   NEWENV ≡ new exceptions(ENV↓,HD)
<u>Test</u> INIT=init ⇒ ISCT∈{cst,lit} ∧ empty(*<handler>*)
        has the rdo prop(DM) ⇒ ¬ empty(*<initialization>*)
        PRE≠none ⇒ is compatible with(DM,PRE),
        has the synchro prop(DM) ⇒ INIT≠none
<u>Let</u>   ∀(i∈L):(T$_i$ ≡ text(<identifier>$_i$),
                N$_i$ ≡ node(<identifier>$_i$),
                D$_i$ ≡ define(T$_i$,N$_i$)),
        RG ≡ regionality(ENV↓),
        [RD,M] ≡ DM,
        PR₁ ≡ loc(RG,stat,refble,RD,M),
        PR₂ ≡ loc(RG,stat,refble,write,M),
        ∀(i∈L):L$_i$ ≡ (<u>Case</u> STATIC=stat:permanent location(V,PRE,PR₁,N$_i$),
                    <u>Case</u> <u>else</u>:unused),
        XM ≡ identify assign exceptions(PRE, PR₂,NEW ENV)

Def   *\<mode denotation\>*.ENV↓ ≡ ENV↓,
     \<initialization\>.ENV↓ ≡ NEWENV,
            "   .HENV↓ ≡ ENV↓,
            "   .POSTMODE↓ ≡ M,

     DECLA↑ ≡ $(\cup(i\in L):D_i)\cup D_1$,

     $\forall(i\in L)$:(N_i.DCAT! ≡ loc,

             N_i.DPREMODE! ≡ PR_1,

             N_i.DIMPLIED! ≡ IMP,

             N_i.DISCT! ≡ (<u>Case</u> STATIC=stat ∨ is program level(ENV↓):cst,

                         <u>Case else</u>:dyn),

             N_i.DLOC! ≡ (<u>Case</u> STATIC=stat:L_i,

                      <u>Case else</u>:none))

Dyn PREELAB=(PE%):
     <u>Step</u> 1 : R(i∈L):
               (L%$_i$ ← (<u>Case</u> STATIC=stat:L_i,

                      <u>Case else</u> : create location(PR_1,PE%)),

                 <u>Case</u> INIT=init: ←assign(V,PRE,L%$_i$,PR_2,{}))

     <u>Step</u> 2 : <u>Let</u>   PE%$_0$ ≡ PE%

              S(i∈L):(PE%$_i$←declare(N_i,L%$_i$,PE%$_{i-1}$))

     ELAB=(E%):
     <u>Step</u> 1: $\forall(i\in L)$:L%$_i$ ← identify(N_i,E%)

     <u>Step</u> 2:
      <u>Case</u> ¬ empty(*\<initialization\>*) ∧ INIT=none:
        (<u>Step</u> 2.1.:V%←*\<initialization\>*.ELAB(E%)
         <u>Step</u> 2.2:R(i∈L):(O%$_i$←assign(V%,PRE,L%$_i$,PR_2,XM),

                            <u>Case</u> exception(X) ≡ O%$_i$:

                                     exit(exception,[X,E%])))

     <u>Step</u> 3 : ← E%

(b1) *\<static\>* → *\<empty\>*
Def   STATIC↑ ≡ none

(b2) *\<static\>* → *STATIC*
Def   STATIC↑ ≡ stat

(c1) *\<initialization\>* → *\<empty\>*
Def   INIT↑ ≡ none,
     ISCT↑ ≡ none,
     VAL↑ ≡ none,
     PREMODE↑ ≡ none,
     HDECLA↑ ≡ {}
Dyn ELAB(E%):unused

(c2) *\<initialization\>*
       → *\<init\>\<assignment symbol\>\<value denotation\>\<handler\>*
With ENV↓,
     HENV↓,
     POSTMODE↓,
     INIT ≡ *\<init\>*.INIT↑,
     PRE ≡ *\<value denotation\>*.PREMODE↑,
     ISCT ≡   "   .ISCT↑,
     VAL ≡   "   .VAL↑,

```
      HD ≡ <handler>.EXCEPT↑
Def   <value denotation>.ENV↓ ≡ ENV↓,
            "          .POSTMODE↓ ≡ POSTMODE↓,
      <handler>.ENV↓ ≡ HENV↓,
      INIT↑ ≡ INIT,
      PREMODE↑ ≡ PRE,
      ISCT↑ ≡ ISCT,
      VAL↑ ≡ VAL,
      HDECLA↑ ≡ HD
Dyn   ELAB(E%):
      Step : ← <value denotation>.ELAB(E%)
```

```
(d1) <init> → <empty>
Def   INIT↑ ≡ none
```

```
(d2) <init> → INIT
Def   INIT↑ ≡ init
```

2.3.2. LOCATION IDENTITY DECLARATIONS

Syntax

(a) *<loc identity declaration>*
        → L(,)*<identifier><mode denotation>*
          LOC *<assignment symbol><location denotation><handler>*

Semantics

```
With  ENV↓,
      DM   ≡ <mode denotation>.DENMODE↑,
      D    ≡         "         .DECLA↑,
      IMP  ≡         "         .IMPLIED↑,
      PRE  ≡ <location denotation>.PREMODE↑,
      ISCT ≡          "          .ISCT↑,
      LOC  ≡          "          .LOC↑,
      HD ≡ <handler>.EXCEPT↑
Let   ∀(i∈L):(T_i ≡ text(<identifier>_i),
             N_i ≡ node(<identifier>_i),
             D_i ≡ define(T_i,N_i)),
      [RD,M] ≡ DM,
      loc(CR,ST,RF,-,M_1) ≡ PRE

Test  is read compatible with(DM,PRE),
      ST=stat
Let   PRE_1 ≡ loc(CR,stat,RF,RD,M),

      NEWENV ≡ new exceptions(ENV↓,HD)
Def   <mode denotation>.ENV↓ ≡ ENV↓,
      <location denotation>.ENV↓ ≡ NEWENV↓,
      <handler>.ENV↓ ≡ ENV↓,
      DECLA↑ ≡ (∪(i∈L):D_i)∪D,

      ∀(i∈L):(N_i.DCAT! ≡ loc,
             N_i.DPREMODE! ≡ PRE_1,
             N_i.DIMPLIED! ≡ IMP,
```

$$N_i.DISCT! \equiv ISCT,$$
$$N_i.DLOC! \equiv LOC)$$

<u>Dyn</u>   ELAB=(E%$_0$):

   <u>Step</u> 1 : L% ← <location denotation>.ELAB(E%$_0$)

   <u>Step</u> 2 : S(i∈L):E%$_i$ ← declare(N$_i$,L$_i$,E%$_{i-1}$)

2.3.3. BASED DECLARATIONS

Syntax

(a) <based declaration>
   (1) → L(,)<identifier><mode denotation> BASED
   (2) | L(,)<identifier><mode denotation>
          BASED (<location identifier>)

Semantics

(a1) <based declaration>
    → L(,) <identifier><mode denotation> BASED

<u>Pass</u> ENV↓
<u>With</u> DM   ≡ <mode denotation>.DENMODE↓,
     D   ≡   "   .DECLA↓,
     IMPL ≡   "   .IMPLIED↓,
     NS   ≡   "   .NODESET↓
<u>Let</u>   ∀(i∈L):(T$_i$ ≡ text(<identifier>$_i$),
           N$_i$ ≡ node(<identifier>$_i$),
           D$_i$ ≡ define(T$_i$,N$_i$))

<u>Test</u> ∀(i∈L):is wellformed(N$_i$,DM)

<u>Def</u>   ∀(i∈L):(N$_i$.DCAT! ≡ mode(syn),
          N$_i$.DDENMODE! ≡ DM,
          N$_i$.DSURR GROUP! ≡ surr group(ENV↓),
          N$_i$.DIMPLIED! ≡ IMPL,
          N$_i$.DNODESET! ≡ NS),

     DECLA↓ ≡ (∪(i∈L):D$_i$)∪D

<u>Dyn</u>   ELAB(E%):
   Step : ← E%

(a2) <based declaration>
    → L(,)<identifier><mode denotation>
          BASED (<location identifier>)

<u>Pass</u> ENV↓
<u>With</u> DM   ≡ <mode denotation>.DENMODE↓,
     D   ≡   "   .DECLA↓,
     IMPL ≡   "   .IMPLIED↓,
     PRE ≡ <location identifier>.PREMODE↓
<u>Test</u> base mode(PRE)=ref(-) ∨ base mode(PRE)=ptr,
<u>Let</u>   ∀(i∈L):(T$_i$ ≡ text(<identifier>$_i$),
           N$_i$ ≡ node(<identifier>$_i$),

$$D_i \equiv \text{define}(T_i, N_i))$$

<u>Test</u> <u>Case</u> base mode(PRE)=ref(-):

        <u>Let</u>   ref(RD_1,M) $\equiv$ base mode(PRE),

           DM_1 $\equiv$ [RD_1,M]

       is read compatible with(DM,DM_1)

<u>Def</u> $\forall(i\epsilon L):(N_i$.DCAT! $\equiv$ based,

         N_i.DPREMODE! $\equiv$ PRE,

         N_i.DIMPLIED! $\equiv$ IMPL,

         N_i.DEREFDM! $\equiv$ DM),

    DECLA$\uparrow$ $\equiv$ ($\cup(i\epsilon L):D_i)\cup D$

<u>Dyn</u> ELAB=($E\%_0$):

    <u>Step</u> 1 : L$ $\leftarrow$ <*location identifier*>.ELAB($E\%_0$)

    <u>Step</u> 2 : S($i\epsilon L$):$E\%_i$ $\leftarrow$ declare(N_i,L$,$E\%_{i-1}$)

3. VALUE DENOTATIONS

Syntax

(a) <value denotation>
    (1) → <expression>
    (2) | <undefined value>
(b) <expression>
    (1) → <primitive value denotation>
    (2) | <formula>
(c) <primitive value denotation>
    (1) → <static primitive value denotation>
    (2) | <dynamic primitive value denotation>
    (3) | (<expression>)
(d) <static primitive value denotation>
    (1) → <synonym identifier>
    (2) | <literal>
    (3) | <tuple>
    (4) | <value string element>
    (5) | <value substring>
    (6) | <value array element>
    (7) | <value subarray>
    (8) | <value structure field>
    (9) | <referenced location>
    (10) | <_value_ procedure call>
    (11) | <_value_ built in routine call>
    (12) | <value conversion>
    (13) | <receive expression>
    (14) | <zeroadic operator>
    (15) | <_static_ delocated location>
    (16) | <start expression>
(e) <dynamic primitive value denotation>
    (1) → <_dynamic_ delocated location>
    (2) | <value string slice>
    (3) | <value array slice>

Semantics

(a1) <value denotation> → <expression>
Pass ENV↓,
      POSTMODE↓,
      PREMODE↑,
      ISCT↑,
      VAL↑,
      NODESET↑
Dyn ELAB=(E%)

(a2) <value denotation> → <undefined value>
Pass ENV↓,
      PREMODE↑,
      ISCT↑,
      VAL↑,
      NODESET↑
Dyn ELAB=(E%)

(b) <expression>
Pass ENV↓,
      POSTMODE↓,

```
        PREMODE↑,
        ISCT↑,
        VAL↑,
        NODESET↑
Def     PRIOR↑ ≡ (Case (b1):highest,
                  Case (b2):<right>.PRIOR↑)
Dyn     ELAB=(E%)
```

(c) *<primitive value denotation>*
```
Pass    ENV↓,
        POSTMODE↓,
        PREMODE↑,
        ISCT↑,
        VAL↑,
        NODESET↑
Dyn     ELAB=(E%)
```

(d) *<static primitive value denotation>*
```
Pass    ENV↓,
        POSTMODE↓,
        PREMODE↑,
        ISCT↑,
        VAL↑,
        NODESET↑
When    (Case(d10,d11):PREMODE↑=val(-),
         Case(d15):PREMODE↑=val(-,-,stat,-))
Def     Case(d3):<right>.STATY↓ ≡ stat
Dyn     (Case(d3):ELAB=(E%,none),
         Case else:ELAB=(E%))
```

(e) *<dynamic primitive value denotation>*
```
Pass    ENV↓,
        PREMODE↑
Def     ISCT↑ ≡ dyn,
        VAL↑ ≡ none,
        NODESET↑ ≡ {}
Dyn     ELAB=(E%)
```


3.1. SYNONYM IDENTIFIER

Syntax

(a) *<synonym identifier>*
        → *<synonym value identifier>*

Semantics

```
Pass    ENV↓,
        PREMODE↑,
        ISCT↑,
        VAL↑,
        NODESET↑
With    CAT↑
When    CAT↑∈{syn,dynsyn}
Test    CAT↑=syn ⇒ VAL↑≠udf
Dyn     ELAB=(E%):
        Step : (Case CAT↑=syn : ← VAL↑,
```

```
            Case CAT+=dynsyn :
                ← <synonym value identifier>.ELAB(E%))
```

3.2. LITERALS

Syntax

(a) *<literal>*
    (1) → *<integer literal>*
    (2) | *<boolean literal>*
    (3) | *<set literal>*
    (4) | *<null literal>*
    (5) | *<procedure literal>*
    (6) | *<string literal>*

Semantics

Pass   ENV↓,
        PREMODE↑,
        VAL↑,
        ISCT↑,
        NODESET↑
Let   BM ≡ base mode(PREMODE↑)
Dyn   ELAB=(E%):
        Step :(Case BM=proc(-):← cluster(VAL↑,E%),
                Case else : ← VAL↑)

3.2.1. INTEGER LITERALS

Syntax

(a) *<integer literal>*
        → <integer literal>

Semantics

Def   PREMODE↑ ≡ dpre(int),
        VAL↑ ≡ <integer literal>.VAL↑,
        NODESET↑ ≡ {},
        ISCT↑ ≡ lit

3.2.2. BOOLEAN LITERALS

Syntax

(a) *<boolean literal>*
    (1) → *TRUE*
    (2) | *FALSE*

Semantics

<u>Def</u>   PREMODE↑ ≡ dpre(bool),
       VAL↑ ≡ (<u>Case</u> (a1):true,
                <u>Case</u> (a2):false),
       NODESET↑ ≡ {},
       ISCT↑ ≡ lit

3.2.3. SET LITERALS

Syntax

(a) *<set literal>*
          → *<<u>set</u> value identifier>*

Semantics

<u>Pass</u> ENV↓,
       PREMODE↑,
       VAL↑,
       ISCT↑,
       NODESET↑
<u>With</u> CAT ≡ *<<u>set</u> value identifier>*.CAT↑
<u>When</u> CAT=lit ∧ base mode(PREMODE↑)=discr(set(-),-,-)

3.2.4. NULL LITERAL

Syntax

(a) *<null literal>*
          → *NULL*

Semantics

<u>Def</u>   PREMODE↑ ≡ val(null,nreg,stat,udf)
       VAL↑ ≡ null,
       NODESET↑ ≡ {},
       ISCT↑ ≡ cst

3.2.5. PROCEDURE LITERALS

Syntax

(a) *<procedure literal>*
          → *<<u>procedure</u> value identifier>*

Semantics

<u>Pass</u> ENV↓,
       PREMODE↑,
       VAL↑,
       ISCT↑,
       NODESET↑

<u>With</u> CAT ≡ <*procedure value identifier*>.CAT↑
<u>When</u> CAT=lit ∧ base mode(PREMODE↑)=proc(-,-,-,general(-))

3.2.6. STRING LITERALS

Syntax

(a) <*string literal*>
    (1) → <*primitive string literal*>
    (2) | <*repeated string literal*>
(b) <*primitive string literal*>
    (1) → <bit string literal>
    (2) | <character string literal>
(c) <*repeated string literal*>
      → (<*integer literal expression*>)
          <*primitive string literal*>

Semantics

(a) <*string literal*>
<u>Pass</u> ENV↓,
     PREMODE↑,
     VAL↑,
     NODESET↑

(b) <*primitive string literal*>
<u>Pass</u> VAL↑,
     NODESET↑
<u>With</u> L ≡ <right>.LENGTH↑
<u>Let</u>   K ≡ (<u>Case</u> b1:bit,
         <u>Case</u> b2:char)
<u>Def</u>   PREMODE↑ ≡ val(dclass,nreg,stat,mode(base,string(K,L))),
     ISCT↑ ≡ (<u>Case</u> L=1:lit,
          <u>Case</u> <u>else</u>:cst)

(c) <*repeated string literal*>
      → (<*integer literal expression*> <*primitive string literal*>
<u>Pass</u> ENV↓,
<u>With</u> PRE₁ ≡ <*integer literal expression*>.PREMODE↑,

     ISCT₁ ≡   "   .ISCT↑,

     VAL₁ ≡   "   .VAL↑,

     NS₁ ≡   "   .NODESET↑

     PRE₂ ≡ <*primitive string literal*>.PREMODE↑,

     ISCT₂ ≡   "   .ISCT↑,

     VAL₂ ≡   "   .VAL↑,

     NS₂ ≡   "   .NODESET↑

<u>Test</u> ISCT₁≠dyn,

     base mode(PRE₁)=discr(int,-,-)

<u>Let</u>   VAL ≡ repeat string(VAL₁,VAL₂,PRE₂),

     val(-,-,-,string(K,L)) ≡ PRE₂,

```
        PRE ≡ val(dclass,nreg,stat,mode(base,string(K,L*VAL₁))
```

$\underline{Def}$ PREMODE↑ ≡ PRE,
      VAL↑ ≡ VAL,
      ISCT↑ ≡ ($\underline{Case}$ L*VAL₁=1:lit,

            $\underline{Case\ else}$:cst),
      NODESET↑ ≡ NS₁∪NS₂

3.3 TUPLES

Syntax

(a) *<tuple>*
      (1) → *<powerset tuple>*
      (2) | *<array tuple>*
      (3) | *<structure tuple>*

Semantics

$\underline{Pass}$ ENV↓,
      POSTMODE↓,
      STATY,
      PREMODE↑,
      ISCT↑,
      VAL↑,
      NODESET↑
$\underline{Dyn}$ ELAB=(E%,N%):
      $\underline{Step}$ ($\underline{Case}$(a1) : ← *<right>*.ELAB(E%),
            $\underline{Case}$ (a2,a3) : ← *<right>*.ELAB(E%,N%)

3.3.1 POWERSET TUPLES

Syntax

(a) *<powerset tuple>*
        → *<u>powerset</u> mode identifier option>* *(:<powerset>:)*
(b) *<powerset>*
      (1) → *<empty>*
      | L(,)*<powerset element>*
(c) *<powerset element>*
      (1) → *<expression>*
      (2) | *<dynamic range>*
(d) *<dynamic range>*
        → *<expression 1>:<expression 2>*
(e) *<mode identifier option>*
      (1) → *<empty>*
      (2) | *<mode identifier>*

Semantics

(a) *<powerset tuple>*
        → *<u>powerset</u> mode identifier option>* *(:<powerset>:)*
$\underline{Pass}$ ENV↓
$\underline{With}$ PM ≡ POSTMODE↓,

```
          DM ≡ <powerset mode identifier option>.DENMODE↑,
          NS ≡              "              .NODESET↑
          ISCT ≡ <powerset>.ISCT↑,
          RANGE ≡       "      .RANGE↑,
          NS' ≡       "      .NODESET↑
```

Test DM=none ⇒ PM≠none

Let M ≡ (Case DM≠none:mode(DM),
            Case else:PM),

When basemode(M)=poset(-)

Let ISCT ≡ compose isct($ISCT_i|i∈L$)

Def <powerset>.PWMODE↑ ≡ M,
     PREMODE↑ ≡ val(vclass,nreg,stat,M),
     ISCT↑ ≡ ISCT,
     VAL↑ ≡ (Case ISCT↑=cst:powerset tuple value(RANGE,M),
             Case else:none),
     NODESET↑ ≡ NS∪NS'

Dyn ELAB=(E$):
     Step 1 : S$ ← <powerset>.ELAB(E$)
     Let S$ ≡ ∪(i∈L):S$_i

     Step 2 : ← powerset tuple value(S$,M)

(b1) <powerset> → <empty>
Def ISCT↑ ≡ cst,
     RANGE↑ ≡ {},
     NODESET↑ ≡ {}
Dyn ELAB=(E$):
     Step : ← {}

(b2) <powerset> → L(,) <powerset element>
Pass ENV↓,
     PREMODE↓
With ∀(i∈L):(ISCT_i ≡ <powerset element>_i.ISCT↑,
            RANGE_i ≡   "   .RANGE↑,
            NS_i ≡   "   .NODESET↑)

Let ISCT ≡ compose isct($ISCT_i≤i∈L$)

Test ISCT=cst ⇒ ∀(i∈L):RANGE_i ⊆ set(member mode(M))

Def ISCT↑ ≡ ISCT,
     RANGE↑ ≡ (Case ISCT=cst:(∪(i∈L):RANGE_i),

             Case else:none)
     NODESET↑ ≡ ∪(i∈L):NS_i

Dyn ELAB=(E$):
     Step 1 : R(i∈L):S$_i ← <powerset element>_i.ELAB(E$)

     Step 2 : ← ∪(i∈L):S$_i

(c1) <powerset element> → <expression>
Pass ENV↓,
     ISCT↑,
     NODESET↑
With PWMODE↓,
     PRE ≡ <expression>.PREMODE↑,
     VAL ≡   "   .VAL↑
Let M ≡ member mode(PWMODE↓),
     XN ≡ identify exception node(text(RANGEFAIL),ENV↓)

Test is compatible with(PRE,M)
Def   RANGE↟ ≡ (<u>Case</u> ISCT≠dyn:{VAL},
                   <u>Case else</u>:none)
<u>Dyn</u>   ELAB=(E%):
      <u>Step</u> 1 : V% ← <*expression*>.ELAB(E%)
      <u>Step</u> 2 : (<u>Case</u> V% ∉ set(M):<u>exit</u>(exception,[XN,E%]),
                   <u>Case else</u> : ← {V%})

(c2) <*powerset element*> → <*dynamic range*>
<u>Pass</u> ENV↓,
      ISCT↟,
      RANGE↟,
      NODESET↟
<u>With</u> PWMODE↓
<u>Def</u>   <*dynamic range*>.RGMODE↓ ≡ member mode(PWMODE↓)
<u>Dyn</u>   ELAB=(E%)

(d) <*dynamic range*> → <*expression 1*>:<*expression 2*>
<u>Pass</u> ENV↓
<u>With</u> RGMODE↓,
      PRE₁ ≡ <*expression 1*>.PREMODE↟,

      ISCT₁ ≡   "   .ISCT↟,

      VAL₁ ≡   "   .VAL↟,

      NS₁   ≡   "   .NODESET↟,

      PRE₂ ≡ <*expression 2*>.PREMODE↟,

      ISCT₂ ≡   "   .ISCT↟,

      VAL₂ ≡   "   .VAL↟,

      NS₂   ≡   "   .NODESET↟,
<u>Let</u>   XN ≡ identify exception node(text(*RANGEFAIL*),ENV↓)
<u>Test</u> is compatible with(RGMODE↓,PRE₁),

      is compatible with(RGMODE↓,PRE₂)

<u>Def</u>   ISCT↟ ≡ (compose isct(⟊ISCT₁,ISCT₂⟊)

      RANGE↟ ≡ (<u>Case</u> ISCT↟=cst:{VAL₁:VAL₂},

                <u>Case else</u>:none),
      NODESET↟ ≡ NS₁∪NS₂
<u>Dyn</u>   ELAB=(E%):
      <u>Step</u> 1 : R(V%₁ ← <*expression 1*>.ELAB(E%),

                  V%₂ ← <*expression 2*>.ELAB(E%))

      <u>Let</u>   T% ≡ V%₁ ∈ set(RGMODE↓) ∧ V%₂ ∈ set(RGMODE↓)

      <u>Step</u> 2 : <u>Case</u> T%=false:<u>exit</u>(exception,[XN,E%])
      <u>Step</u> 3 : ← {V%₁:V%₂}

(e1) <*mode identifier option*> → <empty>
<u>Def</u>   DENMODE↟ ≡ none,
      NODESET↟ ≡ {}

(e2) <*mode identifier option*> → <*mode identifier*>
<u>Pass</u> ENV↓,
      DENMODE↟,
      NODESET↟

3.3.2 ARRAY TUPLES

Syntax

(a) *<array tuple>*
    (1) → *<unlabelled array tuple>*
    (2) | *<labelled array tuple>*
(b) *<unlabelled array tuple>*
        → *<<u>array</u> mode identifier option>*
          (:L(,) <value denotation>:)
(c) *<labelled array tuple>*
        → *<<u>array</u> mode identifier option>*
          (:L(,) {<label subset>:<value denotation>}:)

Semantics

(a) *<array tuple>*
<u>Pass</u> ENV↓,
       POSTMODE↓,
       STATY↓,
       PREMODE↑,
       ISCT↑,
       VAL↑,
       NODESET↑
<u>Dyn</u>   ELAB=(E%,N%)

(b) *<unlabelled array tuple>*
        → *<<u>array</u> mode identifier option>*
          (:L(,)<value denotation>:)

<u>Pass</u> ENV↓
<u>With</u> POSTMODE↓,
       ST=STATY↓,
       DM ≡ *<<u>array</u> mode identifier option>*.DENMODE↑,
       NS ≡   "   .NODESET↑,
       ∀(i∈L) : (PRE_i ≡ *<value denotation>*$_i$.PREMODE↑,

               $ISCT_i$ ≡   "   .ISCT↑,

               VAL_i ≡   "   .VAL↑,

               NS_i ≡   "   .NODESET↑)

<u>Test</u> DM=none ⇒ POSTMODE↓≠none,

      ∃(i∈L):(*<value denotation>*$_i$ $\overset{*}{\Rightarrow}$ *<expression>*,

           PRE_i≠val(all,-,-,-))

<u>Let</u>   M ≡ (<u>Case</u> DM≠none:mode(DM),
           <u>Case else</u>:POSTMODE↓)
<u>When</u> basemode(M)≡array(-)
<u>Let</u>   EM ≡ element mode(M),
       IM ≡ index mode(M),
       ST_1 ≡ (<u>Case</u> DM≠none:stat,

            <u>Case else</u>:ST),
       ISCT ≡ compose isct({ISCT$_i$|i∈L})

<u>Test</u> ∀(i∈L):is compatible with(PRE_i,EM),

      ST_1=stat ⇒ #L=card(IM),

      ST_1=dyn ⇒ #L≤card(IM),

ISCT=cst $\Rightarrow(\forall(i\epsilon L):VAL_i \epsilon$ set(EM))

<u>Let</u>   RG $\equiv$ merged regionality($\{$regionality(PRE$_i$)$|i\epsilon L\}$),

PRE $\equiv$ val(vclass,RG,stat,M),
VALLIST $\equiv \{VAL_i|i\epsilon L\}$,

PMLIST $\equiv \{PRE_i|i\epsilon L\}$,

XN $\equiv$ identify exception node(text(*RANGEFAIL*),ENV$\downarrow$)

<u>Def</u> $\forall(i\epsilon L)$: <*value denotation*>$_i$.POSTMODE$\downarrow \equiv$ EM,

PREMODE$\uparrow \equiv$ PRE,
ISCT$\uparrow \equiv$ compose isct($\{ISCT_i|i\epsilon L\}$

VAL$\uparrow \equiv$ (<u>Case</u> ISCT$\neq$dyn:array tuple value(VALLIST,PMLIST,PRE),
       <u>Case</u> <u>else</u>:none),
NODESET$\uparrow \equiv$ NS$\cup(\cup(i\epsilon L):NS_i)$

<u>Dyn</u>   ELAB=(E%,N%):
<u>Step</u> 1 : R(iϵL) : V%$_i \leftarrow$ <*value denotation*>$_i$.ELAB(E%)

<u>Let</u>   L% $\equiv \{V\%_i|i\epsilon L\}$

<u>Step</u> 2 : <u>Case</u> (ST$_1$=dyn $\wedge$ N%=#L) $\vee$ base mode(EM)=discr(-)

$\wedge \exists(i\epsilon L): V\%_i \notin$ set(EM)):

<u>exit</u>(exception,[XN,E%])
<u>Step</u> 3 : $\leftarrow$ array tuple value(L%,PMLIST,PRE)

(c) <*labelled array tuple*>
      $\rightarrow$ <*array mode identifier option*>
        (:L(,){<*label subset*>:<*value denotation*>}:)

<u>Pass</u> ENV$\downarrow$
<u>With</u> POSTMODE$\downarrow$,
      ST $\equiv$ STATY$\downarrow$,
      DM $\equiv$ <*array mode identifier option*>.DENMODE$\downarrow$,
      NS $\equiv$ .NODESET$\uparrow$
      $\forall(i\epsilon L)$: (PRE$_{1_i}$i $\equiv$ <*label subset*>$_i$.PREMODE$\downarrow$,

                  S$_i$ $\equiv$ "   .SET$\downarrow$,

                  NS$_{1_i}$i $\equiv$ "   .NODESET$\downarrow$,

                  PRE$_{2_i}$i $\equiv$ <*value denotation*>$_i$.PREMODE$\downarrow$,

                  ISCT$_i$ $\equiv$ "   .ISCT$\downarrow$,

                  VAL$_i$ $\equiv$ "   .VAL$\downarrow$,

                  NS$_{2_i}$i $\equiv$ "   .NODESET$\downarrow$)

<u>Test</u> POSTMODE$\downarrow$=none,
      $\exists(i\epsilon L)$:<*value denotation*>$_i \Rightarrow$ <*expression*>
<u>Let</u>   M $\equiv$ (<u>Case</u> DM$\neq$none:mode(DM),
          <u>Case</u> <u>else</u>:POSTMODE$\downarrow$)
      ST$_1$ $\equiv$ (<u>Case</u> DM$\neq$none:stat,

            <u>Case</u> <u>else</u>:ST)
<u>Test</u> basemode(M)=array(-)
<u>Let</u>   EM $\equiv$ element mode(M),
      IM $\equiv$ index mode(M)
<u>Test</u> $\forall(i\epsilon L)$:(is compatible with(EM,PRE$_{2_i}$i),
             VAL$_i \neq$none $\Rightarrow$ VAL$_i \epsilon$set(EM))

<u>Let</u>   RG $\equiv$ compose regionality($\{$regionality(PRE$_i$)$|i\epsilon L\}$),

PRE $\equiv$ val(vclass,RG,ST$_1$,M),

SETLIST $\equiv$ $\{S_i|i\epsilon L\}$,

PSL $\equiv$ $\{PRE_{1_i}i|i\epsilon L\}$,

VALLIST $\equiv$ $\{VAL_i|i\epsilon L\}$,

PMLIST $\equiv$ $\{PRE_{2_i}i|i\epsilon L\}$,

XN $\equiv$ identify exception node(text(*RANGEFAIL*),ENV↓)

<u>Test</u> is coherent array tuple labelling(SETLIST,PSL,PRE)

<u>Def</u> $\forall(i\epsilon L)$: *<value denotation>*$_i$.POSTMODE↓ $\equiv$ EM,

PREMODE↓ $\equiv$ PRE,

ISCT↓ $\equiv$ (<u>Case</u> $\forall(i\epsilon L)$:(ISCT$_i$≠dyn $\lor$ ST$_1$=stat) : cst,

<u>Case</u> else:dyn),

VAL↓ $\equiv$ (<u>Case</u> ISCT↓=cst:

array labelled tuple value(VALLIST,PMLIST,

SETLIST,PSL,PRE,card(IM)),

<u>Case</u> else:none),

NODESET↓ $\equiv$ NS$\cup$($\cup$(iϵL):NS$_{1_i}$i)$\cup$($\cup$(iϵL):NS$_{2_i}$i)

<u>Dyn</u> ELAB=(E%,N%) :

<u>Step</u> 1 : R(iϵL) : V%$_i$ ← *<value denotation>*$_i$.ELAB(E%)

<u>Let</u> N%$_1$ $\equiv$ (<u>Case</u> ST$_1$=stat:card(IM),

<u>Case</u> ST$_1$=dyn:N%)

<u>Step</u> 2 : <u>Case</u> (ST$_1$=dyn

$\land \neg$ is valid number of elements(SETLIST,PSL,PRE,N%$_1$)

$\lor$ ($\exists$(iϵL):V%$_i$ $\notin$ set(EM)):

<u>exit</u>(exception, [XN,E%])

<u>Let</u> VL% $\equiv$ $\{V\%_i|i\epsilon L\}$

<u>Step</u> 3 : ← array labelled tuple value(VL%,PMLIST,SETLIST,PSL,PRE,N%$_1$)

3.3.3 STRUCTURE TUPLES

Syntax

(a) *<structure tuple>*
    (1) → *<unlabelled structure tuple>*
    (2) | *<labelled structure tuple>*
(b) *<unlabelled structure tuple>*
       → *<<u>structure</u> mode identifier option>*
         (:L(,)*<value denotation>*:)
(c) *<labelled structure tuple>*
       → *<<u>structure</u> mode identifier option>*
         (:L(,){*<field list>*:*<value denotation>*}:)
(d) *<field list>*
       → L(,){.*<<u>field</u> identifier>*}

Semantics

(a) *<structure tuple>*
<u>Pass</u> ENV↓,
    POSTMODE↓,
    PREMODE↓,

```
        ISCT↑,
        VAL↑,
        NODESET↑
Dyn     ELAB=(E%,TL%)
```

(b) *<unlabelled structure tuple>*
        → *<structure mode identifier option>*
            (:L(,)*<value denotation>*:)

Pass ENV↓
With POSTMODE↓,
      DM ≡ *<structure mode identifier option>*.DENMODE↑,
      NS ≡   "   .NODESET↑,
      ∀(i∈L) : (PRE$_i$ ≡ *<value denotation>*$_i$.PREMODE↑,
                ISCT$_i$ ≡   "   .ISCT↑,
                VAL$_i$ ≡   "   .VAL↑,
                NS$_i$ ≡   "   .NODESET↑)
Test DM=none ⇒ POSTMODE↓≠none
Let   M ≡ (Case DM≠none:mode(DM),
              Case else:POSTMODE↓),
      mode(NV,BM) ≡ M
When BM=struct(-)
Test ¬ is tag less(BM),
      ∀s:is field selector(s,BM) ⇒ is allowed(S,NV,ENV↓))
Let   VALL ≡ ≬VAL$_i$|i∈L≬,
      PREL ≡ ≬PRE$_i$|i∈L≬,
      SL ≡ selector list(VALL,BM),
      FDL ≡ descriptor list(VALL,BM),
      ML ≡ ≬field mode(S,BM)|S∈SL≬,
      RG ≡ compose regionality(≬regionality(PRE$_i$)|i∈L≬),
      ISCT ≡ compose isct(≬ISCT$_i$|i∈L≬),
      ST ≡ struct staticity(M),
      PRE ≡ val(vclass,RG,ST,M),
      XN$_1$ ≡ identify exception node(text(*RANGEFAIL*),ENV↓),
      XN$_2$ ≡ identify exception node(text(*TAG FAIL*),ENV↓),
      n ≡ #L
Test #SL=n,
      ∀(i∈L):(is tag selector(SL≬i≬,BM) ⇒ ISCT$_i$=lit,
              is compatible with(ML≬i≬,PRE$_i$))
Def   ∀(i∈L):*<value denotation>*$_i$.POSTMODE↓ ≡ ML≬i≬,
      PREMODE↑ ≡ PRE,
      ISCT↑ ≡ ISCT,
      VAL↑ ≡ (Case ISCT=cst:
                structure tuple value(VALLIST,PREL,FDL,PRE),
              Case else:none),
      NODESET↑ ≡ NS ∪(∪(i∈L):NS$_i$
Dyn   ELAB=(E%,TL%):
      Step 1 : R(i∈L) : V%$_i$ ← *<value denotation>*$_i$.ELAB(E%)
      Let   VL% ≡ ≬V%$_i$|i∈L≬
      Step 2 : R(Case is dyn struct(M)
                    ∧ ¬ are parameterization compatible(M,VALL,FDL,TL%):
                        exit(exception, [XN$_2$,E%]),
```
```

$\underline{Case}(\exists(i\epsilon L):V\%_i \notin set(ML\ddagger i\ddagger)):$

$\underline{exit}(exception, [XN_1,E\%]))$

<u>Step</u> 3 : ← structure tuple value(VL%,PREL,FDL,PRE)

(c) *<labelled structure tuple>*
    → *<<u>structure</u> mode identifier option>*
    (:L(,){*<field list>:<value denotation>*}:)

<u>Pass</u> ENV↓
<u>With</u> POSTMODE↓,
       DM ≡ *<<u>structure</u> mode identifier option>*.DENMODE↓,
       NS ≡   "   .NODESET↓,
       ∀(i∊L) : (SL$_i$ ≡ *<field list>*$_i$.SELLIST↓,
                 PRE$_i$ ≡ *<value denotation>*$_i$.PREMODE↓,
                 ISCT$_i$ ≡   "   .ISCT↓,
                 VAL$_i$ ≡   "   .VAL↓,
                 NS$_i$ ≡   "   .NODESET↓)

<u>Test</u> POSTMODE=none ⇒ DM≠none
       ∀(i∊L):*<value denotation>*$_i$ $\overset{*}{\Rightarrow}$ *<expression>*

<u>Let</u> M ≡ (<u>Case</u> DM≠none:mode(DM),
              <u>Case else</u>:POSTMODE↓),
       mode(NV,BM) ≡ M,
       struct(FDL) ≡ BM
<u>Test</u> BM≡struct(-),
<u>Let</u> SLL ≡ ‡SL$_i$|i∊L‡,
       SL ≡ ‖(i∊L):SL$_i$,
       PREL ≡ ‖(i∊L):‡PRE$_i$|s∊SL$_i$‡,
       ISCTL ≡ ‖(i∊L):‡ISCT$_i$|s∊SL$_i$‡,
       VALL ≡ ‖(i∊L):‡VAL$_i$|s∊SL$_i$‡,
       ML ≡ ‡field mode(S,BM)|S∊SL‡,
       n ≡ #SL
<u>Test</u> ∃(v∊set(BM)):SL=selector list(V,BM),
       ∀(i∊{1:n}):(is tag selector(SL‡i‡,BM) ⇒ ISCTL‡i‡ ∊ {cst,lit},
                   is compatible with(ML‡i‡,PREL‡i‡)),
       ∀s:is field selector(s,BM) ⇒ is allowed(S,NV,ENV))
<u>Let</u> RG ≡ compose regionality(‡regionality(PRE)|PRE∊PREL‡),
       ST ≡ struct staticity(M),
       PRE ≡ val(vclass,RG,ST,M),
       ISCT ≡ compose isct(ISCTL),
       FDL ≡ ‡field(A,B,C,D)

               |A∊SL ∧ ∃t∊n³:ijk descriptor(t,FDL)=field(A,B,C,D)‡
       XN$_1$ ≡ identify exception node(text(*RANGE FAIL*),ENV↓),

       XN$_2$ ≡ identify exception node(text(*TAG FAIL*),ENV↓)

<u>Def</u> ∀(i∊L):(*<value denotation>*$_i$.POSTMODE↓ ≡ (<u>Case</u> #SL$_i$=1:ML‡i‡,
                                                  <u>Case else</u>:none)),

       PREMODE↓ ≡ PRE,
       NODESET↓ ≡ NS∪(∪(i∊L):NS$_i$),

       ISCT↓ ≡ ISCT,
       VAL↓ ≡ (<u>Case</u> ISCT=cst ∧ ¬ is dyn struct(M) ∧ is tagless(M)):
              structure tuple value(VALL,PREL,FDL',PRE)

<u>Dyn</u>   ELAB=(E%,TL%):
      <u>Step</u> 1 : R(i∈L) : (V%$_i$ ≡ value denotation$_i$.ELAB(E%))

      <u>Let</u>   L% ≡ ╊V%$_i$|i∈L╊,

             LL% ≡ ‖(i∈L):╊V%$_i$|s∈SL$_i$╊

      <u>Step</u> 2 : R(<u>Case</u> is dyn struct(M)
                      ∧ ¬ are parameterization compatible(M,VALL,FDL',TL%):
                      <u>exit</u> (exception,[XN$_2$,E%]),

                   <u>Case</u> (∃(i∈L):LL%╊i╊ ∉ set(ML╊i╊):
                      <u>exit</u> (exception,[XN$_1$,E%]))

      <u>Step</u> 3 : ← structure labelled tuple value(LL%,PREL,FDL',PRE,TL%)

(d) <i>field list</i>
          → L(,){<u>field</u> identifier>}
<u>With</u> ENV↓
<u>Let</u>   ∀(i∈L):T$_i$ ≡ text(<u>field identifier</u>)
<u>Def</u>   SELLIST↓ ≡ ╊T$_i$|i∈L╊

3.4 VALUE ACCESSING

3.4.1 STRING VALUE ACCESSING

Syntax

(a) <i>value string element</i>
       → <u><i>string</i> expression</u>(<u><i>integer</i> expression</u>)
(b) <i>value substring</i>
    (1) → <u><i>string</i> expression</u>
             (<<i>literal expression <u>1</u></i>>:<<i>literal expression <u>2</u></i>>)
    (2) | <u><i>string</i> expression</u>
             (<<u><i>integer</i> expression</u>> UP <<i>literal expression</i>>)
(c) <i>value string slice</i>
       → <u><i>string</i> expression</u>
             (<<u><i>integer</i> expression <u>1</u></u>>:<<u><i>integer</i> expression <u>2</u></u>>)

Semantics

(a) <i>value string element</i>
       → <u><i>string</i> expression</u> (<u><i>integer</i> expression</u>)
<u>Pass</u> ENV↓
<u>With</u> PRE ≡ <<u>string expression</u>>.PREMODE↑,
      PRE$_1$ ≡ <<u><i>integer</i> expression</u>>.PREMODE↑

<u>When</u> <<u><i>string</i> expression</u>> ≇ <<i>delocated location</i>>,
      base mode(PRE)=string(-)
<u>Test</u> base mode(PRE$_1$)=discr(int,-,-)

<u>Let</u>   XN ≡ identify exception node(text(RANGE FAIL),ENV↓)
<u>Def</u>   <<u>string expression</u>>.POSTMODE↓ ≡ none,
      <<u>integer expression</u>>.POSTMODE↓ ≡ none,
      PREMODE↑ ≡ value substring premode(PRE,1)
      ISCT↓ ≡ dyn,
      VAL↓ ≡ none,

```
                 NODESET↑ ≡ {}
Dyn      ELAB=(E%):
         Step 1 : R(S% ← <string expression>.ELAB(E%),
                     I% ← <integer expression>.ELAB(E%))
         Let   T% ≡ 0 ≤ I% < length(S%,PRE)
         Step 2 : Case T%=false:exit(exception,[XN,E%])
         Step 3 : ← value substring(S%,PRE,I%,I%)
```

(b1) *<value substring>*
         → *<string expression>*
               (<literal expression 1>:<literal expression 2>)

Pass   ENV↓
With   PRE ≡ *<string expression>*.PREMODE↑,
         PRE₁ ≡ *<literal expression 1>*.PREMODE↑,

         V₁   ≡   "   .VAL↑,

         PRE₂ ≡ *<literal expression 2>*.PREMODE↑,

         V₂   ≡   "   .VAL↑

When   *<string expression>* ≵ *<delocated location>*,
         base mode(PRE)=string(-)
Test   base mode(PRE₁)=discr(int,-,-),

         base mode(PRE₂)=discr(int,-,-)

Let   val(-,-,-,mode(-,string(-,L))) ≡ PRE,
         XN ≡ identify exception node(text(*RANGE FAIL*),ENV↓)
Test   0 ≤ V₁ ≤ V₂ < L

Def   *<string expression>*.POSTMODE↓ ≡ none,
         PREMODE↓ ≡ value substring premode(PRE,V₂-V₁+1),

         ISCT↑ ≡ dyn,
         VAL↑ ≡ none,
         NODESET↑ ≡ {}
Dyn   ELAB=(E%):
         Step 1 : S% ← *<string expression>*.ELAB(E%),
         Let   T% ≡ V₂ < length(S%,PRE)

         Step 2 : Case ST=dyn ∧ T%=false:
                         exit(exception,[XN,E%])
         Step 3 : ← value substring(S%,PRE,V₁,V₂)

(b2) *<value substring>*
         → *<string expression>*
               (<integer expression> UP <literal expression>)

Pass   ENV↓
With   PRE ≡ *<string expression>*.PREMODE↑,
         PRE₁ ≡ *<integer expression>*.PREMODE↑,

         PRE₂ ≡ *<literal expression>*.PREMODE↑,

         V₂   ≡   "   .VAL↑

When   *<string expression>* ≵ *<delocated location>*,
         base mode(PRE)=string(-)
Test   base mode(PRE₁)=discr(int,-,-),

         base mode(PRE₂)=discr(int,-,-)

Let   val(-,-,-,mode(-,string(-,L))) ≡ PRE,
         XN ≡ identify exception node(text(*RANGE FAIL*),ENV↓)
```
```

<u>Test</u> $1 \le V_2 \le L$

<u>Def</u> <u>*<string expression>*</u>.POSTMODE↓ ≡ none,
      <u>*<integer expression>*</u>.POSTMODE↓ ≡ none,
      PREMODE↑ ≡ value substring premode(PRE,V_2),

      ISCT↓ ≡ dyn,
      VAL↑ ≡ none,
      NODESET↑ ≡ {}
<u>Dyn</u> ELAB=(E%):
      <u>Step</u> 1 : R(S% ← <u>*<string expression>*</u>.ELAB(E%),
                   V%$_1$ ← <u>*<integer expression>*</u>.ELAB(E%))

      <u>Let</u>   T% ≡ 0 ≤ V%$_1$ ∧(V%$_1$+V_2-1 < length(S%,PRE))

      <u>Step</u> 2 : <u>Case</u> T%=false:<u>exit</u>(exception,[XN,E%])
      <u>Step</u> 3 : ← value substring(S%,PRE,V%$_1$,V%$_1$+V_2-1)

(c) *<value string slice>*
        → <u>*<string expression>*</u>
            (<u>*<integer expression 1>*</u>:<u>*<integer expression 2>*</u>)
<u>Pass</u> ENV↓
<u>With</u> PRE ≡ <u>*<string expression>*</u>.PREMODE↓,
      PRE$_1$ ≡ <u>*<integer expression 1>*</u>.PREMODE↓,

      ISCT$_1$ ≡   "   .ISCT↓,

      PRE$_2$ ≡ <u>*<integer expression 2>*</u>.PREMODE↓,

      ISCT$_2$ ≡   "   .ISCT↓

<u>When</u> ISCT$_1$≠lit ∨ ISCT$_2$≠lit,

      <u>*<string expression>*</u> ≸ *<delocated location>*,
      base mode(PRE)=string(-)
<u>Test</u> base mode(PRE$_1$)=discr(int,-,-),

      base mode(PRE$_2$)=discr(int,-,-)

<u>Let</u> XN ≡ identify exception node(text(*RANGE FAIL*),ENV↓),
<u>Def</u> <u>*<string expression>*</u>.POSTMODE↓ ≡ none,
      <u>*<integer expression 1>*</u>.POSTMODE↓ ≡ none,
      <u>*<integer expression 2>*</u>.POSTMODE↓ ≡ none,
      PREMODE↑ ≡ value string slice premode(PRE),
      ISCT↑ ≡ dyn,
      VAL↓ ≡ none,
      NODESET↑ ≡ {}
<u>Dyn</u> ELAB=(E%):
      <u>Step</u> 1 : R(S% ← <u>*<string expression>*</u>.ELAB(E%),
                   I%$_1$ ← <u>*<integer expression 1>*</u>.ELAB(E%),

                   I%$_2$ ← <u>*<integer expression 2>*</u>.ELAB(E%))

      <u>Let</u>   T% ≡ 0 ≤ I%$_1$ ≤ I%$_2$ < length(S%,PRE)

      <u>Step</u> 2 : <u>Case</u> T%=false:<u>exit</u>(exception,[XN,E%])
      <u>Step</u> 3 : ← value string slice(S%,PRE,I%$_1$,I%$_2$)

3.4.2 ARRAY VALUE ACCESSING

Syntax

(a) <value array element>
→ <array expression>(<discrete expression>)
(b) <value subarray>
(1) → <array expression>
(<literal expression 1>:<literal expression 2>)
(2) | <array expression>
(<discrete expression> UP <literal expression>)
(c) <value array slice>
→ <array expression>
(<discrete expression 1>:<discrete expression 2>)

Semantics

(a) <value array element>
→ <array expression> (<discrete expression>)

Pass ENV↓
With PRE ≡ <array expression>.PREMODE↑,
      PRE₁ ≡ <discrete expression>.PREMODE↑

When base mode(PRE)=array(-),

      <array expression> $\overset{*}{\neq}$ <delocated location>
Let   I ≡ index mode(PRE),
      XN ≡ identify exception node(text(RANGE FAIL),ENV↓)
Test is compatible with(I,PRE₁),

      PRE=val(vclass,-,-,-)
Def   <array expression>.POSTMODE↑ ≡ none,
      <discrete expression>.POSTMODE↑ ≡ none,
      PREMODE↑ ≡ value array element premode(PRE),
      ISCT↑ ≡ dyn,
      VAL↑ ≡ none,
      NODESET↑ ≡ {}
Dyn   ELAB=(E%):
      Step 1 : R(A% ← <array expression>.ELAB(E%),
                 I% ← <discrete expression>.ELAB(E%))
      Let   T% ≡ min(I) ≤ I% ≤ upper(A%,PRE)
      Step 2 : Case T%=false:exit(exception,[XN,E%])
      Step 3 : ← value array element(A%,PRE,I%)

(b1) <value subarray>
→ <array expression>
(<literal expression 1>:<literal expression 2>)

Pass ENV↓
With PRE ≡ <array expression>.PREMODE↑,
      PRE₁ ≡ <literal expression 1>.PREMODE↑,

      V₁ ≡   "   .VAL↑,

      PRE₂ ≡ <literal expression 2>.PREMODE↑,

      V₂ ≡   "   .VAL↑

When base mode(PRE)=array(-),
      <array expression> $\overset{*}{\neq}$ <delocated location>
Let   I ≡ index mode(PRE),
      XN ≡ identify exception node(text(RANGE FAIL),ENV↓)

<u>Test</u> min(I) ≤ V₁ ≤ V₂ ≤ max(I),

  is compatible with(I,PRE₁),

  is compatible with(I,PRE₂),

  PRE=val(vclass,-,-,-)
<u>Def</u> <u>*array expression*</u>.POSTMODE↓ ≡ none,
  PREMODE↑ ≡ value subarray premode(PRE,#{V₁:V₂}),

  ISCT↑ ≡ dyn,
  VAL↑ ≡ none,
  NODESET↑ ≡ {}
<u>Dyn</u> ELAB=(E%):
  <u>Step</u> 1 : A% ← <u>*array expression*</u>.ELAB(E%),
  <u>Let</u> T% ≡ V₂ < upper(A%,PRE)

  <u>Step</u> 2 : <u>Case</u> T%=false:<u>exit</u>(exception,[XN,E%])
  <u>Step</u> 3 : ← value subarray(A%,PRE,V₁,V₂)

(b2) <value subarray>
   → <u>*array expression*</u>
     (<u>*discrete* expression</u> UP <u>*literal expression*</u>)
<u>Pass</u> ENV↓
<u>With</u> PRE ≡ <u>*array expression*</u>.PREMODE↑,
  PRE₁ ≡ <u>*discrete* expression</u>.PREMODE↑,

  PRE₂ ≡ <u>*literal expression*</u>.PREMODE↑,

  V₂ ≡   " .VAL↑
<u>When</u> base mode(PRE)=array(-),

  <u>*array expression*</u> ↯ <delocated *location*>
<u>Let</u> I ≡ index mode(PRE),
  XN ≡ identify exception node(text(*RANGE FAIL*),ENV↓)
<u>Test</u> base mode(PRE₂)=discr(int,-,-),

  1 ≤ V₂ ≤ card(I),

  ~~is compatible with(I,PRE₁),~~

  PRE=val(vclass,-,-,-)
<u>Def</u> <u>*array expression*</u>.POSTMODE↓ ≡ none,
  <u>*discrete* expression</u>.POSTMODE↓ ≡ none,
  PREMODE↑ ≡ value subarray premode(PRE,V₂),

  ISCT↑ ≡ dyn,
  VAL↑ ≡ none,
  NODESET↑ ≡ {}
<u>Dyn</u> ELAB=(E%):
  <u>Step</u> 1 : R(A% ← <u>*array expression*</u>.ELAB(E%),
     V%₁ ← <u>*discrete* expression</u>.ELAB(E%))

  <u>Let</u> T%=min(I) ≤ V%₁ ∧ V%₁+V₂-1 ≤ upper(A%,PRE)

  <u>Step</u> 2 : <u>Case</u> T%=false:<u>exit</u>(exception,[XN,E%])
  <u>Step</u> 3 : ← value subarray(A%,PRE,V%₁,V%₁+V₂-1)

(c) <value array slice>
   → <u>*array expression*</u>
      (<u>*discrete* expression 1</u>:<u>*discrete* expression 2</u>)
<u>Pass</u> ENV↓
<u>With</u> PRE ≡ <u>*array expression*</u>.PREMODE↑,
  PRE₁ ≡ <u>*discrete* expression 1</u>.PREMODE↑,

$ISCT_1 \equiv$ " .ISCT↑,

$PRE_2 \equiv$ *<discrete expression 2>*.PREMODE↓,

$ISCT_2 \equiv$ " .ISCT↓

When $ISCT_1 \neq lit \lor ISCT_2 \neq lit$,

<*array expression*> $\overset{*}{\neq}$ <*delocated location*>,
base mode(PRE)=array(-)

Let $I \equiv$ index mode(PRE),

XN $\equiv$ identify exception node(text(*RANGEFAIL*),ENV↓)

Test is compatible with(I,PRE_1),

is compatible with(I,PRE_2),

PRE=val(vclass,-,-,-)

Def <*array expression*>.POSTMODE↓ $\equiv$ none,
<*discrete expression 1*>.POSTMODE↓ $\equiv$ none,
<*discrete expression 2*>.POSTMODE↓ $\equiv$ none,
PREMODE↑ $\equiv$ value array slice premode(PRE),
ISCT↑ $\equiv$ dyn,
VAL↑ $\equiv$ none,
NODESET↑ $\equiv$ {}

Dyn ELAB=(E%):
Step 1 : R(S% ← <*array expression*>.ELAB(E%),
I%$_1$ ← <*discrete expression 1*>.ELAB(E%),

I%$_2$ ← <*discrete expression 2*>.ELAB(E%))

Let T% $\equiv$ min(I) $\leq$ I%$_1$ $\leq$ I%$_2$ $\leq$ upper(S%,PRE)

Step 2 : Case T%=false:exit(exception,[XN,E%])
Step 3 : ← value array slice(S%,PRE,I%$_1$,I%$_2$)

3.4.3 STRUCTURE VALUE ACCESSING

Syntax

(a) <*value structure field*>
   (1) → <*structure expression*>.<*field* identifier>
   (2) | <*with* value identifier>

Semantics

(a1) <*value structure field*>
    → <*structure expression*>.<*field* identifier>
Pass ENV↓
With PRE $\equiv$ <*structure expression*>.PREMODE↑
Let T $\equiv$ text(<*field* identifier>),
mode(NV,SM) $\equiv$ mode(PRE)

When <*structure expression*> $\overset{*}{\neq}$ <*delocated location*>
Test SM=struct(-),
PRE=val(vclass,-,-,-),
is allowed(T,NV,ENV↓)
Let XN $\equiv$ identify exception node(text(*TAGFAIL*),ENV↓))
Def PREMODE↑ $\equiv$ value field premode(T,PRE),
ISCT↑ $\equiv$ dyn,
VAL↑ $\equiv$ none,
NODESET↑ $\equiv$ {}

<u>Dyn</u>   ELAB=(E%):
    <u>Step</u> 1 : S% ← *<u>structure</u> expression*.ELAB(E%)
    <u>Step</u> 2 : (<u>Case</u> T≠selector list(S%,SM) <u>exit</u>(exception,[XN,E%]))
    <u>Step</u> 3 : ← value field(T,S%,PRE)

(a2) *<value structure field>*
      → *<<u>with</u> value identifier>*
<u>Pass</u> ENV↓
<u>With</u> CAT ≡ *<<u>with</u> value identifier>*.CAT↑,
    T ≡   "   .TEXT↑
<u>When</u> CAT=with(val(-))
<u>Let</u>   with(PRE) ≡ CAT,
    mode(NV,SM) ≡ mode(PRE),
    XN ≡ identify exception node(text(*TAGFAIL*),ENV↓)
<u>Def</u>   PREMODE↑ ≡ value field premode(T,PRE),
    ISCT↑ ≡ dyn,
    VAL↑ ≡ none,
    NODESET↑ ≡ {}
<u>Dyn</u>   ELAB=(E%):
    <u>Step</u> 1 : S% ← *<<u>with</u> value identifier>*.ELAB(E%)
    <u>Step</u> 2 : (<u>Case</u> T≠selector list(S%,SM):<u>exit</u>(exception,[XN,E%]))
    <u>Step</u> 3 : ← value field(T,S%,PRE)

3.5. REFERENCED LOCATIONS

Syntax

(a) *<referenced location>*
     → --> *<location denotation>*

Semantics

<u>Pass</u> ENV↓
<u>With</u> PRE ≡ *<location denotation>*.PREMODE↑,
    ISCT ≡   "   .ISCT↑,
    LOC ≡   "   .LOC↑
<u>Def</u>   PREMODE↑ ≡ reference premode(PRE),
    ISCT↑ ≡ ISCT,
    VAL↑ ≡ (<u>Case</u> ISCT=cst:reference(LOC,PRE),
         <u>Case</u> <u>else</u>:none),
    NODESET↑ ≡ {}
<u>Dyn</u>   ELAB=(E%):
    <u>Step</u> 1 : L% ← *<location denotation>*.ELAB(E%)
    <u>Step</u> 2 : ← reference(L%,PRE)

3.6 VALUE CONVERSIONS

Syntax

(a) *<value conversion>*
     → *<mode identifier>(<expression>)*

Semantics

<u>Pass</u> ENV↓
<u>With</u> DM ≡ <*mode identifier*>.DENMODE↑,
       PRE ≡ <*expression*>.PREMODE,
       ISCT ≡   "   .ISCT↑,
       VAL ≡   "   .VAL↑

<u>When</u> <*expression*> $\overset{*}{\ne}$ <*delocated location*>
<u>Test</u> is value convertible(PRE,DM)
<u>Let</u>   [-,M] ≡ DM,
       val(-,RG,-,-) ≡ PRE,
       RG_1 ≡ compose regionality(RG,DM)

<u>Def</u>   PREMODE↑ ≡ val(vclass,RG_1,stat,M),

       ISCT↑ ≡ ISCT,
       VAL↑ ≡ (<u>Case</u> ISCT≠dyn:value conversion(VAL,PRE,DM),
               <u>Case</u> <u>else</u>:none),
       NODESET ≡ {}
<u>Dyn</u>   ELAB=(E%):
       <u>Step</u> 1 : V% ← <*expression*>.ELAB(E%)
       <u>Step</u> 2 : ← value conversion(V%,PRE,DM)

3.7 CONTENTS OF LOCATIONS

Syntax

(a) <*delocated location*>
        → <*location denotation*>

Semantics

<u>Pass</u> ENV↓
<u>With</u> PRE ≡ <*location denotation*>.PREMODE↑,
<u>Test</u> ¬ has the synchro prop(PRE)
<u>Def</u>   PREMODE↑ ≡ contents premode(PRE),
       ISCT↑ ≡ dyn,
       VAL↑ ≡ none,
       NODESET↑ ≡ {}
<u>Dyn</u>   ELAB=(E%):
       <u>Step</u> 1 : L% ← <*location denotation*>.ELAB(E%)
       <u>Step</u> 2 : ← contents(L%,PRE)

3.8 LITERAL AND CONSTANT EXPRESSIONS

Syntax

(a) <*literal expression*>
        → <*expression*>
(b) <*constant expression*>
        → <*value denotation*>

Semantics

(a) *<literal expression>* → *<expression>*
Pass ENV↓,
     PREMODE↑,
     VAL↑,
     ISCT↑,
     NODESET↑
When ISCT↑=lit

(b) *<constant expression>* → *<value denotation>*
Pass ENV↓,
     PREMODE↑,
     VAL↑,
     ISCT↑,
     NODESET↑
When ISCT↑ ∈ {lit,cst}

3.9 UNDEFINED VALUE

Syntax

(a) *<undefined value>*
    (1) → *
    (2) | *<undefined value identifier>*

Semantics

(a1) *<undefined value>* → *
Def   PREMODE↑ ≡ val(all,-,-,udf)
      ISCT↑ ≡ cst,
      VAL↑ ≡ udf,
      NODESET↑ ≡ {}
Dyn   ELAB=(E%):
      Step : ← udf

(a2) *<undefined value>* → *<undefined synonym value identifier>*
Pass ENV↓,
     PREMODE↑,
     ISCT↑,
     VAL↑,
     NODESET↑
With CAT ≡ *<undefined synonym value identifier>*.CAT↑
When CAT=syn ∧ VAL↑=udf
Dyn   ELAB=(E%)

3.10 VALUE IDENTIFIERS

Syntax

(a) *<value identifier>*
        → <identifier>

Semantics

<u>With</u> ENV↓
<u>Let</u>   T ≡ text(<identifier>),
       N ≡ identify node(T,ENV↓),
       CAT ≡ N.DCAT!
<u>Test</u> N≠udf
<u>When</u> CAT ∈ {syn,lit,dynsyn,with(val(-))}
<u>Def</u>   CAT↑ ≡ CAT
       <u>Case</u> CAT ∈ {syn,dynsyn,lit}:
               (<u>Def</u> PREMODE↑ ≡ N.DPREMODE!,
                      ISCT↑ ≡ N.DISCT!,
                      VAL↑ ≡ N.DVAL!,
                      NODESET↑ ≡ {N}),
       <u>Case</u> CAT=with(-):
               (<u>Def</u>   TEXT↑ ≡ T)
<u>Dyn</u>   ELAB=(E%):
       <u>Case</u> CAT ∈ {with(-),dynsyn}:
               <u>Step</u> : ← identify(N,E%)

4. LOCATION DENOTATIONS

Syntax

(a) *<location denotation>*
    (1) → *<static location denotation>*
    (2) | *<dynamic location denotation>*
(b) *<static location denotation>*
    (1) → *<location identifier>*
    (2) | *<location string element>*
    (3) | *<location substring>*
    (4) | *<location array element>*
    (5) | *<location subarray>*
    (6) | *<location structure field>*
    (7) | *<dereferenced free reference>*
    (8) | *<dereferenced bound reference>*
    (9) | *<location conversion>*
    (10) | *<location procedure call>*
    (11) | *<location built in routine call>*
(c) *<dynamic location denotation>*
    (1) → *<location string slice>*
    (2) | *<location array slice>*
    (3) | *<dereferenced row>*

Semantics

(a) *<location denotation>*
Pass ENV↓,
      PREMODE↑,
      ISCT↑,
      LOC↑
Dyn ELAB=(E%)

(b1) *<static location denotation>* → *<location identifier>*
Pass ENV↓,
      PREMODE↑,
      ISCT↑,
      LOC↑,
With CAT ≡ *<location identifier>*.CAT↑
When CAT ≠ with(-)
Dyn ELAB=(E%)

(b2:b11) *<static location denotation>*
Pass ENV↓,
      PREMODE↑,
      ISCT↑,
      LOC↑
When **Case** (b10:b11):PREMODE↑=loc(-)
Dyn ELAB=(E%)

(c) *<dynamic location denotation>*
Pass ENV↓,
      PREMODE↑
Def ISCT↑ ≡ dyn,
      LOC↑ ≡ none
Dyn ELAB=(E%)

4.1 LOCATION IDENTIFIER

Syntax

(a) <*location identifier*>
        → <<u>*location*</u> identifier>

Semantics

<u>With</u> ENV↓
<u>Let</u>   T ≡ text(<<u>*location*</u> identifier>),
        N ≡ identify node(T,ENV↓),
        CAT ≡ N.DCAT!
<u>Def</u>   CAT↑ ≡ CAT
<u>When</u> CAT ∈ {loc,based,with(loc(-))}
<u>Case</u> CAT=loc:
        <u>Def</u>   PREMODE↑ ≡ N.DPREMODE!,
                ISCT↑ ≡ N.DISCT!,
                LOC↑ ≡ N.DLOC!
        <u>Dyn</u>   ELAB=(E%):
                Step : ← identify(N,E%)
 <u>Case</u> CAT=with(-):
        <u>Def</u>   TEXT↑ ≡ T
        <u>Dyn</u>   ELAB=(E%):
                Step : ← identify(N,E%)
 <u>Case</u> CAT=based
        <u>Let</u>   PRE ≡ N.DPREMODE!,
                DM ≡ N.DREFDM!,
                PRE₁ ≡ contents premode(PRE),

                PRE₂ ≡ dereference premode(PRE₁,DM),

                XM ≡ identify deref exceptions(PRE₁,ENV↓)

        <u>Def</u>   PREMODE↑ ≡ PRE₂,

                ISCT↑ ≡ dyn,
                LOC↑ ≡ none
        <u>Dyn</u>   ELAB=(E%):
                Step 1 : L% ← identify(N,E%)
                Step 2 : P% ← contents(L%,PRE)
                Step 3 : L% ← dereference(P%,PRE₁,DM,XM)

                Step 4 : (<u>Case</u> L%=udf:<u>undefined</u>,
                            <u>Case</u> exception(X) ≡ L%:<u>exit</u>(exception,[X,E%]))
                Step 5 : ← L%

4.2 LOCATION ACCESSING

4.2.1 STRING LOCATION ACCESSING

Syntax

(a) <*location string element*>
        → <<u>*string*</u> location denotation>(<<u>*integer*</u> expression>)
(b) <*location substring*>
    (1) → <<u>*string*</u> location denotation>

```
                    (<literal expression 1>:<literal expression 2>)
    (2) | <string location denotation>
              (<integer expression> UP <literal expression>)
(c) <location string slice>
        → <string location denotation>
              (<integer expression 1>:<integer expression 2>)
```

Semantics

(a) *<location string element>*
      → *<string location denotation>(<integer expression>)*

<u>Pass</u> ENV↓
<u>With</u> PRE   ≡ *<string location denotation>*.PREMODE↑,
      LISCT ≡   "   .ISCT↑,
      LOC   ≡   "   .LOC↑,
      PRE₁ ≡ *<integer expression>*.PREMODE↑,

      VISCT ≡   "   .ISCT↑,
      VAL   ≡   "   .VAL↑
<u>When</u> base mode(PRE)=string(-)
<u>Let</u>   ISCT ≡ compose isct(↕VISCT,LISCT↕)
<u>Test</u> base mode(PRE₁)=discr(int,-,-),

      ISCT=cst ⇒ 0 ≤ VAL < length(LOC,PRE)
<u>Let</u>   XN ≡ identify exception node(text(*RANGEFAIL*),ENV↓),
<u>Def</u>   *<integer expression>*.POSTMODE↓ ≡ none,
      PREMODE↑ ≡ location substring premode(PRE,1),
      ISCT↑ ≡ ISCT,
      LOC↑ ≡ (<u>Case</u> ISCT=cst:location substring(LOC,PRE,VAL,VAL),
               <u>Case else</u>:none)
<u>Dyn</u>   ELAB=(E%):
      <u>Step</u> 1 : R(SL% ← *<string location denotation>*.ELAB(E%),
                I% ← *<integer expression>*.ELAB(E%))
      <u>Let</u>   T% ≡ 0 ≤ I% < length(SL%,PRE)
      <u>Step</u> 2 : <u>Case</u> T%=false:<u>exit</u>(exception,[XN,E%])
      <u>Step</u> 3 : ← location substring(SL%,PRE,I%,I%)

(b1) *<location substring>*
      → *<string location denotation>*
           (<literal expression 1>:<literal expression 2>)
<u>Pass</u> ENV↓
<u>With</u> PRE   ≡ *<string location denotation>*.PREMODE↑,
      LISCT ≡   "   .ISCT↑,
      LOC   ≡   "   .LOC↑,
      PRE₁ ≡ *<literal expression 1>*.PREMODE↑,

      V₁   ≡   "   .VAL↑,

      PRE₂ ≡ *<literal expression 2>*.PREMODE↑,

      V₂   ≡   "   .VAL↑
<u>When</u> base mode(PRE)=string(-)
<u>Test</u> base mode(PRE₁)=discr(int,-,-),

      base mode(PRE₂)=discr(int,-,-)

<u>Let</u>   loc(-,-,-,-,mode(-,string(-,L))) ≡ PRE,
      XN ≡ identify exception node(text(*RANGEFAIL*),ENV↓),
      L₁ ≡ V₂-V₁+1

<u>Test</u> 0 ≤ V₁ ≤ V₂ ≤ L
```
```

<u>Def</u>   PREMODE↑ ≡ location substring premode(PRE,L₁)

ISCT↑ ≡ LISCT,
LOC↑ ≡ (<u>Case</u> LISCT=CST:location substring(LOC,PRE,V₁,V₂),

Case else:none)

<u>Dyn</u>   ELAB=(E%):
Step 1 : SL% ← <u>*string location denotation*</u>.ELAB(E%),
<u>Let</u>   T% ≡ V₂ < length(SL%,PRE)

Step 2 : <u>Case</u> T%=false:<u>exit</u>(exception,[XN,E%])
Step 3 : ← location substring(SL%,PRE,V₁,V₂)

(b2) <u>*location substring*</u>
→ <u>*string location denotation*</u>
(<u>*integer expression*</u> UP <*literal expression*>)

<u>Pass</u>   ENV↓
<u>With</u>   PRE   ≡ <*string location denotation*>.PREMODE↑,
LISCT ≡   "   .LISCT↑,
LOC   ≡   "   .LOC↑,
PRE₁ ≡ <*integer expression*>.PREMODE↑,

VISCT ≡   "   .VISCT↑,
VAL   ≡   "   .VAL↑,
PRE₂ ≡ <*literal expression*>.PREMODE↑,

V₂   ≡   "   .VAL↑

<u>When</u>   base mode(PRE)=string(-)
<u>Test</u>   base mode(PRE₁)=discr(int,-,-),

base mode(PRE₂)=discr(int,-,-)

<u>Let</u>   string(-,L) ≡ basemode(PRE),
XN ≡ identify exception node(text(*RANGEFAIL*),ENV↓),
ISCT ≡ compose isct(‡VISCT,LISCT‡)
<u>Test</u>   1 ≤ V₂ ≤ L,

ISCT=cst ⇒ ((0 ≤ VAL) ∧ (VAL+V₂-1 < L))

<u>Def</u>   <u>*integer expression*</u>.POSTMODE↓ ≡ none,
PREMODE↑ ≡ location substring premode(PRE,V₂),

ISCT↑ ≡ ISCT↑,
LOC↑ ≡ (<u>Case</u> ISCT=cst:location substring(LOC,PRE,VAL,VAL+V₂-1),

Case else:none)

<u>Dyn</u>   ELAB=(E%):
Step 1 : R(SL% ← <u>*string location denotation*</u>.ELAB(E%),
V%₁ ← <u>*integer expression*</u>.ELAB(E%))

<u>Let</u>   T% ≡ 0 ≤ V%₁ ∧ V%₁+V₂-1 < length(SL%,PRE)

Step 2 : <u>Case</u> T%=false:<u>exit</u>(exception,[XN,E%])
Step 3 : ← location substring(SL%,PRE,V%₁,V%₁+V₂-1)

(c) <u>*location string slice*</u>
→ <u>*string location denotation*</u>
(<u>*integer expression 1*</u>:<*integer expression 2*>)

<u>Pass</u>   ENV↓
<u>With</u>   PRE ≡ <*string location denotation*>.PREMODE↑,
PRE₁ ≡ <*integer expression 1*>.PREMODE↑,

ISCT₁ ≡   "   .ISCT↑,

PRE₂ ≡ <*integer expression 2*>.PREMODE↑,

```
        ISCT₂ ≡                 "          .ISCT↑
```

When   ISCT₁≠lit ∨ ISCT₂≠lit,

        base mode(PRE)=string(-)
Test   base mode(PRE₁)=discr(int,-,-),

        base mode(PRE₂)=discr(int,-,-)

Let   XN ≡ identify exception node(text(*RANGEFAIL*),ENV↓)
Def   <*integer expression 1*>.POSTMODE↓ ≡ none,
        <*integer expression 2*>.POSTMODE↓ ≡ none,
        PREMODE↑ ≡ location string slice premode(PRE)
Dyn   ELAB=(E%):
        Step 1 : R(SL% ← <*string location denotation*>.ELAB(E%),
                   I%₁ ← <*integer expression 1*>.ELAB(E%),

                   I%₂ ← <*integer expression 2*>.ELAB(E%))

        Let   T% ≡ 0 ≤ I%₁ ≤ I%₂ < length(SL%,PRE)

        Step 2 : Case T%=false:exit(exception,[XN,E%])
        Step 3 : ← location string slice(SL%,PRE,I%₁,I%₂)

4.2.2 ARRAY LOCATION ACCESSING

Syntax

(a) <*location array element*>
        → <*array location denotation*>(<*discrete expression*>)
(b) <*location subarray*>
    (1) → <*array location denotation*>
               (<*literal expression 1*>:<*literal expression 2*>)
    (2) | <*array location denotation*>
               (<*discrete expression*> UP <*literal expression*>)
(c) <*location array slice*>
        → <*array location denotation*>
               (<*discrete expression 1*>:<*discrete expression 2*>)

Semantics

(a) <*location array element*>
        → <*array location denotation*>(<*discrete expression*>)
Pass   ENV↓
With   PRE   ≡ <*array location denotation*>.PREMODE↑,
        LISCT ≡   "   .ISCT↑,
        LOC   ≡   "   .LOC↑
        PRE₁ ≡ <*discrete expression*>.PREMODE↑

        VISCT ≡   "   .ISCT↑,
        VAL   ≡   "   .VAL↑
When   base mode(PRE)=array(-)
Let   I ≡ index mode(PRE),
        XN ≡ identify exception node(text(*RANGEFAIL*),ENV↓),
        ISCT ≡ compose isct(≹LIST,VISCT≹)
Test   is compatible with(I,PRE₁),

        ISCT=cst ⇒ VAL∈set(I)
Def   <*discrete expression*>.POSTMODE↓ ≡ none,
        PREMODE↑ ≡ location array element premode(PRE),
```
```

```
        ISCT+ ≡ ISCT,
        LOC ≡ (Case ISCT=cst:location array element(LOC,PRE,VAL,PRE₁),

               Case else:none)
Dyn     ELAB=(E%):
        Step 1 : R(SL% ← <array location denotation>.ELAB(E%),
                   I% ← <discrete expression>.ELAB(E%))
        Let   U% ≡ upper(SL%,PRE)
        Step 2 : Case I% < min(I) ∨ I% > U%:
                        exit(exception,[XN,E%])
        Step 3 : ← location array element(SL%,PRE,I%,PRE₁)
```

(b1) *<location subarray>*
       → *<array location denotation>*
            (<literal expression 1>:<literal expression 2>)

```
Pass    ENV+
With    PRE   ≡ <array location denotation>.PREMODE+,
        LISCT ≡              "            .ISCT+,
        LOC   ≡              "            .LOC+,
        PRE₁  ≡ <literal expression 1>.PREMODE+,

        V₁    ≡              "           .VAL+,

        PRE₂  ≡ <literal expression 2>.PREMODE+,

        V₂    ≡              "           .VAL+

When    base mode(PRE)=array(-)
Let     I ≡ index mode(PRE),
        XN ≡ identify exception node(text(MODEFAIL),ENV+)
Test    is compatible with(I,PRE₁),

        is compatible with(I,PRE₂),

        min(I) ≤ V₁ ≤ V₂ ≤ max(I)

Let     L₁ ≡ V₂-V₁+1

Def     PREMODE+ ≡ location subarray premode(PRE,L₁)

        ISCT+ ≡ LISCT,
        LOC+ ≡ (Case LISCT=cst:location subarray(LOC,PRE,V₁,V₂),

                Case else:none
Dyn     ELAB=(E%):
        Step 1 : SL% ← <array location denotation>.ELAB(E%)
        Let   U% ≡ upper(SL%,PRE)
        Step 2 : Case V₂ > U%:exit(exception,[XN,E%])

        Step 3 : ← location subarray(SL%,PRE,V₁,V₂)
```

(b2) *<location subarray>*
       → *<array location denotation>*
            (<discrete expression> UP <literal expression>)

```
Pass    ENV+
With    PRE   ≡ <array location denotation>.PREMODE+,
        LISCT ≡              "            .ISCT+,
        LOC   ≡              "            .LOC+,
        PRE₁  ≡ <discrete expression>.PREMODE+,

        VISCT ≡              "            .ISCT+,
        VAL   ≡              "            .VAL+,
        PRE₂  ≡ <literal expression>.PREMODE+,

        V₂    ≡              "           .VAL+
```

<u>When</u> base mode(PRE)=array(-)
<u>Test</u> base mode(PRE$_2$)=discr(int,-,-)

<u>Let</u>   I ≡ index mode(PRE),
       ISCT ≡ compose isct({VISCT,LISCT}),
       XN ≡ identify exception node(text(*RANGEFAIL*),ENV↓)
       RF$_1$ ≡ subarray refy(array(I,E,R))

<u>Test</u> is compatible with(I,PRE$_1$)

       ISCT=cst ⇒ {VAL:VAL+(V$_2$-1)} ⊆ set(I)

       1 ≤ V$_2$ ≤ card(I)

<u>Def</u>   <u>*discrete expression*</u>.POSTMODE↓ ≡ none,
       PREMODE↓ ≡ location subarray premode(PRE,V$_2$),

       ISCT↑ ≡ ISCT,
       LOC↑ ≡ (<u>Case</u> ISCT=cst:location subarray(LOC,PRE,VAL,VAL+V$_2$=1),

                 <u>Case else</u>:none)
<u>Dyn</u>   ELAB=(E%):
       <u>Step 1</u> : R(SL% ← <u>*array location denotation*</u>.ELAB(E%),
                   V%$_1$ ← <u>*discrete expression*</u>.ELAB(E%))

       <u>Let</u>   U% ≡ upper(SL%,PRE)
       <u>Step 2</u> : <u>Case</u> {V%$_1$:V%$_1$+V$_2$-1} ⊆ {min(I):U%}:<u>exit</u>(exception,[XN,E%])

       <u>Step 3</u> : ← location subarray(SL%,PRE,V%$_1$,V%$_1$+V$_2$-1)

(c) *<location array slice>*
        → *<array location denotation>*
            (*<discrete expression 1>*:*<discrete expression 2>*)
<u>Pass</u> ENV↓
<u>With</u> PRE ≡ <u>*array location denotation*</u>.PREMODE↑,
       PRE$_1$ ≡ <u>*discrete expression 1*</u>.PREMODE↑,

       ISCT$_1$ ≡   "   .ISCT↑,

       PRE$_2$ ≡ <u>*discrete expression 2*</u>.PREMODE↑,

       ISCT$_2$ ≡   "   .ISCT↑

<u>When</u> ISCT$_1$≠lit ∨ ISCT$_2$≠lit,

       base mode(PRE)=array(-)
<u>Let</u>   I ≡ index mode(PRE),
       XN ≡ identify exception node(text(*RANGEFAIL*),ENV↓)
<u>Test</u> is compatible with(I,PRE$_1$),

       is compatible with(I,PRE$_2$)

<u>Def</u>   <u>*discrete expression 1*</u>.POSTMODE↓ ≡ none,
       <u>*discrete expression 2*</u>.POSTMODE↓ ≡ none,
       PREMODE↓ ≡ location array slice premode(PRE)
<u>Dyn</u>   ELAB=(E%):
       <u>Step 1</u> : R(SL% ← <u>*array location denotation*</u>.ELAB(E%),
                   I%$_1$ ← <u>*discrete expression 1*</u>.ELAB(E%),

                   I%$_2$ ← <u>*discrete expression 2*</u>.ELAB(E%))

       <u>Let</u>   T% ≡ min(I) ≤ I%$_1$ ≤ I%$_2$ ≤ upper(SL%,PRE)

       <u>Step 2</u> : <u>Case</u> T%=false:<u>exit</u>(exception,[XN,E%])
       <u>Step 3</u> : ← location array slice(SL%,PRE,I%$_1$,I%$_2$)

4.2.3. STRUCTURE LOCATION ACCESSING

Syntax

(a) *<location structure field>*
    (1) → *<structure location denotation>*.*<field* identifier>
    (2) | *<with location identifier>*

Semantics

(a1) *<location structure field>*
       → *<structure location denotation>*.*<field* identifier>
<u>Pass</u> ENV↓
<u>With</u> PRE ≡ *<structure location denotation>*.PREMODE↑
     LISCT ≡   "   .ISCT↑,
     LOC ≡   "   .LOC↑,
<u>Let</u> T ≡ text(*<field* identifier>),
     mode(NV,SM) ≡ mode(PRE),
     ISCT ≡ (<u>Case</u> LISCT=cst
                     ∧ (is fixed selector(T,SM)
                       ∨ (is parameterizable(SM)
                         ∧ is parameterized(SM)
                         ∧ T∈selector list(LOC,PRE))):cst,
           <u>Case</u> <u>else</u>:dyn)
<u>Test</u> SM=struct(-),
     is allowed(T,NV,ENV↓)
<u>Let</u> XN ≡ identify exception node(text(*TAGFAIL*),ENV↓))
<u>Def</u> PREMODE↑ ≡ location field premode(T,PRE),
     ISCT↑ ≡ ISCT,
     LOC↑ ≡ (<u>Case</u> ISCT=cst:location field(T,LOC,PRE),
            <u>Case</u> <u>else</u>:none)
<u>Dyn</u> ELAB=(E%):
     <u>Step</u> 1 : SL% ← *<structure location denotation>*.ELAB(E%)
     <u>Step</u> 2 : <u>Case</u> T∉selector list(SL%,PRE):<u>exit</u>(exception,[XN,E%])
     <u>Step</u> 3 : ← location field(T,SL%,PRE)

(a2) *<location structure field>* → *<with location identifier>*
<u>Pass</u> ENV↓
<u>With</u> CAT ≡ *<with location identifier>*.CAT↑,
     T ≡   "   .TEXT↑
<u>When</u> CAT=with(loc(-))
<u>Let</u> with(PRE) ≡ CAT,
     mode(NV,SM)) ≡ mode(PRE),
     XN ≡ identify exception node(text(*TAGFAIL*),ENV↓))
<u>Def</u> PREMODE↑ ≡ location field premode(T,PRE),
     ISCT↑ ≡ dyn,
     LOC↑ ≡ none
<u>Dyn</u> ELAB=(E%):
     <u>Step</u> 1 : SL% ← *<with location identifier>*.ELAB(E%)
     <u>Step</u> 2 : (<u>Case</u> T∉selector list(SL%,PRE):<u>exit</u>(exception,[XN,E%])
     <u>Step</u> 3 : ← location field(T,SL%,PRE)

4.3. DEREFERENCED REFERENCES

Syntax

(a) *<dereferenced bound reference>*
          → *<bound reference expression>* -->
                     <mode identifier option>
(b) *<dereferenced free reference>*
          → *<free reference expression>* --> *<mode identifier>*
(c) *<dereferenced row>*
          → *<row expression>* -->

Semantics

(a) *<dereferenced bound reference>*
          → *<bound reference expression>* -->
                     <mode identifier option>

<u>Pass</u> ENV↓
<u>With</u> PRE ≡ *<bound reference expression>*.PREMODE↑,
       DM ≡ *<mode identifier option>*.DENMODE↑
<u>When</u> basemode(PRE)=ref(-)
<u>Let</u>   ref(RD,M) ≡ basemode(PRE),
       XM ≡ identify deref exceptions(PRE,ENV↓)
<u>Test</u> DM≠ none ⇒ is read compatible with(DM,[RD,M]),
       PRE=val(vclass,-,-,-)
<u>Def</u>   *<bound reference expression>*.POSTMODE↑ ≡ none,
       PREMODE↑ ≡ dereference premode(PRE,DM),
       ISCT↑ ≡ dyn,
       LOC↑ ≡ none
<u>Dyn</u>   ELAB=(E%):
       <u>Step</u> 1 : R% ← *<bound reference expression>*.ELAB(E%)
       <u>Step</u> 2 : L% ← dereference(R%,PRE,DM,XM)
       <u>Step</u> 3 : (<u>Case</u> L%=udf:<u>undefined</u>,
                 <u>Case</u> exception(X) ≡ L%:<u>exit</u>(exception,[X,E%])
       <u>Step</u> 4 : ← L%

(b) *<dereferenced free reference>*
          → *<free reference expression>* --> *<mode identifier>*

<u>Pass</u> ENV↓
<u>With</u> PRE ≡ *<free reference expression>*.PREMODE↑,
       DM ≡ *<mode identifier>*.DENMODE↑
<u>When</u> basemode(PRE)=ptr
<u>Test</u> PRE=val(vclass,-,-,-)
<u>Let</u>   XM ≡ identify deref exceptions(PRE,ENV↓)
<u>Def</u>   *<free reference expression>*.POSTMODE↑ ≡ none,
       PREMODE↑ ≡ dereference premode(PRE,DM),
       ISCT↑ ≡ dyn,
       LOC↑ ≡ none
<u>Dyn</u>   ELAB=(E%):
       <u>Step</u> 1 : P% ← *<free reference expression>*.ELAB(E%)
       <u>Step</u> 2 : L% ← dereference(P%,PRE,DM,XM)
       <u>Step</u> 3 : (<u>Case</u> L=udf:<u>undefined</u>,
                 <u>Case</u> exception(X) ≡ L%:<u>exit</u>(exception,[X,E%])
       <u>Step</u> 4 : ← L%

(c) *<dereferenced row>*
          → *<row expression>* -->
<u>Pass</u> ENV↓

<u>With</u>   PRE ≡ <u>row expression</u>.PREMODE↑
<u>When</u>   basemode(PRE)=row(-)
<u>Test</u>   PRE=val(vclass,-,-,-)
<u>Let</u>   XM ≡ identify deref exceptions(PRE,ENV↓)
<u>Def</u>   <u>row expression</u>.POSTMODE↓ ≡ none,
         PREMODE↑ ≡ derow premode(PRE)
<u>Dyn</u>   ELAB=(E%):
         <u>Step</u> 1 : R% ← <u>row expression</u>.ELAB(E%)
         <u>Step</u> 2 : L% ← derow(R%,PRE,XM)
         <u>Step</u> 3 : (<u>Case</u> L%=udf:<u>undefined</u>,
                   <u>Case</u> exception(X) ≡ L%:<u>exit</u>(exception,[X,E%])
         <u>Step</u> 4 : ← L%

4.4 LOCATION CONVERSIONS

Syntax

(a) <i><location conversion></i>
        → <i><mode identifier>(<location denotation>)</i>

Semantics

<u>Pass</u>   ENV↓
<u>With</u>   DM ≡ <mode identifier>.DENMODE↑,
       PRE ≡ <i><location denotation></i>.PREMODE↑,
       ISCT ≡   "   .ISCT↑,
       LOC ≡   "   .LOC↑
<u>Test</u>   size(DM)=size(PRE),
       staticity(PRE)=stat,
       refy(PRE)=refble
<u>Def</u>   PREMODE↑ ≡ location premode(PRE),
       ISCT↑ ≡ ISCT,
       LOC↑ ≡ (<u>Case</u> ISCT=cst:location conversion(LOC,PRE,DM),
               <u>Case</u> <u>else</u>:none)
<u>Dyn</u>   ELAB=(E%):
       <u>Step</u> 1 : L% ← <location denotation>.ELAB(E%)
       <u>Step</u> 2 : ← location conversion(L%,PRE,DM)

5. BUILT-IN ROUTINES AND FORMULAE

5.1 BUILT-IN ROUTINES

Syntax

(a) *<built-in routine call>*
    (1) → *<chill built-in routine call>*
    (2) | *<implementation built-in routine call>*
(b) *<chill built-in routine call>*
    (1)→ *SIZE (<mode identifier>)*
    (2)| *SIZE (<static location denotation>)*
    (3)| *<succ pred> (<expression>)*
    (4)| *NUM (<discrete expression>)*
    (5)| *ABS (<integer expression>)*
    (6)| *CARD (<powerset expression>)*
    (7)| *<min max> (<powerset expression>)*
    (8)| *UPPER (<expression>)*
    (9)| *ADDR (<location denotation>)*
    (10)| *GETSTACK (<mode identifier>)*
    (11)| *GETSTACK (<string mode identifier> (<integer expression>))*
    (12)| *GETSTACK (<array mode identifier> (<expression>))*
    (13)| *GETSTACK (<variant mode identifier>*
                        (L(,)<expression>))
(c) *<succ pred>*
    (1) → *SUCC*
    (2) | *PRED*
(d) *<min max>*
    (1) → *MIN*
    (2) | *MAX*
(e) *<implementation built-in routine call>*

       → *<implemented identifier> (<implemented actual parameter part>)*
Semantics

(a) *<built-in routine call>*
<u>Pass</u> ENV↓,
      PREMODE↑,
      ISCT↑,
      VAL↑,
      NODESET↑
<u>Dyn</u> ELAB=(E%)

(b1) *<chill built-in routine call>* → *SIZE <mode identifier>*
<u>Pass</u> ENV↓,
      NODESET↑
<u>With</u> DM ≡ *<mode identifier>*.DENMODE↑
<u>Def</u>   PREMODE↑ ≡ dpre(int),
      ISCT↑ ≡ cst,
      VAL↑ ≡ size(DM)
<u>Dyn</u> ELAB=(E%):
      <u>Step</u> : ← VAL↑

(b2) *<chill built-in routine call>* → *SIZE (<static location denotation>)*
<u>Pass</u> ENV↓
<u>With</u> PRE ≡ *<static location denotation>*.PREMODE↑
<u>Test</u> PRE=loc(-,stat,refble,-,-)

<u>Def</u>   PREMODE↑ ≡ dpre(int),
       ISCT↑ ≡ cst,
       VAL↑ ≡ size(PRE),
       NODESET↑ ≡ {}
<u>Dyn</u>   ELAB=(E%):
       <u>Step</u> : ← VAL↑

(b3) *<chill built-in routine call>*
         → *<succ pred>* *(<expression>)*

<u>Pass</u>   ENV↓
<u>With</u>   SUCCPRED ≡ *<succ pred>*.FCT↑,
       PRE   ≡ *<expression>*.PREMODE↑,
       ISCT ≡   "   .ISCT↑,
       VAL ≡   "   .VAL↑,
       NS   ≡   "   .NODESET↑
<u>Test</u>   base mode(PRE)=discr(-) ∨ ref(-)
       base mode(PRE)=ref(-) ⇒ PRE=val(vclass,-,-,-),
       ISCT∈{cst,lit} ⇒ apply1(SUCCPRED, VAL,PRE,{})≠exception(-)
<u>Let</u>   XM ≡ identify apply1 exceptions(SUCCPRED,PRE,ENV↓)
<u>Def</u>   PREMODE↑ ≡ apply1 premode(SUCCPRED,PRE),
       ISCT↑ ≡ ISCT,
       VAL↑ ≡ (<u>Case</u> ISCT ∈ {lit,cst}:apply1(SUCCPRED,VAL,PRE,{})
               <u>Case</u> <u>else</u>:none),
       NODESET↑ ≡ NS
<u>Dyn</u>   ELAB=(E%):
       <u>Step</u> 1 : V% ← *<expression>*.ELAB(E%)
       <u>Step</u> 2 : V%₁ ← apply1(SUCCPRED,V%,PRE,XM)

       <u>Step</u> 3 : <u>Case</u> exception(X) ≡ V%₁:

                     <u>exit</u>(exception,[X,E%])
       <u>Step</u> 4 : ← V%₁

(b4) *<chill built-in routine call>*
         → NUM *(<u>discrete</u> expression>)*
<u>Pass</u>   ENV↓,
       NODESET↑
<u>With</u>   PRE ≡ *<u>discrete</u> expression>*.PREMODE↑,
       ISCT ≡   "   .ISCT↑,
       VAL ≡   "   .VAL↑
<u>Test</u>   base mode(PRE)=discr(-)
<u>Def</u>   PREMODE↑ ≡ dpre(int),
       ISCT↑ ≡ ISCT,
       VAL↑ ≡ (<u>Case</u> ISCT ∈ {lit,cst}:num(VAL,PRE),
               <u>Case</u> <u>else</u>:none)
<u>Dyn</u>   ELAB=(E%):
       <u>Step</u> 1 : V% ← *<u>discrete</u> expression>*.ELAB(E%)
       <u>Step</u> 2 : V%₁ ← num(V%,PRE)

(b5) *<chill built-in routine call>*
         → ABS *(<u>integer</u> expression>)*
<u>Pass</u>   ENV↓,
       NODESET↑
<u>With</u>   PRE ≡ *<u>integer</u> expression>*.PREMODE↑,
       ISCT ≡   "   .ISCT↑,
       VAL ≡   "   .VAL↑
<u>Test</u>   base mode(PRE)=discr(int,-,-),
       ISCT∈{cst,dyn} ⇒ apply 1(abs,VAL,PRE,{}) ≠ exception(-)
<u>Let</u>   XM ≡ identify apply1 exceptions(abs,PRE,ENV)

<u>Def</u>   PREMODE↑ ≡ apply1 premode(abs,PRE),
       ISCT↑ ≡ ISCT,
       VAL↑ ≡ (<u>Case</u> ISCT ∈ {lit,cst}:apply(abs,VAL,PRE,{})
              <u>Case</u> <u>else</u>:none)
<u>Dyn</u>   ELAB=(E%):
       <u>Step</u> 1 : V% ← <<u>integer expression</u>>.ELAB(E%)
       <u>Step</u> 2 : V%₁ ← apply1(abs,V%,PRE,XM)

       <u>Step</u> 3 : <u>Case</u> exception(X) ≡ V%₁:<u>exit</u>(exception,[X,E%])

       <u>Step</u> 4 : ← V%₁

(b6) <<u>chill built-in routine call</u>>
         → CARD (<<u>powerset expression</u>>)
<u>Pass</u>   ENV↓,
       NODESET↑
<u>With</u>   PRE ≡ <<u>powerset expression</u>>.PREMODE↑,
       ISCT ≡   "   .ISCT↑,
       VAL ≡   "   .VAL↑
<u>Test</u>   base mode(PRE)=poset(-),
       PRE=val(vclass,-,-,-)
<u>Def</u>   PREMODE↑ ≡ dpre(int)
       ISCT↑ ≡ ISCT,
       VAL↑ ≡ (<u>Case</u> ISCT ∈ {lit,cst}:card(VAL,PRE),
              <u>Case</u> <u>else</u>:none)
<u>Dyn</u>   ELAB=(E%):
       <u>Step</u> 1 : V% ← <<u>powerset expression</u>>.ELAB(E%)
       <u>Step</u> 2 : ← card(V%,PRE)

(b7) <<u>chill built-in routine call</u>>
         → <<u>min max</u>> (<<u>powerset expression</u>>)
<u>Pass</u>   ENV↓
<u>With</u>   MINMAX ≡ <<u>min max</u>>.FCT↑,
       PRE ≡ <<u>powerset expression</u>>.PREMODE↑,
       ISCT ≡   "   .ISCT↑,
       VAL ≡   "   .VAL↑,
       NS   ≡   "   .NODESET↑
<u>Test</u>   base mode(PRE)=poset(-),
       PRE=val(vclass,-,-,-),
       ISCT∈{cst,lit} ⇒ apply1(MINMAX,VAL,PRE,{})
                                  ≠exception(-)
<u>Let</u>   M ≡ member mode(PRE),
       XM=identify apply1 exceptions(MINMAX,PRE,ENV↓)
<u>Def</u>   PREMODE↑ ≡ apply1 premode(MINMAX,PRE),
       ISCT↑ ≡ ISCT,
       VAL↑ ≡ (<u>Case</u> ISCT ∈ {cst,lit}:apply1(MINMAX,VAL,PRE,{}),
              <u>Case</u> <u>else</u>:none),
       NODESET↑ ≡ NS
<u>Dyn</u>   ELAB=(E%):
       <u>Step</u> 1 : V% ← <<u>powerset expression</u>>.ELAB(E%)
       <u>Step</u> 2 : V%₁ ← apply1(MINMAX,V%,PRE,XM)

       <u>Step</u> 3 : <u>Case</u> exception(X) ≡ V%₁:

                    <u>exit</u>(exception,[X,E%])
       <u>Step</u> 4 : ← V%₁

(b8) <<u>chill built-in routine call</u>>
         → UPPER (<<u>expression</u>>)
<u>Pass</u>   ENV↓,

```
        NODESET↑
With    PRE  ≡ <expression>.PREMODE↑,
        ISCT ≡      "      .ISCT↑,
        VAL  ≡      "      .VAL↑
Let     BM ≡ base mode(PRE),
        ISCT ≡ (Case staticity(PRE)=stat:lit,
                 Case else:dyn),
        L ≡ (Case string(-,L₁) ≡ BM:L₁,

             Case array(I,-,-) ≡ BM:card(I))
Test    BM∈{array(-),string(-)},
        BM=array(-) ⇒ PRE=val(vclass,-,-,-)
Def     PREMODE↑ ≡
        (Case array(I,-,-) ≡ BM:val(vclass,nreg,stat,I))
         Case BM=string(-):dpre(int)),
        ISCT↑ ≡ ISCT,
        VAL↑ ≡ (Case ISCT=lit:L,
                 Case else:none)
Dyn     ELAB=(E%):
        Step 1 : V% ← <expression>.ELAB(E%)
        Step 2 : (Case BM=string(-): ← length(V%,PRE)-1,
                   Case BM=array(-) ← upper(V%,PRE))
```

(b9) *<chill built-in routine call>* → *ADDR (<location denotation>)*

```
Pass    ENV↓
With    PRE  ≡ <location denotation>.PREMODE↑,
        ISCT ≡          "           .ISCT↑,
        LOC  ≡          "           .LOC↑
Def     PREMODE↑ ≡ reference premode(PRE),
        ISCT↑ ≡ ISCT,
        VAL↑ ≡ (Case ISCT=cst:reference(LOC,PRE),
                 Case else:none),
        NODESET↑ ≡ {}
Dyn     ELAB=(E%):
        Step 1 : L% ← <location denotation>.ELAB(E%)
        Step 2 : ← reference(L%,PRE)
```

(b10) *<chill built-in routine call>*
            → *GETSTACK (<mode identifier>)*

```
Pass    ENV↓
With    DM ≡ <mode identifier>.DENMODE↑
Let     [RD,M] ≡ DM,
        RG ≡ regionality(ENV↓),
        XN ≡ identify exception node(text(SPACEFAIL),ENV↓),
        PRE= loc(RG, stat, refble, RD, M)
Def     PREMODE↑ ≡ reference premode(PRE),
        ISCT↑ ≡ dyn,
        VAL↑ ≡ none,
        NODESET↑ ≡ {}
Dyn     ELAB=(E%):
        Step 1 : L% ← try and create location(PRE,E%)
        Step 2 : Case L%=udf:exit(exception, [XN,E%])
        Step 3 : ← reference(L%,PRE)
```

(b11) *<chill built-in routine call>*
            → *GETSTACK (<string mode identifier>*
                        (<integer expression>))

```
Pass    ENV↓
With    DM ≡ <string mode identifier>.DENMODE↑,
```

```
        PRE ≡ <integer expression>.PREMODE↑
When    base mode(DM) ≡ string(-)
Test    base mode(PRE) ≡ discr(int,-,-)
Let     [RD,M] ≡ DM
        RG ≡ regionality(ENV↓),
        PRE ≡ loc(RG,dyn,refble,RD,M),
        XN₁ ≡ identify exception node(text(RANGE FAIL),ENV↓),
        XN₂ ≡ identify exception node(text(SPACE FAIL),ENV↓),

        string(-,L) ≡ base mode(M)
Def     PREMODE↑ ≡ reference premode(PRE),
        ISCT↑ ≡ dyn,
        VAL↑ ≡ none,
        NODESET↑ ≡ {}
Dyn     ELAB=(E%):
        Step 1 : N% ← <integer expression>.ELAB(E%)
        Step 2 : Case ¬(1 ≤ N% ≤ L):exit(exception,[XN₁,E%])

        Step 3 : L% ← create dyn string location(PRE,N%,E%)
        Step 4 : Case L%=udf:exit(exception,[XN₂,E%])

        Step 5 : reference(L%,PREMODE↑)


(b12)  <chill built-in routine call>
          → GETSTACK (<array mode identifier> (<expression>))
Pass    ENV↓
With    PRE ≡ <expression>.PREMODE↑,
        DM  ≡ <array mode identifier>.DENMODE↑
When    basemode(DM)=array(-)
Let     [RD,M] ≡ DM,
        I ≡ index mode(M),
        RG ≡ regionality(ENV↓),
        PRE₁ ≡ loc(RG,dyn,refble,RD,M),

        XN₁ ≡ identify exception node(text(RANGEFAIL),ENV↓),

        XN₂ ≡ identify exception node(text(SPACEFAIL),ENV↓)

Test    is compatible with(I,PRE)
Def     PREMODE↑ ≡ reference premode(PRE₁),

        ISCT↑ ≡ dyn,
        VAL↑ ≡ none,
        NODESET↑ ≡ {}
Dyn     ELAB=(E%):
        Step 1 : N% ← <expression>.ELAB(E%)
        Step 2 : Case N% ∉ set(I):exit(exception,[XN₁,E%])

        Step 3 : L% ← create dyn array location(PRE₁,N%,E%)

        Step 4 : Case L%=udf:exit(exception,[XN₂,E%])

        Step 5 : ← reference(L%,PREMODE↑)


(b13)  <chill built-in routine call>
          → GETSTACK (<variant mode identifier>
                      (L(,)<expression>))
Pass    ENV↓
With    DM ≡ <variant mode identifier>.DENMODE↑,
        ∀(i∈L):(PRE_i ≡ <expression>_i.PREMODE↑)

Let     PML ≡ {PRE_i|i∈L},

        PPML ≡ param premodes(DM),
```

        CRD,MJ ≡ DM,
        RG=regionality(ENV↓)
When is variant structure mode(M)
Test are param premodes compatible(PML,M),
        is parameterizable BM ∧ ¬ is parameterized(BM)
Let PRE ≡ loc(RG,dyn,refble,RD,M),
        XN_1 ≡ identify exception node(text(*RANGEFAIL*),ENV↓),

        XN_2 ≡ identify exception node(text(*SPACEFAIL*),ENV↓)

Def PREMODE↑ ≡ reference premode(PRE),
        ISCT↑ ≡ dyn,
        VAL↑ ≡ none,
        NODESET↑ ≡ {}
Dyn ELAB=(E%):
        Step 1 : R(i∈L):($V\%_i$←<*expression*>$_i$.ELAB(E%))

        Let   : VL% ≡ {$V\%_i$|i∈L}

        Step 2 : Case ∃(i∈L):(PPML{i}=val(vclass,-,-,-)
                                ∧ $V\%_i$∉set(PPML{i}):
                                exit(exception,[XN_1,E%])

        Step 3 : L% ← create dyn struct location(PRE,VL%,E%)
        Step 4 : Case L%=udf:exit(exception,[XN_2,E%])

        Step 5 : ← reference(L%,PRE_1)

(c1) <*succ pred*> → *SUCC*
Def FCT↑ ≡ succ

(c2) <*succ pred*> → *PRED*
Def FCT↑ ≡ pred

(d1) <*min max*> → *MIN*
Def FCT↑ ≡ min

(d2) <*min max*> → *MAX*
Def FCT↑ ≡ max

(e) <*implementation built-in routine call*>
        → <*implemented identifier*>
              (<*implemented actual parameter part*>)
{# implementation defined #}

5.2 FORMULAE

Syntax

(a) <*formula*>
    (1) → <*expression 1*><*dyadic operator*><*expression 2*>
    (2) | <*monadic operator*><*expression*>
(b) <*dyadic operator*>
    (1) → <+>
    (2) | <->
    (3) | <*>
    (4) | </>
    (5) | <MOD>
    (6) | <‖>

```
        (7) | <AND>
        (8) | <OR>
        (9) | <XOR>
       (10) | <=>
       (11) | </=>
       (12) | <>>
       (13) | <>=>
       (14) | <<>
       (15) | <<=>
       (16) | <IN>
       (17) | <REM>
(c) <monadic operator>
        (1) → <-->
        (2) | <NOT>
```

Semantics

(a1) *<formula>* → *<expression 1><dyadic operator><expression 2>*
Pass ENV↓
With PRE₁ ≡ *<expression 1>*.PREMODE↑,

  PRIOR₁ ≡   "   .PRIOR,

  ISCT₁ ≡   "   .ISCT↑,

  VAL₁   ≡   "   .VAL↑,

  NS₁   ≡   "   .NODESET↑,

  PRE₂ ≡ *<expression 2>*.PREMODE↑,

  PRIOR₂ ≡   "   .PRIOR↑,

  ISCT₂ ≡   "   .ISCT↑,

  VAL₂   ≡   "   .VAL↑,

  NS₂   ≡   "   .NODESET↑,

  OP   ≡ *<dyadic operator>*.OP↑,
  PRIOR ≡   "   .PRIOR↑
When PRIOR ≤ PRIOR₁ ∧ PRIOR < PRIOR₂

Test is operable(OP,PRE₁,PRE₂)

Let   XM ≡ identify apply2 exceptions(OP,PRE₁,PRE₂,ENV↓),

     ISCT ≡ compose isct(⧼ISCT₁,ISCT₂⧽)

Test ISCT=dyn ⇒ apply2(OP,VAL₁,PRE₁,VAL₂,PRE₂,{})≠exception(-)

Def   PREMODE↑ ≡ apply2 premode(OP,PRE₁,PRE₂),

     PRIOR↑ ≡ PRIOR,
     VAL↑ ≡ (Case ISCT≠dyn:apply2(OP,VAL₁,PRE₁,VAL₂,PRE₂,{})),

          Case else:none),
     NODESET↑ ≡ NS₁ ∪ NS₂
Dyn   ELAB=(E$):
     Step 1 : R(0$₁ ← *<expression 1>*.ELAB(E$),

               0$₂ ← *<expression 2>*.ELAB(E$))

     Step 2 : R$ ← apply2(OP,0$₁,PRE₁,0$₂,PRE₂,XM)

     Step 3 : Case exception(X) ≡ R$:exit(exception,[X,E$])
     Step 4 : ← R$

(a2) *<formula>* → *<monadic operator><expression>*
Pass ENV↓
With PRE   ≡ *<expression>*.PREMODE↑,
      PRIOR ≡   "   .PRIOR↑,
      ISCT ≡   "   .ISCT↑,
      VAL   ≡   "   .VAL↑,
      NS   ≡   "   .NODESET↑,
      OP ≡ *<monadic operator>*.OP↓
When PRIOR=highest
Test is operable(OP,PRE)
Let   XM ≡ identify apply1 exceptions(OP,PRE,ENV↓)
Test ISCT≠dyn ⇒ apply1(OP,VAL,PRE,{})≠exception(-)
Def   PREMODE↑ ≡ apply1 premode(OP,PRE),
      PRIOR↑ ≡ highest,
      ISCT↑ ≡ ISCT,
      VAL↑ ≡ (Case ISCT ∈ {lit,cst}:apply1(OP,VAL,PRE,{}),
                Case else:none),
      NODESET↑ ≡ NS
Dyn   ELAB=(E%):
      Step 1 : O% ← *<expression>*.ELAB(E%)
      Step 2 : R% ← apply1(OP,O%,PRE,XN)
      Step 3 : (Case exception(X) ≡ R%:exit(exception,[X,E%])
      Step 4 : ← R%

(b) *<dyadic operator>*
Pass PRIOR↑,
      OP↑

(c) *<monadic operator>*
Pass PRIOR↑,
      OP↑

6. ACTION STATEMENTS

Syntax

(a) *<action statement list>*
    (1) → *<empty>*
    (2) | *<action statement><action statement list>*
(b) *<action statement>*
    (1) → *<labelling><basic action statement>*
                      <handler><end label>;
    (2) | *<labelling><choice action statement>*
                       <handler><end label>;
    (3) | *<labelling><block action statement>*
                       <handler><end label>;
    (4) | *<module statement>*
(c) *<labelling>*
    (1) → *<empty>*
    (2) | *<label identifier>:*
(d) *<end label>*
    (1) → *<empty>*
    (2) | *<identifier>*
(e) *<handler>*
    (1) → *<empty>*
    (2) | *ON <else handler> END*
    (3) | *ON L <particular handler> <else handler> END*
(f) *<particular handler>*
        → *(L(,)<exception identifier>):*
              <action statement list>
(g) *<else handler>*
    (1) → *<empty>*
    (2) | *ELSE <action statement list>*

Semantics

(a1) *<action statement list>* → *<empty>*
<u>Def</u>   DECLA↑ ≡ {}
<u>Dyn</u>   PREELAB=(PE%):
     <u>Step</u> : ← PE%
     ELAB=(E%,N%)
     <u>Step</u> : ← E%

(a2) *<action statement list>*
          → *<action statement><action statement list>*
<u>Pass</u> ENV↓
<u>With</u> D_1 ≡ *<action statement>*.DECLA↑,

      D_2 ≡ *<action statement list>*.DECLA↑

<u>Def</u>   DECLA↑ ≡ D_1 ∪ D_2

<u>Dyn</u> PREELAB=(PE%):
     <u>Step</u> 1 : $PE\%_1$ ← *<action statement>*.PREELAB(PE%)

     <u>Step</u> 2 : ← *<action statement list>*.PREELAB($PE\%_1$)

     ELAB=(E%,N%):
     (<u>Case</u> N% ∈ labels(D_1) ∨ N%=all :

         (<u>Step</u> 1 : $E\%_1$ ← *<action statement>*.ELAB(E%,N%)

           <u>Step</u> 2 :   ← *<action statement list>*.ELAB($E\%_1$,all)),

<u>Case</u> N% ∈ labels(D₂):

    <u>Step</u> : <*action statement list*>.ELAB(E%,N%))

(b1) <*action statement*>
       → <*labelling*><*basic action statement*>
                <*handler*><*end label*>;

<u>With</u> ENV↓,
     T ≡ <*labelling*>.TEXT↑,
     N ≡   "   .NODE↑,
     HD ≡ <*handler*>.EXCEPT↑,
     ET ≡ <*end label*>.TEXT↑
<u>Test</u> empty(<*handler*>) ⇒ empty(<*end label*>),
     ET≠none ⇒ T=ET
<u>Let</u>   SPP ≡ surrounding proc(ENV↓),
     LD ≡ (<u>Case</u> T≠none:define(T,N),
          <u>Case</u> <u>else</u> : {})
     NEWENV ≡ new exceptions(ENV↓,HD)
<u>Def</u>   <*basic action statement*>.ENV↓ ≡ NEWENV↓,
              "   .HP↓ ≡ ¬ empty(<*handler*>)
     <*handler*>.ENV↓ ≡ ENV↓,
     DECLA↑ ≡ LD,
     N.DCAT! ≡ label(noexit,SPP),
     N.DIMPLIED! ≡ {}
<u>Dyn</u> PREELAB=(PE%):
     <u>Step</u> : ← PE%
     ELAB=(E%,N%):
     <u>Step</u> : ← <*basic action statement*>.ELAB(E%)
     TRAP=(K%,[N%₁,EE%])

         <u>Case</u> K%=exception
              ∧ N%₁ ∈ exception nodes(HD):

              <u>Step</u> : ← N%₁.ELAB(adjust(EE%,E%))

(b2) <*action statement*>
       → <*labelling*><*choice action statement*>
                <*handler*><*end label*>;

<u>With</u> ENV↓,
     T ≡ <*labelling*>.TEXT↑,
     N ≡   "   .NODE↑,
     AD ≡ <*choice action statement*>.DECLA↑,
     HD ≡ <*handler*>.EXCEPT↑,
     ET ≡ <*end label*>.TEXT↑
<u>Test</u> ET≠none ⇒ T=ET
<u>Let</u>   SPP ≡ surrounding proc(ENV↓),
     N₁ ≡ node(<*labelling*>),

     LD ≡ (<u>Case</u> T≠none:define(T,N),
          <u>Case</u> <u>else</u>:{}),
     LDEXIT ≡ (<u>Case</u> T≠none:define(T,N₁),

              <u>Case</u> <u>else</u>:{}),
     NEW ENV ≡ new exceptions(ENV↓,HD),
     NEW ENV₁ ≡ NEW ENV <u>plus</u> LDEXIT,

     NEW ENV₂ ≡ ENV↓ <u>plus</u> LDEXIT
<u>Def</u>   <*choice action statement*>.ENV↓ ≡ NEW ENV₁,

     <*handler*>.ENV↓ ≡ NEW ENV₂,

```
     DECLA↑ ≡ AD ∪ LD,
     N.DCAT! ≡ label(noexit,SPP),
     N.DIMPLIED! ≡ {},
     N₁.DCAT! ≡ label(exitposs,SPP),

     N₁.DIMPLIED! ≡ {}
```

Dyn   PREELAB=(PE%):
      Step : ← <choice action statement>.PREELAB(PE%)
      ELAB=(E%,N%):
      Step : ← <choice action statement>.ELAB(E%,N%)
      TRAP=(K%,[N%₁,EE%]):

          Let   E%₁ ≡ adjust(EE%,E%)

              (Case K%=exception ∧ N%₁ ∈ exception nodes(HD):

                   Step : ← N%₁.ELAB(E%₁)

               Case K%=goto ∧ N%₁=N₁:

                   Step : ← <choice action statement>
                                                    .ELAB(E%₁,all),

               Case K%=exit ∧ N%₁=N₁:

                   Step : ← E%₁)

(b3) <action statement>
        → <labelling><block action statement>
                    <handler><end label>;
With   ENV↓,
       T ≡ <labelling>.TEXT↑,
       N ≡   "   .NODE↑,
       ID ≡ <block action statement>.INDECLA↑,
       OD ≡   "   .OUTDECLA↑,
       HD ≡ <handler>.EXCEPT↑,
       ET ≡ <end label>.TEXT↑
Test   ET≠none ⇒ T=ET,
       is locale(ID)
Let   SPP ≡ surrounding proc(ENV↓),
       N₁ ≡ node(<labelling>),

       LD ≡ (Case T≠none:define(T,N),
                Case else:{}),
       LDEXIT ≡ (Case T≠none:define(T,N₁),

                 Case else:{}),
       NEW ENV₁ ≡ ENV↓ plus LDEXIT,

       NEW ENV₂ ≡ new block env(NEWENV₁,ID ∪ LD,HD),

       NEW ENV₃ ≡ replace exceptions(NEWENV₂,ENV↓),

       XN ≡ identify exception node(SPACEFAIL,ENV↓)
Def   <block action statement>.ENV↓ ≡ NEW ENV₂,

                     "   .EXTENV↓ ≡ ENV↓,
                     "   .HANDLER↓ ≡ HD↓,
       <handler>.ENV↓ ≡ NEW ENV₃,

       DECLA↑ ≡ OD ∪ LD,
       N.DCAT! ≡ label(noexit,SPP),
       N.DIMPLIED! ≡ {},
       N₁.DCAT! ≡ label(exitposs,SPP),

       N₁.DIMPLIED! ≡ {}
```
```

<u>Dyn</u>   PREELAB=(PE%):
       <u>Step</u> : ← PE%
       ELAB=(E%,N%):
       <u>Step</u> 1 : <u>Case</u> the implementation is unable to allocate space for the
                block :
                        :<u>exit</u>(exception,[XN,E%])
       <u>Step</u> 2 : EN% ← new(E%)
       <u>Step</u> 3 : EN%$_1$ ← <block action statement>.PREELAB(EN%)
       <u>Step</u> 4 :   ← <block action statement>.ELAB(EN%$_1$)

       TRAP=(K%,[N%$_1$,EE%]):

          <u>Let</u>   E%$_1$ ≡ adjust(EE%,EN%)

                (<u>Case</u> K%=exception ∧ N%$_1$ ∈ exception nodes(HD):

                    <u>Step</u> : ← N%$_1$.ELAB(E%$_1$)

                  <u>Case</u> K%=goto ∧ N%$_1$=N$_1$:

                    <u>Step</u> : ← <block action statement>.ELAB(E%$_1$),

                  <u>Case</u> K%=exit ∧ N%$_1$=N$_1$:

                    <u>Step</u> : ← E%$_1$)

(b4) <action statement> → <module statement>
<u>Pass</u> ENV↓,
      DECLA↑
<u>Dyn</u>   PREELAB=(PE%)
      ELAB=(E%,N%)

(c1) <labelling> → <empty>
<u>Def</u>   TEXT↑ ≡ none,
      NODE↑ ≡ none

(c2) <labelling> → <<u>label</u> identifier>
<u>Def</u>   TEXT↑ ≡ text(<<u>label</u> identifier>),
      NODE↑ ≡ node(<<u>label</u> identifier>)

(d1) <end label> → <empty>
<u>Def</u>   TEXT↑ ≡ none

(d2) <end label> → <<u>label</u> identifier>
<u>Def</u>   TEXT↑ ≡ text(<<u>label</u> identifier>)

(e1) <handler> → <empty>
<u>Def</u>   EXCEPT↑ ≡ {}

(e2) <handler> → ON <else handler> END
<u>Pass</u> ENV↓,
      EXCEPT↑

(e3) <handler> → ON L<particular handler> <else handler> END
<u>Pass</u> ENV↓
<u>With</u> ∀(i∈L):EXC$_i$ ≡ <particular handler>$_i$.EXCEPT↑,

      EXC ≡ <else handler>.EXCEPT↑
<u>Let</u>   EXCEPT ≡ (∪(i∈L):EXC$_i$)∪EXC
<u>Test</u> is exception locale(EXCEPT)
<u>Def</u>   EXCEPT↑=EXCEPT

(f) *<particular handler>*
       → (L(,)<*exception* identifier>):
                <*action statement list*>

<u>With</u> ENV↓,
      D ≡ <*action statement list*>.DECLA↓
<u>Test</u> is locale(D)
<u>Let</u>   ∀(i∊L):T_i ≡ text(<*exception* identifier>$_i$),
      N ≡ node(<*particular handler*>),
      EXCEPT ≡ ∪(i∊L):define exception(T_i,N),

      NEWENV ≡ new block env(ENV↓,D,{}),
      XN ≡ identify exception node(*SPACEFAIL*,ENV)
<u>Def</u> <*action statement list*>.ENV↓ ≡ NEWENV,
      EXCEPT↓ ≡ EXCEPT
<u>Dyn</u> ELAB=(E%):
    <u>Step</u> 1 : the implementation is unable to allocate space for the handler
                :<u>exit</u>(exception,[XN,E%])
    <u>Step</u> 2 : EN% ← new(E%)
    <u>Step</u> 3 : EN%$_1$ ← <*action statement list*>.PREELAB(EN%)

    <u>Step</u> 4 :   ← <*action statement list*>.ELAB(EN%$_1$,all)

    TRAP=(K%,[N%,EE%]):
        <u>Let</u> E%$_1$ ≡ adjust(EE%,E%)

        <u>Case</u> K=goto ∧ N%∊labels(D):
          <u>Step</u> : ← <*action statement list*>.ELAB(E%$_1$,N%)

(g1) *<else handler>* → <empty>
<u>Def</u> EXCEPT↓ ≡ {}

(g2) *<else handler>* → ELSE <*action statement list*>
<u>With</u> ENV↓,
      D ≡ <*action statement list*>.DECLA↓
<u>Test</u> is locale(D)
<u>Let</u> N ≡ node(<*else handler*>),
      EXCEPT ≡ define exception(else,N),
      NEWENV ≡ new block env(ENV↓,D,{}),
      XN ≡ identify exception node(*SPACEFAIL*,ENV↓)
<u>Def</u> <*action statement list*>.ENV↓ ≡ NEW ENV,
      EXCEPT↓ ≡ EXCEPT
<u>Dyn</u> ELAB=(E%):
    <u>Step</u> 1 : the implementation is unable to allocate space for the handler
                :<u>exit</u>(exception,[XN,E%])
    <u>Step</u> 2 : EN% ← new(E%)
    <u>Step</u> 3 : EN%$_1$ ← <*action statement list*>.PREELAB(EN%)

    <u>Step</u> 4 :   ← <*action statement list*>.ELAB(EN%$_1$,all)

    TRAP=(K%,[N%,EE%]):
        <u>Let</u>   E%$_1$ ≡ adjust(EE%,E%)

        <u>Case</u> K=goto ∧ N%∊labels(D):
          <u>Step</u> : ← <*action statement list*>.ELAB(E%$_1$,N%)

6.1 BASIC ACTION STATEMENTS

Syntax

(a) *<basic action statement>*
    (1) → *<assignment statement>*
    (2) | *<goto statement>*
    (3) | *<exit statement>*
    (4) | *<cause statement>*
    (5) | *<assert statement>*
    (6) | *<empty statement>*
    (7) | *<procedure basic action statement>*
    (8) | *<concurrent basic action statement>*

Semantics

(a)
Pass ENV↓,
    HP↓
Dyn ELAB=(E%)

6.1.1 ASSIGNMENT STATEMENT

Syntax

(a) *<assignment statement>*
    (1) → L(,) *<location denotation>* := *<value denotation>*
    (2) | *<location denotation>* := *<tuple>*
    (3) | *<location denotation>*
           <dyadic operator> := *<value denotation>*

Semantics

(a1) *<assignment statement>*
      → L(,) *<location denotation>*:=*<value denotation>*
Pass ENV↓
With $\forall(i \in L):PRE_i \equiv$ *<location denotation>*$_i$.PREMODE↑,

    PRE ≡ *<value denotation>*.PREMODE↑
Let $\forall(i \in L):XM_i \equiv$ identify assign exceptions(PRE,PRE_i,ENV↓),

Test $\forall(i,j \in L)$:(are equivalent(PRE_i,PRE_j),
          is assignable(PRE,PRE_i))

When #L > 1 ∨ *<value denotation>* $\overset{*}{\not\Rightarrow}$ *<tuple>*
Def *<value denotation>*.POSTMODE↓
        ≡ (Case #L=1:mode(PRE_1)

          Case else:none)
Dyn ELAB=(E%):
    Step 1 : R($\forall(i \in L):L\%_i$ ← *<location denotation>*$_i$.ELAB(E%),

          V% ← *<value denotation>*.ELAB(E%),
          $\forall(i \in L):O\%_i$ ← assign(V%,PRE,$L\%_i$,PRE_i,XM_i),
          $\forall(i \in L)$:Case exception(X) ≡ $O\%_i$:exit(exception,[X,E%]))

    Step 2 : ← E%

(a2) *<assignment statement>*
        → *<location denotation>* := *<tuple>*

<u>Pass</u> ENV↓

<u>With</u> PRE_1 ≡ *<location denotaton>*.PREMODE↑,

        PRE_2 ≡ *<tuple>*.PREMODE↑

<u>Let</u> XM ≡ identify assign exceptions(PRE_2,PRE_1,ENV↓)

<u>Test</u> is assignable(PRE_2,PRE_1)

<u>Def</u> *<tuple>*.POSTMODE↓ ≡ mode(PRE_1),

        "   .STATY↓ ≡ staticity(PRE_1)

<u>Dyn</u> ELAB=(E%):
        <u>Step</u> 1 : L% ← *<location denotation>*.ELAB(E%)
        <u>Let</u> N% ≡ (<u>Case</u> basemode(PRE_1)=array(-):upper(L%,PRE_1),

                      <u>Case</u> basemode(PRE_1)=struct(-):parameterization(L%,PRE_1),

                      <u>Case else</u>:none)
        <u>Step</u> 2 : V% ← *<tuple>*.ELAB(E%,N%)
        <u>Step</u> 3 : 0% ← assign(V%,PRE_2,L%,PRE_1,XM)

        <u>Step</u> 4 : <u>Case</u> exception(X)=0%:<u>exit</u>(exception,[X,E%])
        <u>Step</u> 5 : ← E%

(a3) *<assignment statement>*
        → *<location denotation>*
          <dyadic operator> := *<value denotation>*

<u>Pass</u> ENV↓

<u>With</u> PRE ≡ *<location denotation>*.PREMODE↑,
        OP ≡ *<dyadic operator>*.OP↑,
        PRE_2 ≡ *<value denotation>*.PREMODE↑

<u>Let</u> M_1 ≡ mode(PRE_1),

        CPRE ≡ contents premode(PRE_1),

        RPRE ≡ apply2 premode(OP,CPRE,PRE_2)),

        AXM ≡ identify apply2 exceptions(OP,CPRE,PRE_2,ENV↓),

        BXM ≡ identify assign exceptions(RPRE,PRE_1,ENV↓)

<u>Test</u> is assign'operable(OP↑,PRE_2,PRE_1),

        is assignable(RPRE,PRE_1),

        <value denotation> $\overset{*}{\Rightarrow}$ *<expression>*
<u>Def</u> *<value denotation>*.POSTMODE↓ ≡ M_1

<u>Dyn</u> ELAB=(E%):
        <u>Step</u> 1 : R(L% ← *<location denotation>*.ELAB(E%),
                V% ← *<value denotation>*.ELAB(E%))
        <u>Let</u> C% ≡ contents(L%,PRE_1)

        <u>Step</u> 2 : V% ← apply2(OP,C%,CPRE,V%,PRE_2,AXM)

        <u>Step</u> 3 : <u>Case</u> (exception(AX) ≡ V%):<u>exit</u>(exception,[AX,E%])
        <u>Step</u> 4 : ← assign(V%,RPRE,L%,PRE,BXM)
        <u>Step</u> 5 : <u>Case</u>(exception(BX) ≡ X%) : <u>exit</u>(exception,[BX,E%])
        <u>Step</u> 6 : ← E%

6.1.2 BREAK STATEMENTS

Syntax

(a) *<goto statement>*
     → GOTO *<label* identifier>
(b) *<exit statement>*
     → EXIT *<bracketed statement* identifier>
(c) *<cause statement>*
     → CAUSE *<exception* identifier>

Semantics

(a) *<goto statement>* → GOTO *<label* identifier>
<u>With</u> ENV↓,
      HP↓
<u>Let</u>   T ≡ text(*<label* identifier>),
      N ≡ identify node(T,ENV↓),
      SPP ≡ surrounding proc(ENV↓)
<u>Test</u> N.DCAT!=label(-,SPP),
      ¬ HP↓
<u>Dyn</u> ELAB=(E%):
     <u>Step</u> : ← <u>exit</u>(goto,[N,E%])

(b) *<exit statement>* → EXIT *<bracketed statement* identifier>
<u>With</u> ENV↓,
      HP↓
<u>Let</u>   T ≡ text(*<bracketed statement* identifier>),
      N ≡ identify node(T,ENV↓),
      SPP ≡ surrounding proc(ENV↓)
<u>Test</u> N.DCAT!=label(exit poss,SPP),
      ¬ HP↓
<u>Dyn</u> ELAB=(E%):
     <u>Step</u> : ← <u>exit</u>(exit,[N,E%])

(c) *<cause statement>* → CAUSE *<exception* identifier>
<u>With</u> ENV↓,
      HP↓
<u>Let</u>   T ≡ text(*<exception* identifier>),
      N ≡ identify exception node(T,ENV↓)
<u>Test</u> ¬ HP↓
<u>Dyn</u> ELAB=(E%):
     <u>Step</u> : ← <u>exit</u>(exception,[N,E%])

6.1.3 ASSERT AND EMPTY STATEMENTS

Syntax

(a) *<assert statement>*
     → ASSERT *<boolean* expression>
(b) *<empty statement>*
     → <empty>

Semantics

(a) *<assert statement>* → ASSERT *<u>boolean</u> expression>*
<u>Pass</u> ENV↓
<u>With</u> PRE ≡ *<u>boolean</u> expression>*.PREMODE↑
<u>Test</u> basemode(PRE)=discr(bool,-,-)
<u>Let</u>   XN ≡ identify exception node(text(*ASSERT FAIL*),ENV↓)
<u>Def</u>   *<u>boolean</u> expression>*.POSTMODE↓ ≡ none
<u>Dyn</u>   ELAB=(E%):
        <u>Step</u> 1 : B% ← *<u>boolean</u> expression>*.ELAB(E%)
        <u>Step</u> 2 : (<u>Case</u> B%=true:←E%,
                    <u>Case</u> B%=false:
                         ← <u>exit</u>(exception,[XN,E%]))

(b) *<empty statement>* → *<empty>*
<u>With</u> HP↓
<u>Test</u> ¬ HP↓
<u>Dyn</u>   ELAB=(E%):
        <u>Step</u> : ← E%

6.2 CHOICE ACTION STATEMENTS

Syntax

(a) *<choice action statement>*
        (1) → *<if statement>*
        (2) | *<case statement>*
        (3) | *<concurrent case statement>*

Semantics

<u>Pass</u> ENV↓,
        DECLA↑
<u>Dyn</u>   PREELAB=(PE%)
        ELAB=(E%,N%)

6.2.1 IF STATEMENTS

Syntax

(a) *<if statement>*
        → IF *<conditional part>* FI
(b) *<conditional part>*
        → *<u>boolean</u> expression>* THEN *<action statement list>*
                            <else part>
(c) *<else part>*
        (1) → *<empty>*
        (2) | ELSE *<action statement list>*
        (3) | ELSIF *<conditional part>*

Semantics

(a) *<if statement>*
     → IF *<conditional part>* FI
<u>Pass</u> ENV↓,
       DECLA↑
<u>Dyn</u>   PREELAB=(PE%)
       ELAB=(E%,N%)

(b) *<conditional part>*
         → *<u>boolean</u> expression>* THEN *<action statement list>*
                               <else part>

<u>Pass</u> ENV↓
<u>With</u> PRE ≡ *<u>boolean</u> expression>*.PREMODE↑,
       D₁ ≡ *<action statement list>*.DECLA↑,

       D₂ ≡ *<else part>*.DECLA↑

<u>Test</u> base mode(PRE)=discr(bool,-,-)
<u>Def</u>   *<u>boolean</u> expression>*.POSTMODE↓ ≡ none,
       DECLA↑ ≡ D₁ ∪ D₂

<u>Dyn</u>   PREELAB=(PE%):
       <u>Step 1</u> : E%₁ ← *<action statement list>*.PREELAB(PE%)

       <u>Step 2</u> : ← *<else part>*.PREELAB(E%₁)

       ELAB=(E%,N%):
       <u>Case</u> N%=all:
             <u>Step 1</u> : B% ← *<u>boolean</u> expression>*.ELAB(E%)
             <u>Step 2</u> : (<u>Case</u> B%=true:
                          ← *<action statement list>*.ELAB(E%,all),
                       <u>Case</u> B%=false:
                          ← *<else part>*.ELAB(E%,all)),
       <u>Case</u> N% ∈ labels(D₁):

             <u>Step</u> : ← *<action statement list>*.ELAB(E%,N%),
       <u>Case</u> N% ∈ labels(D₂):

                 <u>Step</u> : ← *<else part>*.ELAB(E%,N%)

(c1) *<else part>* → *<empty>*
<u>Def</u>   DECLA↑ ≡ {}
<u>Dyn</u>   PREELAB=(PE%):
       <u>Step</u> : ← PE%
       ELAB=(E%,N%):
       <u>Step</u> : ← E%

(c2) *<else part>* → ELSE *<action statement list>*
<u>Pass</u> ENV↓,
       DECLA↑
<u>Dyn</u>   PREELAB=(E%)
       ELAB=(E%,N%)

(c3) *<else part>* → ELSIF *<conditional part>*
<u>Pass</u> ENV↓,
       DECLA↑
<u>Dyn</u>   PREELAB=(PE%)
       ELAB=(E%,N%)

6.2.2 CASE STATEMENTS

Syntax

(a) <case statement>
     → CASE <case selector list> OF <range list>
       L <case alternative> <case else part> ESAC
(b) <case selector list>
     → L(,) <u>discrete expression</u>
(c) <range list>
     (1) → <empty>
     (2) | L(,) <discrete mode denotation>;
(d) <case alternative>
     → <decision table selector> :<action statement list>
(e) <case else part>
     (1) → <empty>
     (2) | ELSE <action statement list>

Semantics

(a) <case statement>
     → CASE <case selector list> OF <range list>
       L <case alternative> <case else part> ESAC

Pass ENV↓
With CPL ≡ <case selector list>.PREMODE LIST↑,
       RML ≡ <range list>.MODE LIST↑,
       RD ≡   "   .DECLA↑,
       $\forall(i \in L):(SL_i$ ≡ <case alternative>$_i$.SET LIST↑,
              PML_i ≡   "   .PREMODE LIST↑,
              D_i ≡   "   .DECLA↑),

       D ≡ <case else part>.DECLA↑,
       EL ≡   "   .ELSE LIST↑
Let   DT=∪(i∈L):D$_i$,

       SLL ≡ ⦃SL$_i$|i∈L⦄,

       PMLL ≡ ⦃PML$_i$|i∈L⦄,

       ML ≡ (<u>Case</u> RML=none:⦃mode(p)|p∈CPL⦄
            <u>Case</u> else:RML),
       CSL ≡ case selection list(SLL,PMLL,ML),
       CEP ≡ case else part(SLL,PMLL,ML),
       XN ≡ identify exception node(text(*RANGE FAIL*),ENV↓),
       $\forall(i \in \{1:\#ML\}):RC_i$ ≡ resulting premode(⦃PML$_j$⦃i⦄|j∈L⦄)
Test #ML=#CML,
       $\forall(i \in L):\#PMLL$⦃i⦄=#ML,
       $\forall(i \in \{1:\#CPL\}):$
            are compatible(CPL⦃i⦄,RC$_i$)

         ∧ (RML=none ⇒
                (is compatible with(RML⦃i⦄,CPL⦃i⦄
                 ∧ is compatible with(RML⦃i⦄,RC$_i$)

                 ∧ {s∈SL$_j$⦃i⦄|j∈L} ⊆ set(RML⦃j⦄)))

         ∧ (CPL⦃i⦄=val(vclass,-,-,-) ⇒
                ({s∈SL$_j$⦃i⦄|j∈L} ⊆ set(CPL⦃i⦄)

                 ∧ (RML≠none ⇒ set(RML⦃i⦄) ⊆ set(CPL⦃i⦄))))

```
        EL=none ⇒ CEP={},
        is coherent case selection(SLL,PMLL,ML)
Def     DECLA↑ ≡ DT ∪ D ∪ RD
Dyn     PREELAB=(PE%₀)

        Step 1 : S(i∈ L):(PE%ᵢ ← <case alternative>
                                        .PREELAB(PE%ᵢ₋₁))

        Let   n ≡ #L
        Step 2 : ← <case else part>.PREELAB(PE%ₙ)

        ELAB=(E%,N%):
        (Case N%=all:
             Step 1 : VT% ← <case selector list>.ELAB(E%)
             Step 2 : Case(RML≠none ∧ VT%≠π(i∈{1:#ML}:set(ML↓i↓)):
                                    exit(exception,[XN,E%])

             Step 3 :
                (Case(i such that VT%∈CSL↓i↓:
                             ← <case alternative>ᵢ.ELAB(E%,N%),

                  Case VT%∈CEP:
                             ← <case else part>.ELAB(E%,N%)),
             Case i such that N%∈labels(Dᵢ):

                          Step : ← <case alternative>ᵢ.ELAB(E%,N%),

          Case N%∈labels(D)
             Step : ← <case else part>.ELAB(E%,N%))
```

(b) <case selector list> → L(,) <discrete expression>

Pass ENV↓
With ∀(i∈L):PREᵢ ≡ <discrete expression>ᵢ.PREMODE↑

Test ∀(i∈L):base mode(PREᵢ)=discr(-)

Def ∀(i∈L):<discrete expression>ᵢ.POSTMODE↑ ≡ none,

PREMODE LIST↑ ≡ ↓PREᵢ|i∈L↓

Dyn ELAB=(E%):
Step 1 : R(i∈L):Vᵢ ← <discrete expression>ᵢ.ELAB(E%)

Step 2 : ← [Vᵢ|i∈L]

(c1) <range list> → <empty>
Def MODE LIST↑ ≡ none,
DECLA↑ ≡ {}

(c2) <range list> → L(,) <discrete mode denotation>;
Pass ENV↓
With ∀(i∈L):([-,Mᵢ] ≡ <discrete mode denotation>ᵢ.DENMODE↑,

Dᵢ ≡ " .DECLA↑)

Def MODE LIST↑ ≡ ↓Mᵢ|i∈L↓,

DECLA↑ ≡ ∪(i∈L):Dᵢ

(d) <case alternative>
→ <decision table selector>
:<action statement list>
Pass ENV↓
With SL ≡ <decision table selector>.SET LIST↑,
PML ≡ " .PRE LIST↑,

```
        D ≡ <action statement list>.DECLA↑
Test    SL≠{}
Def     PREMODE LIST ≡ PML,
        SET LIST↑ ≡ SL,
        DECLA↑ ≡ D
Dyn     PREELAB=(PE%):
        Step : ← <action statement list>.PREELAB(PE%)
        ELAB%=(E%,N%):
        Step : ← <action statement list>.ELAB(E%,N%)
```

```
(e1) <case else part> → <empty>
Def     DECLA↑ ≡ {},
        ELSE LIST↑ ≡ none
Dyn     PREELAB=(PE%):
        Step : ← PE%
        ELAB↑(E%):
        Step : ← E%
```

```
(e2) <case else part> → ELSE <action statement list>
Pass    ENV↓,
        DECLA↑
Def     ELSE LIST↑ ≡ else
Dyn     PREELAB=(PE%)
        ELAB=(E%,N%)
```

6.3 BLOCK ACTION STATEMENTS

Syntax

```
(a) <block action statement>
    (1) → <begin end block>
    (2) | <do statement>
```

Semantics

```
Pass    ENV↓,
        EXTENV↓,
        HANDLER↓,
        INDECLA↑,
        OUTDECLA↑
Dyn     PREELAB=(PE%)
        ELAB=(E%)
```

6.3.1 BEGIN END BLOCKS

Syntax

```
(a) <begin end block>
        → BEGIN <data statement list>
                <action statement list> END
```

Semantics

<u>Pass</u>   ENV↓
<u>With</u>   DD ≡ <*data statement list*>.DECLA↑,
        AD ≡ <*action statement list*>.DECLA↑
<u>Def</u>   INDECLA↑ ≡ DD∪AD,
        OUTDECLA↑ ≡ {}
<u>Dyn</u>   PREELAB=(PE$):
        <u>Step</u> 1 : PEN$ ← <*data statement list*>.PREELAB(PE$)
        <u>Step</u> 2 :   ← <*action statement list*>.PREELAB(PEN$)
        ELAB=(E$):
        <u>Step</u> 1 : EN$ ← <*data statement list*>.ELAB(E$)
        <u>Step</u> 2 :   ← <*action statement list*>.ELAB(EN$,all)
        TRAP=(K$,[N$,EE$]):
              <u>Let</u>   EE$$_1$ ≡ adjust(EE$,E$)

              <u>Case</u> K$ ≡ goto ∧ N$∈labels(AD):
                  <u>Step</u> : ← <*action statement list*>.ELAB(EE$$_1$,N$)

6.3.2 DO STATEMENTS

Syntax

(a) <*do statement*>
      (1) → DO <*loop control*> <*do body*> OD
      (2) | DO <*for control*> <*for body*> OD
      (3) | DO <*with control*> <*do body*> OD
(b) <*loop control*>
      (1) → FOR EVER; <*while option*>
      (2) | <*while control*>
(c) <*while option*>
      (1) → <empty>
      (2) | <*while control*>
(d) <*while control*>
          → WHILE <<u>boolean</u> expression>;
(e) <*do body*>
          → <*action statement list*>
(f) <*for control*>
          → FOR L(,) <*iteration*>;
(g) <*for body*>
          → <*while option*> <*do body*>
(h) <*with control*>
      (1) → <empty>
      (2) | WITH L(,) <*object expression*>;
(i) <*object expression*>
      (1) → <*expression*>
      (2) | <*location denotation*>
(j) <*iteration*>
      (1) → <identifier><*value enumeration*>
      (2) | <identifier><*location enumeration*>
(k) <*value enumeration*>
      (1) → := <*start value*><*step*><*way*><*end value*>
      (2) | <*way*> IN <*discrete mode denotation*>
      (3) | <*way*> IN <<u>powerset</u> expression>
(l) <*start value*>
          → <*expression*>
(m) <*step*>
      (1) → <empty>

```
      (2) | BY <integer expression>
(n) <way>
      (1) → <empty>
      (2) | DOWN
(o) <end value>
          → TO <expression>
(p) <location enumeration>
          → <way> IN <array location denotation>
```

Semantics

```
(a1) <do statement>
          → DO <loop control> <do body> OD
Pass  ENV↓
With  D ≡ <do body>.DECLA↑
Def   INDECLA↑ ≡ D,
      OUTDECLA↑ ≡ {}
Dyn   PREELAB=(PE%):
      Step : ← <do body>.PREELAB(PE%)
      ELAB=(E%):
      Step 1 : B% ← <loop control>.ELAB(E%)
      Step 2 :
        (Case B%=true:
            (Step 2.1 : ← <do body>.ELAB(E%)
             Step 2.2 : ← itself.ELAB(E%))
         Case B%=false:
             Step : ← E%)
```

```
(a2) <do statement>
          → DO <for control> <for body> OD
With  ENV↓,
      EXT ENV↓,
      HANDLER↓,
      OD ≡ <for control>.OUTDECLA↑,
      ID ≡          "       .INDECLA↑,
      NL ≡          "       .NODE LIST↑,
      XL ≡          "       .XNODE LIST↑,
      BD ≡ <for body>.DECLA↑
Let   n ≡ #NL,
      ∀(i∈{1:n}):(PRE_i ≡ NL↓i↓.DPREMODE!,

                  PREX_i ≡ (Case XL↓i↓≠none:XL↓i↓.DPREMODE!,

                          Case else:unused),
                  XN_i ≡ (Case XL↓i↓≠none:

                           identify assign exceptions(PRE_i,PREX_i,EXTENV↓),

                          Case else:unused)
Def   <for control>.ENV↓ ≡ EXT ENV↓,
      <for body>.ENV↓ ≡ ENV,
          "      .NODE LIST↓ ≡ NL,
      OUTDECLA↑ ≡ OD,
      INDECLA↑ ≡ ID∪BD
Dyn   PREELAB=(PE%):
      Step 1 ← <for body>.PREELAB(PE%)
      ELAB=(E%):
      Step 1 : LL% ← <for control>.ELAB(peel(E%))
      Step 2 : ← <for body>.ELAB(E%,LL%)
      Step 3 : ∀(i∈{1:n}):
                  Case XL↓i↓≠none:
```

                              the contents of identify(XL⌊i⌋,E%) is undefined
        TRAP=(K%,[N%,EE%]):
        Step 1 : R(i∈{1:n}):
                        (Case XL⌊i⌋≠none:
                          Let   V%$_i$ ≡ identify(NL⌊i⌋,EE%),

                                 L%$_i$ ≡ identify(XL⌊i⌋,EE%)

                          (Case N%∈exception nodes(HANDLER↓):
                            (Step 1.1 : O%$_i$ ← assign(V%$_i$,PRE$_i$,L%$_i$,PREX$_i$,XN$_i$)

                            Step 1.2 : Case exception(X) ≡ O%$_i$:

                                            exit(exception,[X,adjust(EE%,E%)])),
                            Case else : the contents of L%$_i$ is undefined)

        Step 2 : (Case K%≠abnormal :
                        exit(K%,[N%,EE%]),
                  Case else : ← EE%)

(a3) *<do statement>*
        → *DO <with control> <do body> OD*
With   ENV↓,
       EXT ENV↓,
       WD ≡ *<with control>*.DECLA↑,
       D ≡ *<do body>*.DECLA↑
Def   *<with control>*.ENV↓ ≡ EXT ENV↓,
       <do body>.ENV↓ ≡ ENV↓,
       OUTDECLA↑ ≡ {},
       INDECLA↑ ≡ D∪WD
Dyn   PREELAB=(PE%):
       Step : ← *<do body>*.PREELAB(PE%)
       ELAB=(E%):
       Step 1 : E%$_1$ ← *<with control>*.ELAB(E%)

       Step 2 : ← *<do body>*.ELAB(E%$_1$)

(b1) *<loop control>* → *FOR EVER; <while option>*
Pass   ENV↓
Dyn   ELAB=(E%):
       Step : ← *<while option>*.ELAB(E%)

(b2) *<loop control>* → *<while control>*
Pass   ENV↓
Dyn   ELAB=(E%)

(c1) *<while option>* → *<empty>*
Dyn   ELAB=(E%):
       Step : ← true

(c2) *<while option>* → *<while control>*
Pass   ENV↓
Dyn   ELAB=(E%)

(d) *<while control>*
        → *WHILE <boolean expression>;*
Pass   ENV↓
With   PRE ≡ *<boolean expression>*.PREMODE↑
Test   basemode(PRE)=discr(bool,-,-)
Def   POSTMODE↓ ≡ none
Dyn   ELAB=(E%)

(e) *<do body>* → *<action statement list>*
<u>Pass</u> ENV↓,
      DECLA↑
<u>Dyn</u>   PREELAB=(PE%)
      ELAB=(E%):
      <u>Step</u> : *<action statement list>*.ELAB(E%,all)
      TRAP=(K%,[N%,EE%]):
      <u>Case</u> K%=goto ∧ N%∈labels(DECLA↑):
        <u>Step</u> : ← *<action statement list>*
                        .ELAB(adjust(EE%,E%),N%)

(f) *<for control>* → FOR L(,)*<iteration>*;
<u>Pass</u> ENV↓
<u>With</u> ∀(i∈L):(OD$_i$ ≡ *<iteration>*$_i$.OUTDECLA↑,
              ID$_i$ ≡   "   .INDECLA↑,
              N$_i$ ≡   "   .NODE↑,
              X$_i$ ≡   "   .XNODE↑)

<u>Def</u>   OUTDECLA↑ ≡ ∪(i∈L):OD$_i$,
      INDECLA↑ ≡ ∪(i∈L):ID$_i$,
      NODE LIST↑ ≡ {N$_i$|i∈L},
      XNODE LIST↑ ≡ {X$_i$|i∈L}

<u>Dyn</u>   ELAB=(E%):
      <u>Step 1</u> : R(i∈L):L%$_i$ ← *<iteration>*$_i$.ELAB(E%)

      <u>Step 2</u> : ← {L%$_i$|i∈L}

(g) *<for body>* → *<while option>* *<do body>*
<u>Pass</u> ENV↓
<u>With</u> NL ≡ NODE LIST↑
      D ≡ *<do body>*.DECLA↑
<u>Let</u>   n ≡ #NL
<u>Def</u>   DECLA↑ ≡ D
<u>Dyn</u>   PREELAB=(PE%):
      <u>Step</u> : ← *<do body>*.PREELAB(PE%)
      ELAB=(E%,LL%):
      <u>Case</u> (∃(L∈LL%):L={}:
            <u>Step</u> : ← E%
      <u>Case else</u> :
            <u>Let</u>   : E%$_0$=E%

            <u>Step 1</u> : S(i∈{1:n}):
                   E%$_i$ ← declare(NL{i},head(LL%{i},E%$_{i-1}$))

            <u>Step 2</u> : B% ← *<while option>*.ELAB(E%$_n$)

            <u>Step 3</u> :
               (<u>Case</u> B%=true:
                   <u>Step 3.1</u> : ← *<do body>*.ELAB(E%$_n$)

                   <u>Step 3.2</u> : ← <u>itself</u>.ELAB(E%$_0$,{tail(L)|L∈LL%}),

                <u>Case</u> B%=false:
                   <u>Step 3.1</u> : <u>exit</u>(abnormal,unused))

(h1) *<with control>* → *<empty>*
<u>Def</u>   DECLA↑ ≡ {}
<u>Dyn</u>   ELAB=(E%):

      Step : ← E%

(h2) *<with control>* → *WITH* L(,)*<object expression>*
Pass   ENV↓,
With   ∀(i∈L):PRE$_i$ ≡ *<object expression>*$_i$.PREMODE↑

Test   ∀(i∈L):base mode(PRE$_i$)=struct(-)

Let   ∀(i∈L):(mode(NV$_i$,-) ≡ mode(PRE$_i$),
                 SL$_i$ ≡ {s|is field selector(S,PRE$_i$)
                             ∧ is allowed(S,NV$_i$,ENV)}

Let   ∀(i∈L):
          (N$_i$ ≡ node(*<object expression>*$_i$),
           D$_i$ ≡ ∪(s∈SL$_i$):define(s,N$_i$))
Def   DECLA↑ ≡ ∪(i∈L)D$_i$,
       ∀(i∈L):N$_i$.DCAT!=with(PRE$_i$)

Dyn   ELAB=(E%$_0$):
       Step 1 : R(i∈L):S%$_i$ ← *<object expression>*$_i$.ELAB(E%)
       Step 2 : S(i∈L):(E%$_i$ ← declare(N$_i$,S%$_i$,E%$_{i-1}$)

(i1) *<object expression>* → *<expression>*
Pass   ENV↓,
       PREMODE↑,

When   *<expression>* $\overset{*}{\neq}$ *<delocated location>*
Test   PREMODE↑=val(vclass,-,-,-)
Def   *<expression>*.POSTMODE↓ ≡ none
Dyn   ELAB=(E%)

(i2) *<object expression>* → *<location denotation>*
Pass   ENV↓,
       PREMODE↑
Dyn   ELAB=(E%)

(j1) *<iteration>*
          → *<identifier> <value enumeration>*
Pass   ENV↓
With   PRE ≡ *<value enumeration>*.PREMODE↑,
       D₁ ≡   "   .DECLA↑

Let   T ≡ text(*<identifier>*),
       N ≡ node(*<identifier>*),
       XX ≡ identify node(T,ENV↓),
       X ≡ (Case XX≠udf ∧ XX.DCAT!=loc:XX,
            Case else:none),
       D₂ ≡ define(T,N)

Test   X≠none ⇒ is assignable(PRE,X.DPREMODE!)
Def   OUTDECLA↑ ≡ D₁,

       INDECLA↑ ≡ D₂,

       NODE↑ ≡ N,
       XNODE↑ ≡ X,
       N.DCAT! ≡ dynsyn,
       N.DPREMODE! ≡ PRE
Dyn   ELAB=(E%):

<u>Step</u> : ← <value enumeration>.ELAB(E%)

(j2) <iteration>
                → <identifier> <location enumeration>
<u>Pass</u> ENV↓
<u>With</u> PRE ≡ <location enumeration>.PREMODE↑
<u>Let</u>   T ≡ text(<identifier>),
       N ≡ node(<identifier>)
<u>Def</u>   OUTDECLA↑ ≡ {},
       INDECLA↑ ≡ define(T,N),
       NODE↑ ≡ N,
       XNODE↑ ≡ none,
       N.DCAT! ≡ loc,
       N.DPREMODE! ≡ PRE
<u>Dyn</u>   ELAB=(E%):
       <u>Step</u> : ← <location enumeration>.ELAB(E%)

(k1) <value enumeration>
            → := <start value><step><way><end value>
<u>Pass</u> ENV↓
<u>With</u> W ≡ <way>.WAY,
       PRE₁ ≡ <start value>.PREMODE↑,

       PRE₂ ≡ <step>.PREMODE↑,

       PRE₃ ≡ <end value>.PREMODE↑

<u>Let</u>   PREL ≡ {PRE_i|i∈{1:3} ∧ PRE_i ≠ none},

       PRE ≡ resulting premode(PREL)
<u>Test</u> are compatible(PREL)
<u>Def</u>   PREMODE↑ ≡ PRE,
       DECLA↑ ≡ {}
<u>Dyn</u>   ELAB=(E%):
       <u>Step 1</u> : R(L% ← <start value>.ELAB(E%),
                 S% ← <step>.ELAB(E%),
                 U% ← <end value>.ELAB(E%))
       <u>Step 2</u> : (<u>Case</u> W=up:
                   VL% ← {V%|j∈{0:maxint}∧V%=L%+j*S%
                              ∧ V%∈{L%:U%}},
                 <u>Case</u> W=down:
                   VL% ← {V%|j∈{0:maxint}∧V%=L%-j*S%
                              ∧ V%∈{U%:L%}})
       <u>Step 3</u> : ← VL%

(k2) <value enumeration>
            → <way> IN <discrete mode denotation>
<u>Pass</u> ENV↓
<u>With</u> W ≡ <way>.WAY↑,
       DM ≡ <discrete mode denotation>.DENMODE↑,
       D ≡   "   .DECLA↑
<u>Let</u>   [-,M] ≡ DM,
       L ≡ {V|V∈{min(M):max(M)}}
<u>Def</u>   PREMODE↑ ≡ val(vclass,nreg,stat,M),
       DECLA↑ ≡ D
<u>Dyn</u>   ELAB=(E%):
       <u>Step</u> : (<u>Case</u> W=up:← L,
              <u>Case</u> W=down:← reverse(L))

(k3) <value enumeration>
            → <way> IN <u>powerset</u> expression>

<u>Pass</u> ENV↓
<u>With</u> W ≡ <*way*>.WAY↑,
       PRE₁ ≡ <*powerset expression*>.PREMODE↑

<u>Test</u> base mode(PRE₁)=poset(-)

<u>Let</u>   PRE₂ ≡ val(vclass,nreg,stat,member mode(PRE₁)),

       B ≡ member mode(PRE₁)

<u>Def</u> PREMODE↑ ≡ PRE₂,

       DECLA↑ ≡ {}
<u>Dyn</u> ELAB=(E%):
       <u>Step 1</u> : S% ← <*powerset expression*>.ELAB(E%)
       <u>Let</u>   L% ≡ ↯V%|V%∈{min(B):max(B)} ∧ V%∈S%↯
       <u>Step 2</u> : (<u>Case</u> W=up : ← L%,
                   <u>Case</u> W=down : ← reverse(L%))

(1) <*start value*> → <*expression*>
<u>Pass</u> ENV↓
<u>With</u> PRE ≡ <*expression*>.PREMODE↑
<u>Test</u> base mode(PRE)=discr(-)
<u>Def</u> <*expression*>.POSTMODE↓ ≡ none,
       PREMODE↑ ≡ PRE
<u>Dyn</u> ELAB=(E%)

(m1) <*step*> → <empty>
<u>Def</u> PREMODE↑ ≡ none
<u>Dyn</u> ELAB=(E%):
       <u>Step</u> : ← 1

(m2) <*step*> → BY <*integer expression*>
<u>Pass</u> ENV↓
<u>With</u> PRE ≡ <*integer expression*>.PREMODE↑
<u>Test</u> base mode(PRE)=discr(int,-,-)
<u>Let</u>   XN ≡ identify exception node(text(*RANGEFAIL*),ENV↓),
<u>Def</u> <*integer expression*>.POSTMODE↓ ≡ none,
       PREMODE↑ ≡ PRE
<u>Dyn</u> ELAB=(E%):
       <u>Step 1</u> : V% ← <*integer expression*>.ELAB(E%)
       <u>Step 2</u> : <u>Case</u> V%≤0 : <u>exit</u>(exception,[XN,E%])
       <u>Step 3</u> : ← V%)

(n1) <*way*> → <empty>
<u>Def</u> WAY↑ ≡ up

(n2) <*way*> → DOWN
<u>Def</u> WAY↑ ≡ down

(o) <*end value*> → TO <*expression*>
<u>Pass</u> ENV↓
<u>With</u> PRE ≡ <*expression*>.PREMODE↑
<u>Test</u> base mode(PRE)=discr(-)
<u>Def</u> <*expression*>.POSTMODE↓ ≡ none,
       PREMODE↑ ≡ PRE
<u>Dyn</u> ELAB=(E%):
       <u>Step</u> : ← <*expression*>.ELAB(E%)

(p) <*location enumeration*>
        → <*way*> IN <*array* location denotation>

<u>Pass</u> ENV↓
<u>With</u> W ≡ <*way*>.WAY↑,
       PRE ≡ <*array location denotation*>.PREMODE↑
<u>Test</u> base mode(PRE)=array(-)
<u>Def</u>   PREMODE↑ ≡ location array element premode(PRE)
<u>Dyn</u>   ELAB=(E%):
       <u>Step</u> 1 : L% ← <*array location denotation*>.ELAB(E%)
       <u>Step</u> 2 : (<u>Case</u> W=up : ← L%,
                     <u>Case</u> W=down : ← reverse(L%))

7. MODULES, CRITICAL REGIONS AND VISIBILITY

7.1 MODULES

Syntax

(a) *<module statement>*
      → *<labelling><module><handler><end label>*;
(b) *<module>*
      → MODULE ∟*<module data statement list>*
           <action statement list>
        END
(c) *<module data statement list>*
    (1) → <empty>
    (2) | ∟*<module data statement>*
(d) *<module data statement>*
    (1) → *<data statement>*
    (2) | *<visibility statement>*

Semantics

(a) *<module statement>*
      → *<labelling><module><handler><end label>*;

With   ENV↓,
      T ≡ *<labelling>*.TEXT↑,
      N ≡   "   .NODE↓,
      ID ≡ *<module>*.INDECLA↑,
      OD ≡   "   .OUTDECLA↑,
      MN ≡   "   .MODNODE↓,
      HD ≡ *<handler>*.EXCEPT↑,
      ET ≡ *<end label>*.TEXT↑
When   ET≠none ⇒ T=ET
Test   is locale(ID)
Let   SPP ≡ surrounding proc(ENV↓),
      N_1 ≡ node(*<labelling>*),

      MN ≡ node(*<module>*),
      LD ≡ (**Case** T≠none:define(T,N),
          Case else:{}),
      LDEXIT ≡ (**Case** T≠none:define(T,N_1),

             Case else:{}),
      $NEWENV_1$ ≡ ENV↓ **plus** LDEXIT,

      $NEWENV_2$ ≡ new modulion env($NEWENV_1$,module(MN),ID,HD)

      $NEWENV_3$ ≡ replace exceptions($NEWENV_2$,ENV↓)

Def   *<module>*.ENV↓ ≡ $NEWENV_2$,

       "   .EXTENV↓ ≡ ENV↓,
     <handler>.ENV↓ ≡ $NEWENV_3$,

      DECLA↑ ≡ ODuLD,
      N.DCAT! ≡ label(module(MN),SPP),
      N.DIMPLIED! ≡ {},
      N_1.DCAT! ≡ label(exitposs,SPP),

      N_1.DIMPLIED! ≡ {}

Dyn   PREELAB=(PE%):

Step 1 : ← <module>.PREELAB(PE%)
ELAB=(E%,N%):
Step : ← <module>.ELAB(E%,N%)
TRAP=(K%,[N%$_1$,EE%]):

Let   E%$_1$ ≡ adjust(EE%,E%)

  (Case K%=exception ∧ N%$_1$ ∈ exception nodes(HD):

        Step : N%.ELAB(E%$_1$)

   Case K%=goto ∧ N%$_1$=N$_1$:

        Step : ← <module>.ELAB(E%$_1$,all),

   Case K%=exit ∧ N%$_1$=N$_1$:

        Step : ← E%$_1$)

(b) <module> → MODULE L <module data statement list>
                 <action statement list>
                 END

Pass ENV↓
With EXTENV↓,
      AD ≡ <action statement list>.DECLA↑,
      DD ≡ <module data statement list>.DECLA↑,
      GD ≡   "   .GDECLA↑,
      SD ≡   "   .SDECLA↑)
Let   SEIZABLE ENV ≡ seizable env(EXTENV↓,GD,N),
      INTERNAL DECLA ≡ DD∪AD∪SD,
      N ≡ node(<module>),
      GRANTABLE ENV ≡ grantable env(ENV↓,SD,N)
Def   <module data statement list>.SENV↓ ≡ SEIZABLE ENV,
                      "   .GENV↓ ≡ GRANTABLE ENV,
      OUTDECLA↑ ≡ GD ∪ forbid fields(ENV↓),
      INDECLA↑ ≡ INTERNAL DECLA,
      N.DCAT! ≡ module,
      N.DWINDOW! ≡ GD,
      N.DIMPLIED! ≡ {}
Dyn   PREELAB(PE%):
      Step 1 : PE% ← <module data statement list> .PREELAB(PE%)
      Step 2 : ← <action statement list>.PREELAB(PE%$_1$)

      ELAB(E%,N%):
      (Case N%=all:
            Step 1 : E% ← <module data statement list>.ELAB(E%)
            Step 2 : ← <action statement list>.ELAB(E%$_1$,all)

       Case N% ∈ labels(AD):
            Step : ← <action statement list>.ELAB(E%,N%))
      TRAP(K%,[N%$_1$,EE%])

      Let   EE%$_1$ ≡ adjust(EE%,E%)

      Case K%=goto ∧ N%$_1$∈labels(AD):

            Step : ← <action statement list>.ELAB(EE%$_1$,N%$_1$)

(c1) <module data statement list> → <empty>
Def   DECLA↑ ≡ {},
      GDECLA↑ ≡ {},
      SDECLA↑ ≡ {}
Dyn   PREELAB=(PE%):
      Step : ← PE%

```
          ELAB=(E%):
          Step : ← E%
```

(c2) *<module data statement list>* → L*<module data statement>*

<u>Pass</u> ENV↓,
       SENV↓,
       GENV↓

<u>With</u> $\forall(i \in L):(D_i \equiv$ *<module data statement>*$_i$.DECLA↑,

           $GD_i \equiv$ "   .GDECLA↑,

           $SD_i \equiv$ "   .SDECLA↑)

<u>Def</u> DECLA↑ $\equiv \cup(i \in L):D_i$,

     GDECLA↑ $\equiv \cup(i \in L):GD_i$,

     SDECLA↑ $\equiv \cup(i \in L):SD_i$

<u>Dyn</u> PREELAB=$(PE\%_0)$:

     $S(i \in L):PE\%_i \leftarrow$ *<module data statement>*$_i$.PREELAB$(PE\%_{i-1})$

     ELAB=$(E\%_0)$:

     $S(i \in L):E\%_i \leftarrow$ *<module data statement>*$_i$.ELAB$(E\%_{i-1})$

(d1) *<module data statement>* → *<data statement>*

<u>Pass</u> ENV↓,
       DECLA↑

<u>Def</u> SDECLA↑ $\equiv$ {},
     GDECLA↑ $\equiv$ {}

<u>Dyn</u> PREELAB=(PE%)
     ELAB=(E%)

(d2) *<module data statement>* → *<visibility statement>*

<u>Pass</u> ENV↓,
       SENV↓,
       GENV↓,
       DECLA↑,
       SDECLA↑,
       GDECLA↑

<u>Dyn</u> PREELAB(PE%):
     Step : ← PE%
     ELAB(E%):
     Step : ← E%

7.2. CRITICAL REGIONS

Syntax

(a) *<critical region>*
    → *<labelling><region> <handler> <end label>*
(b) *<region>*
    (1) → REGION END
    (2) | REGION L*<region data statement>* END
(c) *<region data statement>*
    (1) → *<declaration statement>*;
    (2) | *<definition statement>*;
    (3) | *<visibility statement>*

Semantics

(a) *<critical region>* → *<labelling><region> <handler> <end label>*
<u>With</u> ENV↓,
     T ≡ *<labelling>*.TEXT↑,
     N ≡   "   .NODE↑,
     ID ≡ *<region>*.INDECLA↑,
     OD ≡   "   .OUTDECLA↑,
     N₁ ≡   "   .REGNODE↓,

     HD ≡ *<handler>*.EXCEPT↑,
     ET ≡ *<end label>*.TEXT↑
<u>When</u> ET≠none ⇒ T=ET
<u>Let</u> SPP ≡ surrounding proc(ENV↓)
<u>Test</u> is region allowed(ENV↓),
     is locale(ID)
<u>Let</u> LD ≡ (<u>Case</u> T≠none:define(T,N),
          <u>Case</u> <u>else</u> : {}),
     NEW ENV₁ ≡ new modulion env(ENV↓,region(N),ID,HD),

     NEW ENV₂ ≡ replace exceptions(NEW ENV₁,ENV↓)
<u>Def</u> *<region>*.ENV↓ ≡ NEW ENV₁,

          "   .EXTENV↓ ≡ ENV↓,
     <handler>.ENV↓ ≡ NEW ENV₂,

     DECLA↑ ≡ OD ∪ LD,
     N.DCAT! ≡ label(region(N₁),SPP),

     N.DIMPLIED! ≡ {}
<u>Dyn</u> PREELAB=(PE%):
     <u>Step</u> : ← *<region>*.PREELAB(PE%)
     ELAB=(E%):
     <u>Step</u> : ← *<region>*.ELAB(E%)
     TRAP=(K%,[N%,EE%]):
     <u>Let</u>   EE%₁ ≡ adjust(EE%,E%)

     <u>Case</u> K%=exception ∧ N∈exception nodes(HD):
          <u>Step</u> : ← N%.ELAB(EE%₁)

(b1) *<region>* → REGION END
<u>Let</u> N=node(*<region>*)
<u>Def</u> OUTDECLA↑ ≡ {},
     INDECLA↑ ≡ {},
     REGNODE↑ ≡ N,
     N.DCAT↑ ≡ region,
     N.DWINDOW↓ ≡ {},
     N.DIMPLIED↑ ≡ {}
<u>Dyn</u> PREELAB=(PE%):
     <u>Step</u> : ← PE%
     ELAB=(E%):
     <u>Step</u> : ← E%

(b2) *<region>* → REGION L*<region data statement>* END
<u>With</u> ENV↓,
     EXTENV↓,
     DD ≡ ∪(i∈L):*<region data statement>*ᵢ.DECLA↑,

     GD ≡ ∪(i∈L):   "   .GDECLA↑,
     SD ≡ ∪(i∈L):   "   .SDECLA↑
<u>Let</u> N ≡ node(*<region>*)

```
        GP ≡ ∪(d∈GD):granted procs(d),
        SEIZABLE ENV ≡ seizable env(EXT ENV,GD,N),
        INTERNAL DECLA ≡ DD ∪ SD ∪ GP,
        GRANTABLE ENV ≡ grantable env(ENV↓,SD,N)
Def   ∀(i∈L):(<region data statement>_i.ENV↓ ≡ ENV↓,
                           "         .SENV↓ ≡ SEIZABLE ENV,
                           "         .GENV↓ ≡ GRANTABLE ENV),
        OUTDECLA↑ ≡ GD ∪ forbid fields(ENV↓),
        INDECLA↑ ≡ INTERNAL DECLA,
        REGNODE↑ ≡ N,
        N.DCAT! ≡ region,
        N.DWINDOW! ≡ GD,
        N.DIMPLIED! ≡ {}
Dyn   PREELAB=(PE%_0):
```

Step : $S(i \in L)$:
$$PE\%_i \leftarrow <region\ data\ statement>_i.PREELAB(PE\%_{i-1})$$

$ELAB=(E\%_0)$:

Let n=#L
Step 1 : enter and lock(N)
Step 2 : $S(i \in L):E\%_i \leftarrow <region\ data\ statement>_i.ELAB(E\%_{i-1})$

Step 3 : ← Exit(N)
Step 4 : ← E%n
TRAP=(K%,[X%,EE%]):
Step 1 : ← exit(N)
Step 2 : exit(K%,[X%,EE%])

(c1,c2) <region data statement>
Pass ENV↓,
      DECLA↑
Def   GDECLA↑ ≡ {},
      SDECLA↑ ≡ {}
Dyn   PREELAB=(PE%)
      ELAB=(E%)

(c3) <region data statement> → <visibility statement>
Pass ENV↓,
      SENV↓,
      GENV↓,
      DECLA↑,
      GDECLA↑,
      SDECLA↓
Dyn   PREELAB=(PE%)
      ELAB=(E%)

7.3 VISIBILITY

Syntax

(a) <visibility statement>
    (1) → <grant statement>;
    (2) | <seize statement>;
(b) <grant statement>
    (1) → GRANT <grant window>
    (2) | GRANT <grant window> PERVASIVE

(c) *<grant window>*
   (1) → *ALL*
   (2) | L(,) *<granted element>*
(d) *<granted element>*
   (1) → *<identifier>*
   (2) | *<mode* identifier*> <forbid clause>*
(e) *<forbid clause>*
   (1) → *FORBID ALL*
   (2) | *FORBID* (L(,) *<field* identifier*>*)
(f) *<seize statement>*
     → *SEIZE <seize window>*
(g) *<seize window>*
   (1) → *ALL*
   (2) | L(,) *<seized element>*
(h) *<seized element>*
   (1) → *<identifier>*
   (2) | *<module or region* identifier*> ALL*

Semantics

(a1) *<visibility statement>* → *<grant statement>;*
Pass GENV↓,
      GDECLA↑
Def   DECLA↑ ≡ {},
      SDECLA↑ ≡ {}

(a2) *<visibility statement>* → *<seize statement>;*
Pass SENV↓,
      SDECLA↑
Def   DECLA↑ ≡ {},
      GDECLA↑ ≡ {}

(b) *<grant statement>*
Pass GENV↓,
      GDECLA↑
Let   WTYPE=(**Case**(b1):nperv,
            Case(b2):perv)
Def   <right>.WINDOWTYPE↓ ≡ WTYPE

(c1) *<grant window>* → *ALL*
With GENV↓,
      WT ≡ WINDOWTYPE↓
Let   GD ≡ grant all(GENV↓,WT)
Test ∀(d∈GD):is grantable(d,GENV↓)
Def   GDECLA↑ ≡ GD

(c2) *<grant window>* → L(,) *<granted element>*
Pass GENV↓,
      WINDOWTYPE↓
With ∀(i∈L):D_i ≡ *<granted element>*_i.DECLA↑
Def   GDECLA↑ ≡ ∪(i∈L):D_i

(d1) *<granted element>* → *<identifier>*
With ENV↓,
      WT ≡ WINDOW TYPE↓
Let   T ≡ text(<identifier>),
      D ≡ identify decla(T,GENV↓)
      WD ≡ grant(D,WT)

<u>Test</u> is grantable(D,GENV↓)
<u>Def</u>   DECLA↑ ≡ WD

(d2) *<granted element>* → *<<u>mode</u> identifier> <forbid clause>*
<u>With</u> GENV↓,
      WT ≡ WINDOW TYPE↓,
      FF ≡ *<forbid clause>*.FORBIDDEN FIELDS↑
<u>Let</u>   T ≡ text(<identifier>),
      D ≡ identify decla(T,ENV↓),
      N ≡ identify node(T,ENV↓),
      N ≡ mode(N.DDENMODE!),
      WD ≡ grant(D,WT),
      MD ≡ surr group(GENV↓),
      N₁ ≡ (<u>Case</u> module(N₂) ≡ MD:N₂,

                <u>Case</u> region(N₂) ≡ MD:N₂)

<u>Test</u> N.DCAT!=mode(new),
      is grantable(D,GENV↓),
      N.DSURRGROUP!=N₁,

      M=struct(-)
<u>Def</u>   *<forbid clause>*.MODE↓ ≡ M,
      DECLA↑ ≡ WD ∪ FF

(e1) *<forbid clause>* → *FORBID ALL*
<u>With</u> M ≡ MODE↓
<u>Let</u>   FF ≡ {forbid(T,M)|is field selector(T,M)}
<u>Def</u>   FORBIDDEN FIELDS↑ ≡ FF

(e2) *<forbid clause>* → *(L(,)<<u>field</u> identifier>)*
<u>With</u> M ≡ MODE↓,
<u>Let</u>   ∀(i∈L):T_i ≡ text(*<<u>field</u> identifier>*),

      FF ≡ {forbid(T_i,M)|i∈L},

<u>Test</u> ∀(i∈L):is field selector(T_i,M)

<u>Def</u>   FORBIDDEN FIELDS ≡ FF

(f) *<seize statement>* → *SEIZE <seize window>*
<u>Pass</u> SENV↓,
      SDECLA↑

(g1) *<seize window>* → *ALL*
<u>With</u> SENV↓
<u>Let</u>   SD ≡ seize all(SENV↓)
<u>Test</u> ∀(d∈SD):is seizable(d,SENV↓)
<u>Def</u>   SDECLA↑ ≡ SD

(g2) *<seize window>* → *L(,) <seized element>*
<u>Pass</u> SENV↓
<u>With</u> SD ≡ ∪(i∈L):*<seized element>*_i.SDECLA↑

<u>Def</u>   SDECLA↑ ≡ SD

(h1) *<seized element>* → *<identifier>*
<u>With</u> SENV↓
<u>Let</u>   T ≡ text(<identifier>,
      D ≡ identify decla(T,SENV↓),
      SD ≡ seize(D)
<u>Test</u> is seizable(D,SENV↓)

<u>Def</u>   SDECLA↑ ≡ SD

(h2) *<seized element>* → *<module or region* identifier> *ALL*
<u>With</u>   SENV↓
<u>Let</u>   T ≡ text(*<module or region* identifier>),
       N ≡ identify node(T,SENV↓)
<u>Test</u>   N.DCAT! ∈ {label(region(-)), label(module(-))}
<u>Let</u>   SD ≡ seizable and granted(N,SENV↓)
<u>Def</u>   SDECLA↑ ≡ SD ∪ identify decla(T,SENV↓)

8. PROCEDURES

8.1 PROCEDURE DEFINITIONS

Syntax

(a) *<procedure definition statement>*
     → *<routine>*
(b) *<routine>*
        → *<procedure* identifier> : *PROC*
              (<formal parameter part>)
              <result> <exceptions>
              <procedure attribute>;
              <data statement list>
              <procedure action statement list>
           END <handler> <end label>
(c) *<formal parameter part>*
        (1) → *<empty>*
        (2) | L(,) *<formal parameter>*
(d) *<formal parameter>*
        → L(,) *<formal* identifier>
                    <mode denotation>
                    <parameter attribute>
                    <register specification>
(e) *<procedure attribute>*
        (1) → *<empty>*
        (2) | *GENERAL <recursive>*
        (3) | *SIMPLE <recursive>*
        (4) | *INLINE*

(f) *<procedure action statement list>*
        (1) → *<action statement list>*
        (2) | *<action statement list><entry statement>*
                 <procedure action statement list>
(g) *<entry statement>*
        → *<entry* identifier> : *ENTRY*

Semantics

(a) *<procedure definition statement>* → *<routine>*
<u>Pass</u> ENV↓,
       DECLA↑
<u>Dyn</u>   PREELAB=(PE%):
       <u>Step</u> : ← *<routine>*.PREELAB(PE%)

(b) *<routine>* → *<procedure* identifier> : *PROC*
                        (<formal parameter part>)
                        <result> <exceptions>
                        <procedure attribute>;
                        <data statement list>
                        <procedure action statement list>
                     END <handler> <end label>
<u>With</u> ENV↓,
       PLAN ≡ *<formal parameter part>*.PLAN↑,
       PD   ≡   "   .DECLA↑,
       RD ≡ *<result>*.DECLA↑,
       RS ≡   "   .RESULT↑,
       RI ≡   "   .IMPLIED↑,

```
         EEXC ≡ <exceptions>.EXCEPT↑,
         PAT ≡ <procedure attribute>.AT↑,
         DD ≡ <data statement list>.DECLA↑,
         AD ≡ <procedure action statement list>.DECLA↑,
         HD ≡ <handler>.EXCEPT↑,
         ET ≡ <end label>.TEXT↑
   Let   T ≡ text(<procedure identifier>),
         N ≡ node(<procedure identifier>),
         NR ≡ node(<routine>),
         BD ≡ DD ∪ AD,
         IED ≡ internal entries(NR,BD),
         RG ≡ proc regionality(NR,ENV↓),
         ENVN ≡ new proc env(ENV↓,proc(NR),PD∪BD,EEXC,HD),
         PRDECLA ≡ define(T,N),
         EEXCI ≡ {T|except(T,-)∈EEXC}
         PROC MODE ≡ mode(base,proc(PLAN,RS,EEXCI,PAT)),
         RM ≡ (Case RS=none:none,
              Case[loc,[-,MODE],-] ≡ RS:mode(base,descr(MODE)),
              Case[nloc,[-,MODE],-] ≡ RS:MODE),
         RLM ≡ loc(nreg,stat,refble,write,RM)
   Test  is implementable(PROC MODE),
         is locale(PD∪BD),
         RG=reg ⇒ PAT≠general(-),
         regionality(ENV↓)=reg ∧ RG=nreg
                  ⇒ (PAT=inline ∨ PAT=simple(nrec)),
         ET≠none ⇒ ET=T
   Def   DECLA↑ ≡ RD ∪ PRDECLA ∪ IED,
         <formal parameter part>.ENV↓ ≡ ENVN,
         <result>.ENV↓ ≡ ENV↓,
         <data statement list>.ENV↓ ≡ ENVN,
         <procedure action statement list>.ENV↓ ≡ ENVN,
         <handler>.ENV↓ ≡ replace exceptions(ENVN,ENV↓),
         N.DCAT! ≡ lit,
         N.DVAL! ≡ entry(NR,all),
         N.DISCT! ≡ cst,
         N.DIMPLIED! ≡ RI,
         N.DPREMODE! ≡ val(dclass,RG,stat,PROC MODE),
         NR.DPREMODE! ≡ val(dclass,RG,stat,PROC MODE),
         NR.DBN! ≡ block number(ENV↓),
         NR.DIMPLIED! ≡ RI,
         NR.DIDENNODE! ≡ N,
         NR.DCAT! ≡ procedure,
         NR.DREGNODE! ≡ surr region(ENV↓)
   Dyn   PREELAB=(PE%):
         (Case PATTR ∈ {inline,simple(nrec),general(nrec)}:
               Step 1 : ← initialize recursivity test(N,PE%),
               Step 2 : ← PE%
          Case else :
               Step : ← PE%)
         ELAB=(E%,A%,EP%):
         Step 1 : EN%₁ ← <formal parameter part>.ELAB(E%,A%)

         Step 2 : (Case RM≠none:
                        Step 2.1 : RESLOC% ← create location(RML,EN%₁)

                        Step 2.2 : EN%₂ ← declare(NR,RESLOC%,EN%₁),

                   Case else :
                        Step : EN%₂ ← EN%₁)

         Step 3 : EN%₃ ← <data statement list>.PREELAB(EN%₂)
```

Step 4 : EN%₄ ← <procedure action statement list>.PREELAB(EN%₃)

Step 5 : (Case EP%=all:
                Step : EN%₅ ← <data statement list>.ELAB(EN%₄),

          Case else :
                Step : EN%₅ ← EN%₄

Step 6 : EN%₆ ← <procedure action statement list>.ELAB(EN%₅,entry,EP%)

Step 7 : (Case RM=none:
                Step : R% ← none,
            Case base mode(RM)=descr(-):
                Step : R% ← dedescr(contents(RESLOC%,RLM),RM)
            Case else:
                Step : R% ← contents(RESLOC%,RLM))
Step 8 : UL% ← <formal parameter part>.POSTELAB(EN%₆)

Step 9 : ← [R%,UL%]
TRAP=(K%,[N%,EE%]):
(Case K%=return:
    Step 1 : (Case base mode(RM)=descr(-):
                    Step : S% ← none,
                Case RM=descr(-):
                    Step : S% ← dedescr(contents(RESLOC%,RLM),RM),
                Case else:
                    Step : S% ← contents(RESLOC%,RLM))
        Step 2 : UN% ← <formal parameter part>.POSTELAB(EN%₅)

        Step 3 : ← [S%,UN%],
  Case K%=exception ∧ N% ∈ exception nodes(HD):
      Step 1 : ← N%.ELAB(adjust(EE%,E%))
      Step 2 : (Case RM=none:
                    Step : T% ← none,
                Case base mode(RM)=descr(-):
                    Step : T% ← dedescr(contents(RESLOC%,RLM),RM),
                Case else :
                    Step : T% ← contents(RESLOC%,RLM))
        Step 3 : UM% ← <formal parameter part>.POSTELAB(EN%₂)

        Step 4 : ← [T%,UM%]
  Case K%=exception ∧ except(-,N%) ∈ EEXC:
      Let   t% such that except(t%,N%) ∈ EEXC
      Step : ← [exception,t%],
  Case K%=goto ∧ N% ∈ labels(AD):
      Step : ← <procedure action statement list>
                .ELAB(adjust(EE%,EN%₂),label,N%))

(c1) <formal parameter part> → <empty>
Def   PLAN↑ ≡ ↔
      DECLA↑ ≡ {}
Dyn   ELAB=(E%,A%):
      Step : ← E%
      POSTELAB=(PE%):
      Step : ← ↔

(c2) <formal parameter part> → L(,) <formal parameter>
Pass   ENV↓,
With   ∀(i∈L):(Pᵢ ≡ <formal parameter>ᵢ.PLAN↑,
           Dᵢ ≡   "   .DECLA↑,
           Nᵢ ≡   "   .NUMBER↑)

```
        PLAN↑ ≡ ||(i∈L):P_i,
        DECLA↑ ≡ ∪(i∈L):D_i
```

<u>Dyn</u> ELAB=(E%₀,A%):

    <u>Let</u> $N_0 \equiv 0$,

$$\forall(i\in L):(a_i \equiv 1+\Sigma(k\in\{0:i-1\}):N_k,$$
$$b_i \equiv a_i+N_i-1)$$

    <u>Step</u> : ← S(i∈L):(E%_i ← formal parameter_i.ELAB(E%_{i-1},A%⟨a_i:b_i⟩))

    POSTELAB=(PE%):

    <u>Step</u> 1 : R(i∈L):x_i ← formal parameter_i.POSTELAB(PE%)

    <u>Step</u> 2 : ← ||(i∈L):x_i

(d) <formal parameter>
        → L(,) <<u>formal</u> identifier>
                        <mode denotation>
                        <parameter attribute>
                        <register specification>

<u>Pass</u> ENV↓,

<u>With</u> DM ≡ <mode denotation>.DENMODE↑,
      D ≡   "   .DECLA↑,
      I ≡   "   .IMPLIED↑,
      AT ≡ <parameter attribute>.AT↑,
      R ≡ <register specification>.REG↑

<u>Test</u> has the synchro prop(DM) ⊃ AT=loc

<u>Let</u> $\forall(i\in L):(T_i \equiv$ text(<<u>formal</u> identifier>_i),

              $N_i \equiv$ node(<<u>formal</u> identifier>_i)),

      PDECLA ≡ ∪(i∈L):define(T_i,N_i),

      [RD,M] ≡ DM,
      proc(NR) ≡ surrounding proc(ENV↓),
      RG ≡ regionality(NR.DPREMODE!),
      PRL ≡ loc(RG,stat,refble,RD,M),
      PRV ≡ contents premode(PRL),
      XM ≡ identify assign exceptions(PRV,PRL,ENV↓),
      n ≡ #L

<u>Def</u> PLAN↑ ≡ ⟨[DM,AT,R]|i∈L⟩,
      DECLA↑ ≡ PDECLA ∪ D,
      NUMBER↑ ≡ n,
      ∀(i∈L):(N_i.DCAT! ≡ loc,

               N_i.DPREMODE! ≡ PRL,

               N_i.DIMPLIED! ≡ I)

<u>Dyn</u> ELAB=(E%₀,A%):

  (<u>Case</u> AT=loc:
      <u>Step</u> 1 : S(i∈L):E%_i ← declare(N_i,A%⟨i⟩,E%_{i-1})
        <u>Step</u> 2 : ← E%_n,

    <u>Case</u> AT≠loc:
      <u>Step</u> 1 : R(i∈L):L%_i ← create location(PRL,E%₀)

      <u>Step</u> 2 :
        (<u>Case</u> AT ∈ {in,inout}:
          <u>Step</u> 2.1 :
             R(i∈L):O%_i ← assign(A%⟨i⟩,PRV,L%_i,PRL,XM)

Step 2.2 : Case $\exists(i\epsilon L):exception(X\%) \equiv 0\%_i$:

exit(exception,$[X\%,E\%_0]$)

Step 3 : $S(i\epsilon L):E\%_i \leftarrow declare(N_i,L\%_i,E\%_{i-1})$

Step 4 : $\leftarrow E\%_n$

POSTELAB=(PE%):

Case AT ϵ {out,inout}:

Step $\leftarrow$ {contents($L\%_i$,PRL)$|i\epsilon L$}

Case else : Step $\leftarrow$ {unused$|i\epsilon L$}

(e1) *<procedure attribute>* $\rightarrow$ *<empty>*
Def   AT$\uparrow$ $\equiv$ {# implemented procedure attribute #}
(e2) *<procedure attribute>* $\rightarrow$ *GENERAL <recursive>*
With REC $\equiv$ *<recursive>*.REC$\uparrow$
Def   AT$\uparrow$ $\equiv$ general(REC)
(e3) *<procedure attribute>* $\rightarrow$ *SIMPLE <recursive>*
With REC $\equiv$ *<recursive>*.REC$\uparrow$
Def   AT$\uparrow$ $\equiv$ simple(REC)
(e4) *<procedure attribute>* $\rightarrow$ *INLINE*
Def   AT$\uparrow$ $\equiv$ inline

(f1) *<procedure action statement list>*
     $\rightarrow$ *<action statement list>*
Pass ENV$\downarrow$,
      DECLA$\uparrow$
Dyn   PREELAB=(PE%)
      ELAB=(E%,K%,N%):
      Step : $\leftarrow$ *<action statement list>*.ELAB(E%,N%)

(f2) *<procedure action statement list>*
     $\rightarrow$ *<action statement list> <entry statement>*
                <procedure action statement list>
Pass ENV$\downarrow$
With $D_1 \equiv$ *<action statement list>*.DECLA$\uparrow$,

      $D_2 \equiv$ *<entry statement>*.DECLA$\uparrow$,

      $D_3 \equiv$ *<procedure action statement list>*.DECLA$\uparrow$

Let   proc(NR) $\equiv$ surr group(ENV$\downarrow$)
Def   DECLA$\uparrow$ $\equiv$ $D_1 \cup D_2 \cup D_3$

Dyn   PREELAB=(PE%):
      Step 1 : $PE\%_1 \leftarrow$ *<action statement list>*.PREELAB(PE%)

      Step 2 : $\leftarrow$ *<procedure action statement list>*.PREELAB($PE\%_1$)

      ELAB=(E%,K%,N%):
      Case N%=all:
        (Step 1 : $E\%_1 \leftarrow$ *<action statement list>*.ELAB(E%,all)

         Step 2 : $\leftarrow$ *<procedure active statement list>*.ELAB($E\%_1$,K%,all))

      Case K%=label $\land$ N%ϵlabels(D_1):

        (Step 1 : $E\%_1 \leftarrow$ *<action statement list>*.ELAB(E%,N%)

         Step 2 : $\leftarrow$ *<procedure action statement list>*.ELAB($E\%_1$,K%,all))

      Case K%=entry $\land$ N%ϵentries(NR,D_2):

        Step : $\leftarrow$ *<procedure action statement list>*.ELAB(E%,K%,all)
      Case else :

   <u>Step</u> : ← *<procedure action statement list>*.ELAB(E%,K%,N%)

(g) *<entry statement>*
     → *<<u>entry</u> identifier>* : *ENTRY*
<u>With</u> ENV↓,
<u>Let</u> proc(NR) ≡ surr group(ENV↓),
   NE ≡ node(*<<u>entry</u> identifier>*),
   T ≡ text(*<<u>entry</u> identifier>*),
   PRE ≡ NR.DPREMODE!,
   D ≡ define(T,NE)
<u>Def</u> DECLA↑ ≡ D,
   NE.DCAT! ≡ lit,
   NE.DISCT! ≡ true,
   NE.DVAL! ≡ entry(NR,NE),
   NE.DIMPLIED! ≡ NR.DIMPLIED!,
   NE.DPREMODE! ≡ PRE

8.2 PROCEDURE CALLS

Syntax

(a) *<procedure call>*
    → *<<u>procedure</u> expression>* (*<actual parameter part>*)
(b) *<actual parameter part>*
   (1) → *<empty>*
   (2) | L(,) *<actual parameter>*
(c) *<actual parameter>*
   (1) → *<value denotation>*
   (2) | *<location denotation>*
Semantics

(a) *<procedure call>*
    → *<<u>procedure</u> expression>* (*<actual parameter part>*)
<u>With</u> ENV↓,
   PRE ≡ *<<u>procedure</u> expression>*.PREMODE↑,
   NB ≡ *<actual parameter part>*.NUMBER↑
<u>Test</u> base mode(PRE) ≡ proc(-)
<u>Let</u> proc(-,-,XN,-) ≡ base mode(PRE),
   RPRE ≡ result premode(PRE),
   RG ≡ regionality(PRE),
   ARGSPECS ≡ arg specs(PRE),
   ENVN ≡ new dummy env(ENV↓)
   XM ≡ {[X→identify exception node(X,ENV↓)]|X∈XN},
   X_1 ≡ identify exception node(text(*EMPTY*),ENV↓),
   X_2 ≡ identify exception node(text(*SPACEFAIL*),ENV↓),
   X_3 ≡ identify exception node(text(*RECURSEFAIL*),ENV↓),
<u>Test</u> NB=#ARGSPECS
<u>Def</u> *<<u>procedure</u> expression>*.ENV↓ ≡ ENV↓,
     "   .POSTMODE↓ ≡ none,
   <actual parameter part>.ENV↓ ≡ ENVN,
     "   .ARGSPECS↓ ≡ ARGSPECS↓,
     "   .RG↓ ≡ RG,
   PREMODE↑ ≡ RPRE↑,
   ISCT ≡ dyn,
   VAL↑ ≡ none,

```
         NODESET↑ ≡ {},
         LOC↑ ≡ none
Dyn     ELAB=(E%):
         Step 1 : P% ← <procedure expression>.ELAB(E%)
         Step 2 : Case P%=NULL:exit(exception,[X₁,E%])

         Step 3 : Case the implementation is unable to allocate space for the
                       routine : exit(exception,[X₂,E%])

         Step 4 : E%₁ ← new(E%)

         Step 5 : A% ← <actual parameter part>.ELAB(E%₁)

         Let   I% ≡ {i|[i,-]∈A%},
               O% ≡ {o|[-,o]∈A%},
               [NR%,NE%,D%] ≡ P%,
               NI% ≡ NR%.DIDENNODE!,
               REG% ≡ NR%.DREGNODE!
         Step 6 : Case REG%≠none:Enter and lock(REG%)
         Step 7 : C% ← check recursivity(NI%,E%₁)

         Step 8 : Case C%=rec ∧ recursivity(PRE)=nrec:
                           exit(exception,[X₃,E%₁])

         Step 9 : E%₂ ← new call env(E%₁,D%)

         Step 10 : [R%,UL%] ← NR%.ELAB(E%₂,I%,NE%)

         Step 11 : (Case R%=exception:
                       Step 11.1 : X% ← XM[UL%]
                       Step 11.2 : exit(exception,[X%,E%]),
                     Case else:
                       Step 11.1 : ← <actual parameter part>.POSTELAB(E%₂,O%,UL%)

         Step 12 : Case REG%≠none:Exit(REG%)
         Step 13 : ← R%
         TRAP=(K%,[N%,EE%]):
         Case REG%≠none:
               (Step 1 : ← Exit(REG%)
                Step 2 : exit(K%,[N%,EE%])
```

(b1) <actual parameter part> → <empty>
With ARGSPECS↑
Test ARGSPECS↑ ≡ {}
Def   NUMBER↑ ≡ 0,
      DECLA↑ ≡ {}
Dyn   ELAB=(E%):
      Step : ← {}
      POSTELAB=(E%,-,-):
      Step : ← E%

(b2) <actual parameter part> → L(,) <actual parameter>
Pass ENV↓
With ARGSPECS↑
Test # ARGSPECS↑=#L
Def   ∀(i∈L):<actual parameter>ᵢ.ARGSPEC↓ ≡ ARGSPECS↓{i},

      NUMBER↑ ≡ #L
Dyn   ELAB=(E%):
      Step 1 : R(i∈L):[I%ᵢ,O%ᵢ] ← <actual parameter>ᵢ.ELAB(E%)

      Step 2 : ← {[I%ᵢ,O%ᵢ]|i∈L}

```
       POSTELAB=(E%,OL%,UL%):
       Step : R(i∈L): ← <actual parameter>_i.POSTELAB(E%,OL%↓i↓,UL%↓i↓)
```

(c1) <actual parameter> → <value denotation>
Pass ENV↓
With ARGSPEC↓,
      RG↓,
      PRE ≡ <value denotation>.PREMODE↑

When <value denotation> ≱ <delocated location>
Test is argument(PRE,ARGSPEC↓,RG↓)
Let   [[RD,MODE],-,AT,REG] ≡ ARGSPEC↓,
      PREL ≡ loc(RG↓,stat,refble,write,MODE),
      XM ≡ identify assign exceptions(PRE,PREL,ENV↓)
Def   <value denotation>.POSTMODE↓ ≡ MODE
Dyn   ELAB=(E%):
      Step 1 : V% ← <value denotation>.ELAB(E%)
      Step 2 : (Case AT=loc:
                      Step 2.1 : L% ← create location(PREL,E%)
                      Step 2.2 : O% ← assign(V%,PRE,L,PREL,XM)
                      Step 2.3 : Case exception(X) ≡ O%:exit(exception,[X,E%])
                      Step 2.4 : ← [L%,unused]
                  Case AT=in:
                      (Step 2.1 : O% ← in param exception(V%,PRE,PREL,XM)
                       Step 2.2 : Case exception(X) ≡ O%:exit(exception,[X,E%]
                       Step 2.3 : ← [V%,unused]
      POSTELAB=(E%,-,-):
      Step : ← E%

(c2) <actual parameter> → <location denotation>
Pass ENV↓
With ARGSPEC↓,
      RG↓,
      DECLA ≡ <location denotation>.DECLA↑,
      PRE   ≡   "   .PREMODE↑
Let   [[RD,MODE],AT,REG] ≡ ARGSPEC↓,
      CPRE ≡ contents premode(PRE),
      PRE_1 ≡ (Case AT=in:CPRE,

             Case else:PRE),
      PREL ≡ loc(RG↓,stat,refble,write,MODE),
      PREV ≡ contents premode(PREL),
      XMF ≡ identify assign exceptions(CPRE,PREL,ENV↓),
      XMB ≡ identify assign exceptions(PREV,PRE,ENV↓)
Test is argument(PRE,ARGSPEC↓,RG),
Dyn   ELAB=(E%):
      Step 1 : L%.← <location denotation>.ELAB(E%)
      Step 2 : (Case AT=loc:
                      Step : ← [L%,unused],
                  Case AT∈{in,inout}:
                      Let V% ≡ contents(L%,PRE)
                      Step 2.1 : O% ← in param exception(V%,CPRE,PREL,XMF)
                      Step 2.2 : Case exception(X) ≡ O%:exit(exception,[X,E%])
                      (Case AT=in:
                           Step 2.3 : ← [V%,unused],
                       Case AT=inout:
                           Step 2.3 : ← [V%,L%]),
                  Case AT =out
                      Step : ← [unused,L%])
```
```

```
    POSTELAB=(PE%,PL%,V%)
    (Case PL%=unused:Step : skip,
     Case else :
        Step 1 : O% ← assign(V%,PREV,PL%,PRE,XMB)
        Step 2 : Case exception(X) ≡ O%:exit(exception,[X,PE%])
        Step 3 : ← PE%
```

8.3 PROCEDURE BASIC STATEMENTS

Syntax

(a) *<procedure basic action statement>*
    (1) → *<call statement>*
    (2) | *<return statement>*
    (3) | *<result statement>*

Semantics

(a)
Pass ENV↓,
      HP↓
Def   DECLA↑ ≡ {}
Dyn   ELAB=(E%)

8.3.1 CALL STATEMENT

Syntax

(a) *<call statement>*
        → *<call option> <procedure call>*
(b) *<call option>*
    (1) → *<empty>*
    (2) | *CALL*

Semantics

(a) *<call statement>*
Pass ENV↓
With PRE ≡ *<procedure call>*.PREMODE↑
Def   PREMODE↑ ≡ PRE
Dyn   ELAB=(E%)

8.3.2 RESULT AND RETURN STATEMENTS

Syntax

(a) *<result statement>*
    (1) → *RESULT <value denotation>*
    (2) | *RESULT <location denotation>*
(b) *<return statement>*
    (1) → *RETURN*
    (2) | *RETURN <value denotation>*
    (3) | *RETURN <location denotation>*

Semantics

(a1) <result statement> → RESULT <value denotation>
Pass ENV↓
With PRE ≡ <value denotation>.PREMODE↑
Let   NR ≡ surrounding proc(ENV↓),
      RSPEC ≡ result spec(NR.DPREMODE!),
      RG ≡ regionality(NR.DPREMODE!)
When RSPEC≠[loc,-,-]
Test is result(PRE,RSPEC,RG),
      NR≠udf,
      NR.DCAT!≠process
Let   [LOC,DM,REG] ≡ RSPEC,
      M ≡ mode(DM),
      PREL ≡ loc(RG,stat,refble,write,M),
      XM ≡ identify assign exceptions(PRE,PREL,ENV↓)
Def   <value denotation>.POSTMODE↓ ≡ M
Dyn   ELAB=(E%):
      Step : V% ← <value denotation>.ELAB(E%)
      Step 2 : LR% ← identify(NR,E%)
      Step 3 : O% ← assign(V%,PRE,LR%,PREL,XM)
      Step 4 : Case exception(X) ≡ O%:exit(exception,[X,E%])
      Step 5 : ← E%

(a2) <result statement> → RESULT <location denotation>
Pass ENV↓
With PRE ≡ <location denotation>.PREMODE↑
Let   NR ≡ surrounding proc(ENV↓),
      RSPEC ≡ result spec(NR.DPREMODE!),
      RG ≡ regionality(NR.DPREMODE!)
When RSPEC=[loc,-,-]
Test is result(PRE,RSPEC,RG),
      NR≠udf,
      NR.DCAT!≠process
Let   [LOC,DM,REG] ≡ RSPEC,
      M ≡ mode(DM),
      PRELR ≡ loc(RG,stat,refble,write,mode(base,descr(M))),
      DELRM ≡ contents premode(PRELR)
Dyn   ELAB=(E%):
      Step 1 : L% ← <location denotation>.ELAB(E%)
      Step 2 : LR% ← identify(NR,E%)
      Step 3 : ← assign(descr(L%,PRE),DELRM,LR%,PRELR,XM)
      Step 4 : ← E%

(b1) <return statement> → RETURN
With HP↓
Let   NR ≡ surrounding proc(ENV↓)
Test ¬ HP↓,
      NR≠udf,
      NR.DCAT!≠process
Dyn   ELAB=(E%):
      Step 1 : exit(return,[none,E%])

(b2) <return statement>
          → RETURN <value denotation>
Pass ENV↓
With PRE ≡ <value denotation>.PREMODE↑
Let   NR ≡ surrounding proc(ENV↓),
      RSPEC ≡ result spec(NR.DPREMODE!),

```
          RG ≡ regionality(NR.DPREMODE!)
When   RSPEC≠[loc,-,-]
Test   is result(PRE,RSPEC,RG),
          NR≠udf,
          NR.DCAT!≠process
Let    [LOC,DM,REG] ≡ RSPEC,
          M ≡ mode(DM),
          PREL ≡ loc(RG,stat,refble,write,M),
          XM ≡ identify assign exceptions(PRE,PREL,ENV↓)
Def    <value denotation>.POSTMODE↑ ≡ M
Dyn    ELAB=(E%):
          Step 1 : V% ← <value denotation>.ELAB(E%)
          Step 2 : LR% ← identify(NR,E%)
          Step 3 : O% ← assign(V%,PRE,LR%,PREL,XM)
          Step 4 : Case exception(X) ≡ O%:exit(exception,[X,E%])
          Step 5 : exit(return,[none,E%])
```

(b3) *<return statement>* → *RETURN <location denotation>*

```
Pass   ENV↓
With   PRE ≡ <location denotation>.PREMODE↑
Let    NR ≡ surrounding proc(ENV↓),
          RSPEC ≡ result spec(NR.DPREMODE!),
          RG ≡ regionality(NR.DEPREMODE!)
When   RSPEC=[loc,-,-]
Test   is result(PRE,RSPEC,RG)
          NR≠udf,
          NR.DCAT!≠process
Let    [LOC,UM,REG] ≡ RSPEC,
          M ≡ mode(DM),
          PRELR ≡ loc(RG,stat,refble,write,mode(base,M))),
          DELRM ≡ contents premode(PRELR)
Dyn    ELAB=(E%):
          Step 1 : L% ← <location denotation>.ELAB(E%)
          Step 2 : LR% ← identify(NR,E%)
          Step 3 : ← assign(descr(L%,PRE),DELRM,LR%,PRELR,XM)
          Step 4 : exit(return,[none,E%])
```

9. CONCURRENT PROCESSING

Syntax

(a) *<concurrent mode denotation>*
    (1) → *<instance mode denotation>*
    (2) | *<synchro mode denotation>*
(b) *<synchro mode denotation>*
    (1) → *<event mode denotation>*
    (2) | *<buffer mode denotation>*
(c) *<concurrent definition statement>*
    (1) → *<process definition statement>*
    (2) | *<signal definition statement>*
(d) *<concurrent basic action statement>*
    (1) → *<start statement>*
    (2) | *<stop statement>*
    (3) | *<send buffer statement>*
    (4) | *<send signal statement>*
    (5) | *<delay statement>*
    (6) | *<continue statement>*
(e) *<concurrent case statement>*
    (1) → *<delay case statement>*
    (2) | *<receive buffer case statement>*
    (3) | *<receive signal case statement>*
(f) *<priority value>*
       → *<u>integer</u> literal expression>*

Semantics

(a,b)
<u>Pass</u> ENV↓,
      DENMODE↑,
      DECLA↑,
      IMPLIED↑,
      NODESET↑

(c) *<concurrent definition statement>*
<u>Pass</u> ENV↓,
      DECLA↑

(d) *<concurrent basic action statement>*
<u>Pass</u> ENV↓,
      HP↓
<u>Dyn</u>   ELAB(E%)

(e) *<concurrent case statement>*
<u>Pass</u> ENV↓,
      DECLA↑
<u>Dyn</u>   PREELAB=(PE%)
      ELAB=(E%,N%)

(f) *<priority value>* → *<u>integer</u> literal expression>*
<u>Pass</u> ENV↓
<u>With</u> V   ≡ *<u>integer</u> literal expression>*.VAL↑,
      PRE ≡   "   .PREMODE↑
<u>Test</u> base mode(PRE)=descr(int,-,-),
      V↑ ≡ 0
<u>Def</u>   PRIOR↑ ≡ V

9.1 PROCESSES

9.1.1 PROCESS DEFINITIONS

Syntax

(a) *<process definition statement>*
    → *<process>*
(b) *<process>*
    → *<process* identifier> : *PROCESS*
       (<formal parameter part>):
       <data statement list>
       <action statement list>
       END <handler> <end label>

Semantics

(a) *<process definition statement>* → *<process>*
<u>Pass</u> ENV↓,
       DECLA↑

(b) *<process>* → *<process* identifier> : *PROCESS*
                   (<formal parameter part>):
                   <data statement list>
                   <action statement list>
                   END <handler> <end label>
<u>With</u> ENV↓,
       PLAN ≡ *<formal parameter part>*.PLAN↑,
       PD   ≡   "   .DECLA↑,
       DD ≡ *<data statement list>*.DECLA↑,
       AD ≡ *<action statement list>*.DECLA↑,
       HD ≡ *<handler>*.EXCEPT↑,
       ET ≡ *<end label>*.TEXT↑
<u>Let</u>   T ≡ text(*<process* identifier>),
       N ≡ node(*<process* identifier>),
       NP ≡ node(*<process>*),
       BD ≡ DD ∪ AD,
       PRDECLA ≡ define(T,N),
       INDECLA ≡ PD ∪ DD ∪ AD,
       ENVN ≡ new proc(ENV↓,process(HP),INDECLA,{},HD)
<u>Test</u> ET≠none ⇒ ET=T,
       is locale(INDECLA),
       is process plan(PLAN),
       is process allowed(ENV↓)
<u>Def</u>   *<formal parameter part>*.ENV↓ ≡ ENVN,
       <data statement list>.ENV↓ ≡ ENVN,
       <action statement list>.ENV↓ ≡ ENVN,
       <handler>.ENV↓ ≡ ENVN \ exceptions(ENVN),
       DECLA↑ ≡ PRDECLA,
       N.DCAT! ≡ process,
       N.DPROCESS IDEN! ≡ T,
       N.DIMPLIED! ≡ {},
       N.DPLAN! ≡ PLAN,
       NP.DCAT! ≡ process
<u>Dyn</u>   ELAB=(E%,A%):
       <u>Step</u> 1 : EN%₁ ← *<formal parameter part>*.ELAB(E%,A%)

<u>Step</u> 2 : EN%$_2$ ← *<data statement list>*.PREELAB(EN%$_1$)

<u>Step</u> 3 : EN%$_3$ ← *<action statement list>*.PREELAB(EN%$_2$)

<u>Step</u> 4 : EN%$_4$ ← *<data statement list>*.ELAB(EN%$_3$)

<u>Step</u> 5 :   ← *<action statement list>*.ELAB(EN%$_4$,all)

<u>Step</u> 6 : <u>end</u>()
TRAP=(K%,[N%,EE%])
(<u>Case</u> K%=exception ∧ N% ∈ exception node(HD)
        <u>Step</u> 1 : ← N%.ELAB(adjust(EE%,E%))
        <u>Step</u> 2 : <u>end</u>(),
  <u>Case</u> K%=goto ∧ N% ∈ labels(AD):
        <u>Step</u> 1 : ← *<action statement list>*
                        .ELAB(adjust(EE%,EN%$_1$),N%)

        <u>Step</u> 2 : <u>end</u>(),
  <u>Case</u> K%=stop ∧ N%=NP
        <u>Step</u> : <u>end</u>()
  <u>Case</u> <u>else</u>:
        {# implementation defined : the program is in error #}

9.1.2 INSTANCE MODE DENOTATIONS

Syntax

(a) *<instance mode denotation>*
    (1) → *<read> INSTANCE*
    (2) | *<u>instance</u> derived mode denotation>*

Semantics

(a1) *<instance mode denotation>*
         → *<read> INSTANCE*
<u>Pass</u> ENV↓
<u>With</u> RD ≡ *<read>*.READ↑
<u>Let</u>   DM ≡ [RD,mode(base,inst)]
<u>Def</u>   DENMODE↑ ≡ DM,
      DECLA↑ ≡ {},
      IMPLIED↑ ≡ {}
      NODESET↑ ≡ {}

(a2) *<instance mode denotation>*
         → *<u>instance</u> derived mode denotation>*
<u>Pass</u> ENV↓,
      DENMODE↓,
      IMPLIED↓,
      NODESET↓
<u>Test</u> base mode(DENMODE↓) ≡ inst
<u>Def</u>   DECLA ≡ {}

9.1.3 INSTANCE BASIC ACTION STATEMENTS

Syntax

(a) *<start statement>*
    → *<start expression> <instance initialization>*
(b) *<start expression>*
    → START *<process identifier>* *(<actual parameter part>)*
(c) *<instance initialization>*
    (1) → *<empty>*
    (2) | SET *<instance location denotation>*
(d) *<stop statement>*
    → STOP

Semantics

(a) *<start statement>*
    → *<start expression> <instance initialization>*

Pass ENV↓
With PRE₁ ≡ *<start expression>*.PREMODE↑,

      PRE₂ ≡ *<instance initialization>*.PREMODE↑

Dyn ELAB=(E%):
    Step 1 : R(I% ← *<start expression>*.ELAB(E%),
             L% ← *<instance initialization>*.ELAB(E%))
    Step 2 : (Case PRE₂≠none:

               ← assign(I%,PRE₁,L%,PRE₂,{})

    Step 3 : ← E%

(b) *<start expression>*
    → START *<process identifier>* *(<actual parameter part>)*

With ENV↓,
      NB ≡ *<actual parameter part>*.NUMBER↑
Let T ≡ text(*<process identifier>*),
      PN ≡ identify node(T,ENV↓),
      P ≡ PN.DPLAN!
Test PN.DCAT! ≡ process
Let ENVN ≡ new dummy env(ENV↓),
      XN ≡ identify exception node(*SPACEFAIL*,ENV↓)
Test #P ≤ NB
Def *<actual parameter part>*.ENV↓ ≡ ENVN,
                "   .ARGSPECS↓ ≡ ARGSPECS,
      PREMODE↑ ≡ val(dclass,nreg,stat,inst),
      ISCT↑ ≡ dyn,
      VAL↑ ≡ none,
      NODESET↑ ≡ {}
Dyn ELAB=(E%):
    Step 1 : Case the implementation is unable to allocate space for the
               process : exit(exception,[XN,E%])
    Step 2 : E%₁ ← new process dyn env(E%)

    Step 3 : A% ← *<actual parameter part>*.ELAB(E%₁)

    Step 4 : ← create and start(PN,A%,E%₁)

(c1) *<instance initialization>* → *<empty>*
Def PREMODE↑ ≡ none

<u>Dyn</u>   ELAB=(E%):
         <u>Step</u> : ← none

(c2) *<instance initialization>*
              → *SET <u>instance</u> location denotation>*
<u>Pass</u>   ENV↓
<u>With</u>   PRE ≡ *<instance location denotation>*.PREMODE↑
<u>Test</u>   ¬ has the rdo prop(PRE),
         base mode(PRE)=instance
<u>Def</u>   PREMODE↑ ≡ PRE
<u>Dyn</u>   ELAB=(E%):
         <u>Step</u> : ← *<u>instance</u> location denotation>*.ELAB(E%)

(d) *<stop statement>* → *STOP*
<u>With</u>   ENV↓,
         HP↓
<u>Test</u>   ¬ HP↓
<u>Let</u>   P ≡ surr process(ENV↓)
<u>Dyn</u>   ELAB=(E%):
         <u>Step</u> : <u>exit</u>(stop,[P,E%])

9.1.4 INSTANCE EXPRESSIONS

Syntax

(a) *<zeroadic operator>* → *THIS*

Semantics

<u>With</u>   ENV↓
<u>Def</u>   PREMODE↑ ≡ val(dclass,nreg,stat,mode(base,inst)),
         ISCT↑ ≡ dyn,
         VAL↑ ≡ none,
         NODESET↑ ≡ {}
<u>Dyn</u>   ELAB=(E%):
         <u>Step</u> : ← descr(<u>myself</u>)

9.2 EVENTS

Syntax

(a) *<event mode denotation>*
      (1) → *<read> EVENT <queue length>*
      (2) | *<u>event</u> derived mode denotation>*
(b) *<queue length>*
      (1) → *<empty>*
      (2) | *(<length>)*
(c) *<delay statement>*
              → *DELAY (<u>event</u> location denotation> <priority>)*
(d) *<priority>*
      (1) → *<empty>*
      (2) | *PRIORITY <priority value>*
(e) *<continue statement>*
              → *CONTINUE (<u>event</u> location denotation>)*
(f) *<delay case statement>*

```
                    → DELAY CASE <instance intialization>
                      <semicolon 1> <priority> <semicolon 2>
                      L{(<event list>):<action statement list>}
                      ESAC
(g) <event list>
                    → L(,)<event location denotation>
(h) <semicolon>
    (1) → <empty>
    (2) | ;
```

Semantics

(a1) *<event mode denotation>*
         → *<read>* EVENT *<queue length>*

Pass ENV↓
With RD ≡ *<read>*.READ↑,
      L ≡ *<queue length>*.LENGTH↑,
      NS ≡   "   .NODESET↑

Test L≠none ⇒ L>0
Let   DM ≡ [RD,mode(base,event(L))]
Def   DENMODE↑ ≡ DM,
      DECLA↑ ≡ {},
      IMPLIED↑ ≡ {},
      NODESET↑ ≡ NS

(a2) *<event mode denotation>*
         → *<event* derived mode denotation>

Pass ENV↓,
      DENMODE↑,
      IMPLIED↑,
      NODESET↑
Test base mode(DENMODE↑)=event(-)
Def   DECLA↑ ≡ {}

(b1) *<queue length>* → *<empty>*
Def   LENGTH↑ ≡ none,
      NODESET↑ ≡ {}

(b2) *<queue length>* → (*<integer literal expression>*)
Pass ENV↓
With PRE ≡ *<integer literal expression>*.PREMODE↑,
      VAL ≡   "   .VAL↑,
      NS ≡   "   .NODESET↑
Test VAL ≥ 0,
      base mode(PRE)=discr(int,-,-)
Def   LENGTH↑ ≡ VAL,
      NODESET↑ ≡ NS

(c) *<delay statement>*
         → DELAY (*<event location denotation><priority>*)
Pass ENV↓
With PRE ≡ *<event location denotation>*.PREMODE↑,
      P   ≡ *<priority>*.PRIOR↑
Let   XN ≡ identify exception node(text(DELAYFAIL),ENV↓)
Test basemode(PRE)=event(-)
Dyn   ELAB=(E%):
      Step 1 : L% ← *<event location denotation>*.ELAB(E%)
      Step 2 : K% ← Delay until event(⎨L%⎬,⎨PRE⎬,⎨P⎬,none,unused)
      Step 3 : (Case K%=exception(delayfail) :exit(exception,[XN,E%])
```
```

$\underline{\text{Case}}$ $\underline{\text{else}}$: ← E%)

(d1) *<priority>* → *<empty>*
$\underline{\text{Def}}$ PRIOR↑ ≡ 0

(d2) *<priority>* → *PRIORITY <priority value>*
$\underline{\text{Pass}}$ ENV↓,
       PRIOR↑

(e) *<continue statement>*
            → *CONTINUE (<event location denotation>)*
$\underline{\text{Pass}}$ ENV↓
$\underline{\text{With}}$ PRE ≡ *<event location denotation>*.PREMODE↑,
$\underline{\text{Test}}$ basemode(PRE)=event(−)
$\underline{\text{Dyn}}$ ELAB=(E%):
       $\underline{\text{Step}}$ 1 : L% ← *<event location denotation>*.ELAB(E))
       $\underline{\text{Step}}$ 2 : ← $\underline{\text{Wake up}}$ (L%,PRE)
       $\underline{\text{Step}}$ 3 : ← E%

(f) *<delay case statement>*
            → *DELAY CASE <instance initialization>*
            <semicolon 1> <priority> <semicolon 2>
            L{(*<event list>*): *<action statement list>*}
            ESAC

$\underline{\text{Pass}}$ ENV↓
$\underline{\text{With}}$ PR ≡ *<priority>*.PRIOR↑,
       ∀(i∈L):(PREL$_i$ ≡ *<event list>*$_i$.PREMODE LIST↑,
                AD$_i$ ≡ *<action statement list>*$_i$.DECLA↑)

$\underline{\text{When}}$ empty(*<instance initialization>*) ⇔ empty(*<semicolon 1>*),
       empty(*<priority>*) ⇔ empty(*<semicolon 2>*)
$\underline{\text{Let}}$ R$_0$ ≡ {0:0},

       ∀(i∈L):(N$_i$ ≡ #PREL$_i$,

                R$_i$ ≡ {1+max(R$_{i-1}$):N$_i$+max(R$_{i-1}$)}),

       PREL ≡ ∥(i∈L):PREL$_i$,

       PL ≡ ⫓PR|p∈PREL⫓,
       D ≡ ∪(i∈L):AD$_i$,

       XN ≡ identify exception node(text(*DELAYFAIL*),ENV↓),
$\underline{\text{Def}}$ DECLA↑ ≡ D
$\underline{\text{Dyn}}$ PREELAB=(PE%):
       $\underline{\text{Step}}$: ← S(i∈L):(PE%$_i$ ← *<action statement list>*$_i$.PREELAB(PE%$_{i-1}$)
       ELAB=(E%,N%):
       ($\underline{\text{Case}}$ N%=all:
            $\underline{\text{Step}}$ 1 : L% ← *<instance initialization>*.ELAB(E%)
            $\underline{\text{Step}}$ 2 : R(i∈L):EVL%$_i$ ← *<event list>*.ELAB(E%)

            $\underline{\text{Let}}$ EVL% ≡ ∥(i∈L):EVL%$_i$

            $\underline{\text{Step}}$ 3 : K% ← Delay until event(EVL%,PREL,PL,L%)
            $\underline{\text{Step}}$ 4 : ($\underline{\text{Case}}$ K% ∈ {1:#PREL}:
                            ($\underline{\text{Choice}}$ (i∈L):K%∈R$_i$):

                                $\underline{\text{Step}}$: ← *<action statement list>*$_i$

                                            .ELAB(E%,all)),
                        $\underline{\text{Case}}$ K%=exception(delayfail)
                                $\underline{\text{Step}}$: $\underline{\text{exit}}$(exception,[XN,E%]))),
       $\underline{\text{Case}}$ N%∈labels(D):

$$\underline{(\text{Choice}}\ (i\epsilon L):N\%\epsilon \text{labels}(AD_i):$$

$$\underline{\text{Step}} : \leftarrow <action\ statement\ list>_i.\text{ELAB}(E\%,N\%)))$$

(g) *<event list>*
    → L(,) *<event location denotation>*

Pass ENV↓

With ∀(iεL):PRE_i ≡ *<event location denotation>*$_i$.PREMODE↑

Test ∀(iεL):base mode(PRE_i)=event(-)

Def   PREMODE LIST↑ ≡ $\{PRE_i|i\epsilon\{1:L\}\}$

Dyn   ELAB=(E%):
          $\underline{\text{Step}}\ 1 : R(i\epsilon L):EV\%_i \leftarrow$ *<event location denotation>*$_i$

                                              .ELAB(E%)

          $\underline{\text{Step}}\ 2 : \leftarrow \{EV\%_i|i\epsilon L\}$

9.3 BUFFERS

Syntax

(a) *<buffer mode denotation>*
    (1) → *<read>* BUFFER *<queue length>* *<mode denotation>*
    (2) | *<buffer derived mode denotation>*
(b) *<receive expression>*
        → RECEIVE (*<buffer location denotation>*)
(c) *<send buffer statement>*
        → SEND *<buffer location denotation>*
        (*<value denotation>*) *<priority>*
(d) *<receive buffer case statement>*
        → RECEIVE CASE *<instance initialization>*
        L(,){(*<buffer location denotation>* IN
              <old or new identifier>):*<do body>*}
        <else option> ESAC
(e) *<old or new identifier>*
        → <identifier>
(f) *<else option>*
    (1) → <empty>
    (2) | ELSE *<do body>*

Semantics

(a1) *<buffer mode denotation>*
        → *<read>* BUFFER *<queue length>* *<mode denotation>*

When successor(BUFFER)="(" ⇒ ¬ empty(*<queue length>*)

Pass ENV↓

With RD ≡ *<read>* ≡ READ↑
          L ≡ *<queue length>*.LENGTH↑,
          NS_1 ≡   "   .NODESET↑,

          DM ≡ *<mode denotation>*.DENMODE↑,
          D   ≡   "   .DECLA↑,
          IMPL ≡   "   .IMPLIED↑,
          NS_2 ≡   "   .NODESET↑

Test ¬ has the synchro prop(DM)

Def   DENMODE↑ ≡ [RD,buffer(L,DM)],

```
        DECLA↑ ≡ D,
        IMPLIED↑ ≡ IMPL,
        NODESET↑ ≡ NS₁∪NS₂
```

(a2) *<buffer mode denotation>*
           → *<buffer derived mode denotation>*

<u>Pass</u> ENV↓
        DENMODE↑,
        IMPLIED↑,
        NODESET↑
<u>Test</u> base mode(DENMODE↑)=buffer(-)
<u>Def</u>   DECLA↑ ≡ {}

(b) *<receive expression>*
           → RECEIVE(*<buffer location denotation>*)

<u>Pass</u> ENV↓
<u>With</u> PRE ≡ *<buffer location denotation>*.PREMODE↑
<u>Let</u>   PRIOR ≡ 0,
        buffer(-,[-,M]) ≡ basemode(PRE)
<u>Test</u> base mode(PRE)=buffer(-)
<u>Def</u>   PREMODE↑ ≡ val(vclass,nreg,stat,M),
        ISCT↑ ≡ dyn,
        VAL↑ ≡ none,
        NODESET↑ ≡ {}
<u>Dyn</u>   ELAB=(E%):
        <u>Step</u> 1 : B% ← *<buffer location denotation>*
        <u>Step</u> 2 : [V%,-] ← <u>Try to get msg from buflist</u>
                               (↓B%↑,↓PRE↑,↓PRIOR↑,none,none)
        <u>Step</u> 3 : ← V%

(c) *<send buffer statement>*
           → SEND *<buffer location denotation>*
                          (*<value denotation>*) *<priority>*

<u>Pass</u> ENV↓
<u>With</u> BPRE ≡ *<buffer location denotaton>*.PREMODE↑,
        MPRE ≡ *<value denotation>*.PREMODE↑,
        PRIOR ≡ *<priority>*.PRIOR↑
<u>Let</u>   buffer(-,[-,M]) ≡ base mode(BPRE),
        PREL ≡ loc(nreg,stat,refble,write,M),
        XM ≡ identify assign exceptions(MPRE,PREL,ENV↓)
<u>Test</u> is compatible with(M,MPRE)
        regionality(MPRE)=nreg,
        buffer(-)=basemode(BPRE)
<u>Def</u>   *<value denotation>*.POSTMODE↑ ≡ M
<u>Dyn</u>   ELAB=(E%):
        <u>Step</u> 1 : R(B% ← *<buffer location denotation>*.ELAB(E%),
                 V% ← *<value denotation>*.ELAB(E%))
        <u>Step</u> 2 : O% ← in param exception(V%,MPRE,PREL,XM)
        <u>Step</u> 3 : <u>Case</u> exception(X) ≡ O%:<u>exit</u>(exception,[X,E%])
        <u>Step</u> 4 : ← <u>Try to put msg in buffer</u>(B%,BPRE,V%,MPRE,PRIOR)
        <u>Step</u> 5 : ← E%

(d) *<receive buffer case statement>*
           → RECEIVE CASE *<instance initialization>*
             L(,){(*<buffer location denotation>*IN
                <old or new identifier>):*<do body>*}
             <else option> ESAC
<u>With</u> ENV↓,
```
```

        ILP ≡ <instance initialization>.PREMODE↑,
        ∀(i∈L):(PRE_i ≡ <u>buffer location denotation</u>_i.PREMODE↑,

                D_i ≡ <old or new identifier>_i.DECLA↑,
                DD_i ≡ <do body>_i.DECLA↑)

        D ≡ <else option>.DECLA↑
Test   ∀(i∈L):is locale(DD_i∪D_i),

        is locale(D)
Let   ∀(i∈L):(buffer(-,[-,M_i]) ≡ base mode(PRE_i),

                ENVN_i ≡ new block env(ENV↑,DD_i∪D_i,{}),

        ENVN ≡ new block env(ENV↑,D,{}),
        PREL ≡ ∤PRE_i|i∈L∤,

        PL ≡ ∤0|i∈L∤,
        XN ≡ identify exception node(SPACEFAIL,ENV↑)
Def   <instance initialization>.ENV↑ ≡ ENV↑,
        ∀(i∈L):(<<u>buffer</u> location denotation>_i.ENV↑ ≡ ENV↑,

                <old or new identifier>_i.ENV↑ ≡ ENVN_i,
                        "   .OUTENV↑ ≡ ENV↑,
                        "   .MODE↑ ≡ M_i

                <do body>_i.ENV↑ ≡ ENVN_i),

        <else option>.ENV↑ ≡ ENVN,
        DECLA↑ ≡ {}
Dyn   PREELAB=(PE$):
        <u>Step</u> : ← PE$
        ELAB=(E$,-):
        <u>Step</u> 1 : L$ ← <instance initialization>.ELAB(E$)
        <u>Step</u> 2 : R(i∈L):B$_i ← <u>buffer location denotation</u>_i.ELAB(E$)

        Let   BL$ ≡ ∤B$_i|i∈L∤

        <u>Step</u> 3 :
            (<u>Case</u> ¬ empty(<else option>):
                <u>Step</u> :
                [V$,K$] ← get msg from buflist(BL$,PREL,PL,L$,ILP),
            <u>Case</u> empty(<else option>):
                <u>Step</u> :
                [V$,K$] ← <u>Try to get msg from buflist</u>(BL$,PREL,PL,L$,IPL))
        <u>Step</u> 4 :   <u>Case</u> the implementation is unable to allocate space for
                            the body : <u>exit</u>(exception,[XN,E$])
        <u>Step</u> 5 : EN$ ← new(E$)
        <u>Step</u> 6 :
            (<u>Case</u> K$=no msg:
                ←<else option>.ELAB(EN$),
            <u>Case</u> K$ ∈ L:
                (<u>Choice</u> (i∈L):K$=i):
                    (<u>Step</u> 5.1 : E$_i ← <old or new identifier>_i.ELAB(EN$,V$)
                        <u>Step</u> 5.2 : ← <do body>_i.ELAB(E$_i))))

(e) <old or new identifier> → <identifier>
<u>With</u> ENV↑,
      OUTENV↑,
      M ≡ MODE↑
<u>Let</u>   T ≡ text(<identifier>),
      N ≡ node(<identifier>),

```
        D ≡ define(T,N),
        PREV ≡ val(class,nreg,stat,M),
              (Case identify node(T,ENV↓)=udf:
                              (ON ≡ none,
                               PREL ≡ unused,
                               XM ≡ unused),
                  Case else :(ON ≡ identify node(T,ENV↓),
                              PREL ≡ ON.DPREMODE!,
                              XM ≡ identify assign exceptions(PREV,PREL,ENV↓))
Test    ON≠none ⇒ (ON.DCAT!=loc ∧ is assignable(PREV,PREL))
Def     DECLA↑ ≡ D
        N.DCAT! ≡ dyn syn,
        N.DPREMODE! ≡ PREV
Dyn     ELAB=(E%,V%):
        Step 1 : (Case ON≠none:
                      (Step 2.1 : L% ← identify(ON,E%)
                       Step 2.2 : O% ← assign(V%,PREV,L%,PREL,XM),
                       Step 2.3 : Case exception(X) ≡ O%:exit(exception,[X,E%]))
        Step 2 : ← declare(N,V%,E%)
```

(f1) *<else option>* → *<empty>*
Def   DECLA↑ ≡ {}
Dyn   ELAB=(E%):
        unused

(f2) *<else option>* → *ELSE <do body>*
Pass   ENV↓,
        DECLA↑
Dyn   ELAB=(E%)

9.4. SIGNALS

Syntax

(a) *<signal definition statement>*
        → *SIGNAL* L(,)*<signal definition>*
(b) *<signal definition>*
        → *<identifier> <signal mode list> <signal receiver>*
(c) *<signal mode list>*
        (1) → *<empty>*
        (2) | =(L(,)*<mode denotation>*)
(d) *<signal receiver>*
        (1) → *<empty>*
        (2) | *TO <process identifier>*
(e) *<send signal statement>*
        → *SEND <signal identifier> <signal list>*
                <receiving process instance> <priority>
(f) *<signal list>*
        (1) → *<empty>*
        (2) | (L(,) *<value denotation>*)
(g) *<receiving process instance>*
        (1) → *<empty>*
        (2) | *TO <instance expression>*
(h) *<receive signal case statement>*
        → *RECEIVE CASE <instance initialization>*
        L(,){(*<signal identifier>*
                    <list of old or new identifiers>):

```
                    <do body>}
                 <else option> ESAC
(i) <list of old or new identifiers>
    (1) → <empty>
    (2) | IN L(,)<old or new identifier>
```

Semantics

(a) *<signal definition statement>*
     → *SIGNAL* L(,) *<signal definition>*

<u>Pass</u> ENV↓

<u>With</u> $\forall (i \in L): D_i \equiv$ *<signal definition>*$_i$.DECLA↑

<u>Def</u>   DECLA↑ $\equiv \cup(i \in L): D_i$

(b) *<signal definition>*
    → *<identifier> <signal mode list> <signal receiver>*

<u>Pass</u> ENV↓

<u>With</u> $D_1 \equiv$ *<signal mode list>*.DECLA↑,

     ML $\equiv$ "   .MODE LIST↑,

     IMP $\equiv$ "   .IMPLIED↑,

     P $\equiv$ *<signal receiver>*.PROCESS↑

<u>Let</u>   T $\equiv$ text(*<identifier>*),

     N $\equiv$ node(*<identifier>*),

     $D_2 \equiv$ define(T,N)

<u>Def</u>   DECLA↑ $\equiv D_1 \cup D_2$,

     N.DCAT! $\equiv$ signal(ML,P),

     N.DIMPLIED! $\equiv$ IMP,

(c1) *<signal mode list>* → *<empty>*

<u>Def</u>   DECLA↑ $\equiv$ {},

     MODE LIST↑ $\equiv$ {},

     IMPLIED↑ $\equiv$ {}

(c2) *<signal mode list>* → =(L(,) *<mode denotation>*)

<u>Pass</u> ENV↓

<u>With</u> $\forall (i \in L): (D_i \equiv$ *<mode denotation>*$_i$.DECLA↑,

      $DM_i \equiv$ "   .DENMODE↑,

      $IMP_i \equiv$ "   .IMPLIED↑)

<u>Test</u> $\forall (i \in L): \neg$ has the synchro prop(DM_i)

<u>Def</u>   DECLA↑ $\equiv \cup(i \in L): D_i$,

     MODELIST↑ $\equiv \{M_i \mid i \in L \wedge [-,M_i]=DM_i\}$,

     IMPLIED↑ $\equiv \cup(i \in L): IMP_i$

(d1) *<signal receiver>* → *<empty>*

<u>Def</u>   PROCESS↑ $\equiv$ any

(d2) *<signal receiver>* → *TO <u>process</u> identifier>*

<u>With</u> ENV↓

<u>Let</u>   T $\equiv$ text(*<u>process</u> identifier>*),

     N $\equiv$ identify node(T,ENV↓)

<u>Test</u> N.DCAT!=process

<u>Def</u>   PROCESS↑ $\equiv$ N

(e) *<send signal statement>*
         → SEND *<signal identifier> <signal list>*
                    <receiving process instance> <priority>

<u>Pass</u> ENV↓
<u>With</u> PREL ≡ *<signal list>*.PREMODE LIST↑,
       PR ≡ *<priority>*.PRIOR↑
<u>Let</u>   T ≡ text(*<signal identifier>*),
       N ≡ identify node(T,ENV↓),
       signal(ML,R) ≡ N.DCAT!,
       n ≡ #PREL,
       XN_1 ≡ identify exception node(text(*EMPTY*),ENV↓),

       XN_2 ≡ identify exception node(text(*EXTINCT*),ENV↓),

       XN_3 ≡ identify exception node(text(*MODEFAIL*),ENV↓),

       ∀(i∈{1:n}):(PRE_i ≡ loc(nreg,stat,refble,write,ML,↓i↓),

                    XM_i ≡ identify assign exceptions(PREL↓i↓,PRE_i,ENV↓)),
<u>Test</u> #ML=n,
       ∀(i∈{1:n}):(is compatible with(ML↓i↓,PREL↓i↓),
                    regionality(PREL↓i↓)=nreg)
<u>Def</u>   *<signal list>*.MODELIST↓ ≡ ML
<u>Dyn</u>   ELAB=(E%):
       <u>Step 1</u> : R(VL% ← *<signal list>*.ELAB(E%),
                    I% ← *<receiving process instance>*.ELAB(E%))
       <u>Step 2</u> : (<u>Case</u> I%=null:<u>exit</u>(exception,[XN_1,E%]))

       <u>Step 3</u> : <u>Case</u> I%≠any:
              <u>Let</u> N% ≡ process node(instance(I%))
              <u>Step 3.1</u> : <u>Case</u> is dead(I%): <u>exit</u>(exception,[XN_2,E%])

              <u>Step 3.2</u> : <u>Case</u> R≠any ∧ N%≠R:<u>exit</u>(exception,[XN_3,E%]))

       <u>Step 4</u> : R(i∈L):$O\%_i$ ← in param exception(VL%↓i↓,PREL↓i↓,PRE_i,XM_i))

       <u>Step 5</u> : <u>Case</u> exception(X) ≡ $O\%_i$:<u>exit</u>(exception,[X,E%])

       <u>Step 6</u> : O% ← <u>Send msg to signal</u>(sign(N),signal(ML,R),VL%,PREL,I%,PR)
       <u>Step 7</u> : ← E%

(f1) *<signal list>* → *<empty>*
<u>Def</u>   PREMODE LIST↑ ≡ ↓↓
<u>Dyn</u>   ELAB=(E%):
       <u>Step</u> : ← ↓↓

(f2) *<signal list>*
         → L(,) *<value denotation>*
<u>Pass</u> ENV↓
<u>With</u> ML ≡ MODELIST↓,
       ∀(i∈L):PRE_i ≡ *<value denotation>*$_i$.PREMODE↑
<u>Def</u>   PREMODE LIST↑ ≡ ↓PRE_i|i∈L↓,

       ∀(i∈L):*<value denotation>*$_i$.POSTMODE↓ ≡ ML↓i↓
<u>Dyn</u>   ELAB=(E%):
       <u>Step 1</u> : R(i∈L):V_i ← *<value denotation>*$_i$.ELAB(E%)
       <u>Step 2</u> : ← ↓V_i|i∈L↓

(g1) *<receiving process instance>* → *<empty>*
<u>Dyn</u>   ELAB=(E%):
       <u>Step</u> : ← any

(g2) *<receiving process instance>* → *TO <instance expression>*
Pass ENV↓
With PRE ≡ *<instance expression>*.PREMODE↑
Test basemode(PRE)=instance
Def *<instance expression>*.POSTMODE↓ ≡ none
Dyn ELAB=(E%)

(h) *<receive signal case statement>*
      → *RECEIVE CASE <instance initialization>*
         L(,){(*<signal* identifier>
               <list of old or new identifiers>):*<do body>*}
         <else option> ESAC
With ENV↓,
    IPL ≡ *<instance initialization>*.PREMODE,
    ∀($i \in L$):(D_i ≡ *<list of old or new identifiers>*$_i$.DECLA↑,

           DD_i ≡ *<do body>*$_i$.DECLA↑),

    D ≡ *<else option>*.DECLA↑
Test ∀($i \in L$):is locale($D_i \in DD_i$),

    is locale(D)
Let ∀($i \in L$):(T_i ≡ text(*<signal* identifier>$_i$),

         N_i ≡ identify node(T_i,ENV↓),

         signal(ML_i,R_i) ≡ N_i.DCAT↑,

         $ENVN_i$ ≡ new block env(ENV↓,$D_i \cup DD_i$,{}))),

    ENVN ≡ new block env(ENV↓,D,{}),
    CATL ≡ ⫲N_i.DCAT↑|$i \in L$⫲,

    PL ≡ ⫲0|$i \in L$⫲,
    SL ≡ ⫲sign(N_i)|$i \in L$⫲,

    XN ≡ identify exception node(*SPACEFAIL*,ENV↓)
Def *<instance initialization>*.ENV↓ ≡ ENV↓,
    ∀($i \in L$):(*<list of old or new dentifiers>*$_i$.ENV↓ ≡ $ENVN_i$,
                       "   .OUTENV↓ ≡ ENV↓,
                       "   .MODEL↓ ≡ ML_i,

         <do body>$_i$.ENV↓ ≡ $ENVN_i$),

    <else option>.ENV↓ ≡ ENVN,
    DECLA↑ ≡ {}
Dyn PREELAB=(PE%):
    <u>Step</u> : ← PE%
    ELAB=(E%,-):
    <u>Step</u> 1 : L% ← *<instance initialization>*.ELAB(E%)
    <u>Step</u> 2 :
      (<u>Case</u> ¬ empty(*<else option>*):
         [VL%,K%] ← get msg from sgn list(SL,CATL,PL,L%,IPL)
       <u>Case</u> empty(*<else option>*):
         [VL%,K%] ← <u>Try to get msg from sgn list</u>(SL,CATL,PL,L%,IPL)
    <u>Step</u> 3 : the implementation is unable to allocate space for the block :
                        exit(exception,[XN,E%])
    <u>Step</u> 4 : EN% ← new(E%)
    <u>Step</u> 5 :
      (<u>Case</u> K%=no msg:← *<else option>*.ELAB(EN%)
       <u>Case</u> K%$\in$L:(<u>Choice</u> ($i \in L$):K%=i):
           (<u>Step</u> 5.1 :
               $E\%_i$ ← *<list of old or new identifiers>*$_i$.ELAB(EN%,VL%)

$\underline{Step}$ 5.2 : ← *<do body>*$_i$.ELAB(E%$_i$))))

(11) *<list of old or new identifiers>* → *<empty>*
$\underline{With}$ MODEL↓
$\underline{Test}$ MODEL↓=↓↓
$\underline{Def}$ DECLA↑ ≡ {}
$\underline{Dyn}$ PREELAB=(PE%):
         $\underline{Step}$: ← PE%
         ELAB=(E%):
         $\underline{Step}$: ← E%

(12) *<list of old or new identifiers>*
         → *IN* L(,)*<old or new identifier>*
$\underline{With}$ ENV↓,
         OUTENV↓,
         ML ≡ MODEL↓,
         ∀(i∈L):D$_i$ ≡ *<old or new identifier>*$_i$.DECLA↑

$\underline{Test}$ #ML=#L
$\underline{Def}$ ∀(i∈L):(*<old or new identifier>*$_i$.ENV↓ ≡ ENV↓,
                        "   .OUTENV↓ ≡ OUTENV↓,
                        "   .MODE↓ ≡ ML↓i↓),
         DECLA↑ ≡ ∪(i∈L):D$_i$
$\underline{Dyn}$ ELAB=(E%$_0$,VL%):

         $\underline{Step}$: S(i∈L):E%$_i$ ← *<old or new identifier>*$_i$.ELAB(E%$_{i-1}$,VL%↓i↓)

10. PROGRAM STRUCTURE

Syntax

(a) *<program>*
        → L*<program element>*
(b) *<program element>*
    (1) → *<module statement>*
    (2) | *<critical region>*

Semantics

(a) *<program>* → L*<program element>*
<u>With</u> $\forall(i\epsilon L):D_i \equiv$ *<program element>*$_i$.DECLA↑

<u>Let</u>   NP ≡ node(*<program>*,
        ENVP ≡ program env(D,program(NP)),
        n ≡ #L
<u>Def</u> $\forall(i\epsilon L):$*<program element>*$_i$.ENV↓ ≡ ENVP,

        NP.DCAT↓=program
<u>Dyn</u>   ELAB=(PE%):
        {# PE%$_0$=preenv%, see I-0.3(7) #}

        <u>Step</u> 1 : $S(i\epsilon L):$PE%$_i$ ← *<program element>*$_i$.PREELAB(PE%$_{i-1}$)

        <u>Let</u>   E%$_0$ ≡ PE%$_n$

        <u>Step</u> 2 : $S(i\epsilon L):$E%$_i$ ← *<program element>*$_i$.ELAB(E%$_{i-1}$,all)

        <u>Step</u> 3 : <u>program end</u> ()
        TRAP=(K%,[N%,EE%]):
        (<u>Case</u> K%=goto:
                <u>Choice</u> $\forall(i\epsilon L):$N%ϵlabels(D_i):

                        <program element>$_i$.ELAB(adjust(EE%,E%),N%)

            <u>Case</u> <u>else</u> : implemented)

(b) *<program element>*
<u>Pass</u> ENV↓,
        DECLA↑
<u>Dyn</u>   PREELAB=(PE%)
        ELAB=(E%,N%):
                (<u>Case</u> (b1):<right>.ELAB(E%,N%),
                 <u>Case</u> (b2):<right>.ELAB(E%))

BIBLIOGRAPHY

[1]   *"CHILL Language Definition"*, CCITT proposed recommendation Z200,
        Study group XI, Period 1977-1980.

[2]   *"Proposal for a Recommendation for a CCITT High Level Language : Blue
        document"*, CCITT Study group XI, HLL Implementors Forum, February
        1979.

[3]   D.E. KNUTH, *"Semantics of Context-Free Languages"*, Math. Syst.
        Theory, Vol. 2.1, 1968.

[4]   D. BJORNER, C.B. JONES (Editors), *"The Vienna Development Method :
        The Metalanguage"*, LNCS 61, Springer Verlag 1978.

[5]   P. BRANQUART, G. LOUIS, P. WODON, *"A Software Programming Language"*,
        PRL Brussels, Report R388, January 1979.

[6]   F. HEYMANS and R. VANTILBORGH, *"Paper and Document Generator (PDG)"*,
        PRL Brussels, Technical Note N108, September 1976.

[7]   P. BRANQUART, J.P. CARDINAEL, J. LEWI, J.P. DELESCAILLE, M. VANBEGIN,
        "An Optimized Translation Process and its Application to Algol 68",
        LNCS 38, Springer Verlag 1976.

[8]   M. BOUCKAERT, A. PIROTTE, M. SNELLING, P. WODON, D. WYBAUX,
        "Utilisation des attributs dans un systeme d'ecriture de software",
        Seminaire IRIA, Structure et programmation des calculatrices, 1973.

[9]   *Specification for the Computer Programming Language Pascal*, Draft
        Proposal ISO/DP 7185, Jan. 1981.

[10]   C.A.R. HOARE, N. WIRTH, *"An Axiomatic Definition of the Algorithmic
        Language Pascal"*, Acta Informatica, 2-4, 1973.

INDEX OF TECHNICAL TERMS

INDEX OF SPECIAL TYPE FONT NOTATIONS

INDEX OF FUNCTIONS

INDEX OF SYNTACTIC UNITS[1]

---

[1]Defining occurrences are underlined, all references concern Part II.

Vol. 77: G. V. Bochmann, Architecture of Distributed Computer Systems. VIII, 238 pages. 1979.

Vol. 78: M. Gordon, R. Milner and C. Wadsworth, Edinburgh LCF. VIII, 159 pages. 1979.

Vol. 79: Language Design and Programming Methodology. Proceedings, 1979. Edited by J. Tobias. IX, 255 pages. 1980.

Vol. 80: Pictorial Information Systems. Edited by S. K. Chang and K. S. Fu. IX, 445 pages. 1980.

Vol. 81: Data Base Techniques for Pictorial Applications. Proceedings, 1979. Edited by A. Blaser. XI, 599 pages. 1980.

Vol. 82: J. G. Sanderson, A Relational Theory of Computing. VI, 147 pages. 1980.

Vol. 83: International Symposium Programming. Proceedings, 1980. Edited by B. Robinet. VII, 341 pages. 1980.

Vol. 84: Net Theory and Applications. Proceedings, 1979. Edited by W. Brauer. XIII, 537 Seiten. 1980.

Vol. 85: Automata, Languages and Programming. Proceedings, 1980. Edited by J. de Bakker and J. van Leeuwen. VIII, 671 pages. 1980.

Vol. 86: Abstract Software Specifications. Proceedings, 1979. Edited by D. Bjørner. XIII, 567 pages. 1980

Vol. 87: 5th Conference on Automated Deduction. Proceedings, 1980. Edited by W. Bibel and R. Kowalski. VII, 385 pages. 1980.

Vol. 88: Mathematical Foundations of Computer Science 1980. Proceedings, 1980. Edited by P. Dembiński. VIII, 723 pages. 1980.

Vol. 89: Computer Aided Design - Modelling, Systems Engineering, CAD-Systems. Proceedings, 1980. Edited by J. Encarnacao. XIV, 461 pages. 1980.

Vol. 90: D. M. Sandford, Using Sophisticated Models in Resolution Theorem Proving. XI, 239 pages. 1980

Vol. 91: D. Wood, Grammar and L Forms: An Introduction. IX, 314 pages. 1980.

Vol. 92: R. Milner, A Calculus of Communication Systems. VI, 171 pages. 1980.

Vol. 93: A. Nijholt, Context-Free Grammars: Covers, Normal Forms, and Parsing. VII, 253 pages. 1980.

Vol. 94: Semantics-Directed Compiler Generation. Proceedings, 1980. Edited by N. D. Jones. V, 489 pages. 1980.

Vol. 95: Ch. D. Marlin, Coroutines. XII, 246 pages. 1980.

Vol. 96: J. L. Peterson, Computer Programs for Spelling Correction: , 213 pages. 1980.

Vol. 97: S. Osaki and T. Nishio, Reliability Evaluation of Some Fault-Tolerant Computer Architectures. VI, 129 pages. 1980.

Vol. 98: Towards a Formal Description of Ada. Edited by D. Bjørner and O. N. Oest. XIV, 630 pages. 1980.

Vol. 99: I. Guessarian, Algebraic Semantics. XI, 158 pages. 1981.

Vol. 100: Graphtheoretic Concepts in Computer Science. Edited by Noltemeier. X, 403 pages. 1981.

Vol. 101: A. Thayse, Boolean Calculus of Differences. VII, 144 pages. 1981.

Vol. 102: J. H. Davenport, On the Integration of Algebraic Functions. 197 pages. 1981.

Vol. 103: H. Ledgard, A. Singer, J. Whiteside, Directions in Human Factors of Interactive Systems. VI, 190 pages. 1981.

Vol. 104: Theoretical Computer Science. Ed. by P. Deussen. VII, pages. 1981.

Vol. 105: B. W. Lampson, M. Paul, H. J. Siegert, Distributed Systems – Architecture and Implementation. XIII, 510 pages. 1981.

Vol. 106: The Programming Language Ada. Reference Manual. X, pages. 1981.

Vol. 107: International Colloquium on Formalization of Programming Concepts. Proceedings. Edited by J. Diaz and I. Ramos. VII, 478 pages. 1981.

Vol. 108: Graph Theory and Algorithms. Edited by N. Saito and T. Nishizeki. VI, 216 pages. 1981.

Vol. 109: Digital Image Processing Systems. Edited by L. Bolc and Zenon Kulpa. V, 353 pages. 1981.

Vol. 110: W. Dehning, H. Essig, S. Maass, The Adaptation of Virtual Man-Computer Interfaces to User Requirements in Dialogs. X, 142 pages. 1981.

Vol. 111: CONPAR 81. Edited by W. Händler. XI, 508 pages. 1981.

Vol. 112: CAAP '81. Proceedings. Edited by G. Astesiano and C. Böhm. VI, 364 pages. 1981.

Vol. 113: E.-E. Doberkat, Stochastic Automata: Stability, Nondeterminism, and Prediction. IX, 135 pages. 1981.

Vol. 114: B. Liskov, CLU, Reference Manual. VIII, 190 pages. 1981.

Vol. 115: Automata, Languages and Programming. Edited by S. Even and O. Kariv. VIII, 552 pages. 1981.

Vol. 116: M. A. Casanova, The Concurrency Control Problem for Database Systems. VII, 175 pages. 1981.

Vol. 117: Fundamentals of Computation Theory. Proceedings, 1981. Edited by F. Gécseg. XI, 471 pages. 1981.

Vol. 118: Mathematical Foundations of Computer Science 1981. Proceedings, 1981. Edited by J. Gruska and M. Chytil. XI, 589 pages. 1981.

Vol. 119: G. Hirst, Anaphora in Natural Language Understanding: A Survey. XIII, 128 pages. 1981.

Vol. 120: L. B. Rall, Automatic Differentiation: Techniques and Applications. VIII, 165 pages. 1981.

Vol. 121: Z. Zlatev, J. Wasniewski, and K. Schaumburg, Y12M Solution of Large and Sparse Systems of Linear Algebraic Equations. IX, 128 pages. 1981.

Vol. 122: Algorithms in Modern Mathematics and Computer Science. Proceedings, 1979. Edited by A. P. Ershov and D. E. Knuth. XI, 487 pages. 1981.

Vol. 123: Trends in Information Processing Systems. Proceedings, 1981. Edited by A. J. W. Duijvestijn and P. C. Lockemann. XI, 349 pages. 1981.

Vol. 124: W. Polak, Compiler Specification and Verification. XIII, 269 pages. 1981.

Vol. 125: Logic of Programs. Proceedings, 1979. Edited by E. Engeler. V, 245 pages. 1981.

Vol. 126: Microcomputer System Design. Proceedings, 1981. Edited by M. J. Flynn, N. R. Harris, and D. P. McCarthy. VII, 397 pages. 1982.

Voll. 127: Y. Wallach, Alternating Sequential/Parallel Processing. X, 329 pages. 1982.

Vol. 128: P. Branquart, G. Louis, P. Wodon, An Analytical Description of CHILL, the CCITT High Level Language. VI, 277 pages. 1982.